The Stalin
Phenomenon

The Stalin Phenomenon

GIUSEPPE BOFFA

Translated by Nicholas Fersen

A BOOK FROM THE WILLIAMS COLLEGE CENTER
FOR THE HUMANITIES AND SOCIAL SCIENCES

CORNELL UNIVERSITY PRESS

ITHACA AND LONDON

First published 1992 by Cornell University Press.

International Standard Book Number 0-8014-2576-x (cloth)
International Standard Book Number 0-8014-9799-x (paper)
Library of Congress Catalog Card Number 91-813

Printed in the United States of America

*Librarians: Library of Congress cataloging information appears on the
last page of the book.*

⊗The paper in this book meets the minimum requirements of the
American National Standard for Information Sciences—Permanence of
Paper for Printed Library Materials, ANSI Z39.48-1984.

Contents

Preface to the American Edition

This book appeared for the first time in the spring of 1982 in Italy. I am happy that it can now become available to American readers interested in the kind of problems with which it deals. These readers will, I hope, share my conviction that we cannot reconstruct our century's history accurately if we do not understand the complex phenomenon known as Stalinism.

I began writing this book after I had completed a much larger project, a two-volume history of the Soviet Union, to which I had devoted several years. Stalinism turned out to be the most important historical phenomenon I had to deal with in the course of my research. For this reason I became convinced that a comparative study of the various ways in which historians have interpreted Stalinism, as I had encountered them during my work on the earlier project, might well yield further insights into the phenomenon.

As the American edition was being prepared for publication, a new dimension was added to the picture. By 1988 the turnabout provoked by Mikhail Gorbachev's *perestroika* had unleashed passionate arguments in the Soviet Union, and for the first time ever Stalinism became a subject of heated debate across the land. So I brought the book up to date by adding a chapter devoted to an analysis of the debates that have taken place in the Soviet Union during recent years. At the same time, a careful review of the original text convinced me that even when these new facts are taken into consideration, the earlier chapters need no revision save a few stylistic adjustments. The reader will decide whether or not I made the right decision.

It is particularly gratifying to me that the American edition happens to coincide with the publication in Moscow of a Russian translation of my *History of the Soviet Union*, which was banned there in the past. Even in those difficult decades I never doubted that it was necessary and possible to produce a truthful account of the events in our century despite the deep divisions that set one group of nations at odds with another. To this end I always sought encounters and exchanges of ideas with scholars in the USSR and the United States, in addition to those in my own country and the rest of Europe.

In the original edition of my book I appealed directly to the leaders in Moscow, challenging them to make the information that sheds light on their history available to scholars. I wrote:

> The seals on the archives, legacies of Stalinism preserved intact, are still seen in the USSR as instruments to protect the official interpretation of history which has become an integral part of state ideology. The inevitable consequence is the increasing sterility of that ideology. If Moscow thinks the secrecy with which it shrouds the sources is enough to block the development of new interpretations, the least one can say is that the results certainly are not brilliant. Nor could they be, even if the purpose were only to hide the sad pages of the past. More basically, one detects a desire to prevent new knowledge or new readings of the motherland's history from seeping into the country's consciousness. But these prophylactic precautions are of little use because pressures for a better understanding of the nation's history are rising within Soviet society. The problem, of course, does not concern historical research alone; it covers the whole spectrum of cultural activity. Yet history is not simply a matter of parochial interest, of concern only to its devotees. It is the biography of an entire people. A country that deprives itself of the tools needed for a continuous meditation on its own nature is a country handicapped.

I knew at the time, and I said as much, that my challenge would fall on deaf ears among Soviet officialdom. And so I added that the lack of a response from Moscow was no excuse for us to stop using all the means at our disposal to continue our own research and reflection. Today, as new Soviet scholarship and debate steadily increase the flow of information we can make our own, that resolve becomes even more essential and I can only rejoice at the thought that my views were privately shared by so many Soviet scholars during those dark days, and that eventually such views were heeded by the country's leadership.

With the highest esteem and affection I thank Nicholas Fersen, the translator of these pages, for his considerable contribution to our enterprise. Without his initiative and fervent involvement in becoming the link, as it were, between myself, my text, and the American publishing world, this volume in the English language would not have seen the light of day. To me Professor Fersen, in his life and in his ideas, personifies that profound faith in a culture capable of growing beyond all geographical, historical, linguistic, and ideological borders which is so urgently needed by the world we live in. We cannot help, it seems to me, but be grateful to him for this.

GIUSEPPE BOFFA

Rome

Translator's Acknowledgments

My gratitude goes first of all to Senator Giuseppe Boffa for allowing me to translate his book. I was captivated by his writings long before I met him and his talented wife, Laura. The impulse that pushed me to knock at their door will remain among the most felicitous of my inspirations. Sincere thanks go also to John G. Ackerman, director of Cornell University Press, and to his editorial staff, all of whom I have pursued in my quest for the "editable copy" Grail; but above all others to Barbara H. Salazar, without whose flair, perspicacity, and professionalism "the road that leads to the Temple" (to borrow an expression found in this book) would certainly have remained unpaved for a long, long time. Thanks to Marc Taylor and Jean-Bernard Bucky at the Williams College Center for the Humanities and Social Sciences for their solidarity and encouragement. To the Reference Department staff at the John E. Sawyer Library, Williams College: cheerful, helpful, and efficient, they always made me feel at home in their midst. To Kurt P. Tauber of the Political Science Department for his inexhaustible willingness to listen, then advise and inspire. To my wife, Nina: this time, as every other time, she was there, oblivious of her needs when my needs were at stake; sharp-eyed scanner of catalog cards, bibliographies, page proofs; patient, intelligent, fun; Nina, thank you. To Apricot, feline paperweight par excellence, who steadfastly sat on top of the "Boffa file" and kept it from blowing away in the Green Mountain breezes.

N. F.

The Stalin
Phenomenon

Some say he's mad; others that lesser hate him
Do call it valiant fury; but, for certain,
He cannot buckle his distemper'd cause
Within the belt of rule.

Macbeth, Act V, scene 2

But cruel are the times, when we are traitors
And do not know ourselves, when we hold rumour
From what we fear, yet know not what we fear,
But float upon a wild and violent sea
Each way and move.

Macbeth, Act IV, scene 2

1 The Problem of Stalinism

"Stalinism" is a controversial term, one of the most controversial in the vocabularies of politics and the social sciences. It has been frequently used, and still is. One can sketch a short history of this term, but its legitimacy and its usefulness continue to be debated. Even those who accept the term as legitimate do not agree on its meaning. To different writers it covers different ground. So much disagreement might lead one to discard a word whose bounds are so uncertain. And yet the very fact that the debate drags on seems to demonstrate a widespread, if vague, realization that we are dealing here with one of those moments in history which, no matter what we choose to call it, lives on as one of the most important in our century. And the very disagreements over the value of the term "Stalinism" already foreshadow the clashes over its interpretation.

In the Soviet Union during the Stalin era—the real core of the phenomenon we are examining—no one ever spoke of Stalinism. Such silence ought to indicate that even the leading players were unaware of either its existence or its uniqueness. Yet during that period we find an abundance of derivative expressions and circumlocutions that mean the same thing. The adjective *stalinskii* and the noun *stalinist* were commonly used, and not only in the press. One of Stalin's closest collaborators, and therefore one of the principal Soviet leaders of the time, spoke of him as the "builder of a new human society." The same man used such expressions as "the *stalinskie* five-year plans," "the *stalinskaia* peace policy," and "*stalinskaia* military science."[1] As others followed the example set by the ruling elites, such locutions became ever more common in the press, at congresses, at public gatherings. The 1936 Constitution, which remained in effect in the Soviet Union until 1977, was known from the start, according to one of the most hallowed publications of the day, as "the Stalin [*stalinskaia*] Constitution, in honor of its maker."[2] With the onset of the war one finds repeated references to a "*stalinskaia* science of victory"—a phrase that in its vagueness connoted more than just military triumph.[3]

The contrast between the obsessive repetition of such expressions and the resolute avoidance of the word "Stalinism" was so pronounced that one scholar wrote that the word was officially "banned" from the Soviet vocabulary.[4] We have a curiously apropos anecdote related in 1956 by Nikita Khrushchev to a foreign visitor. Lazar Kaganovich, one of Stalin's principal collaborators, a rigid member of Stalin's faction in the Bolshevik party since the early 1920s, one day told the leader that it seemed to him the time had come to stop talking simply of "Marxism-Leninism" and to start referring instead to "Marxism-Leninism-Stalinism." Stalin, who among his intimates liked to use what is known as virile language, replied: "How can you compare a prick to a fire lookout tower!"[5] Was Stalin being touchingly modest? It's difficult to think so when one remembers that Stalin took good care of his public image and never hesitated to encourage the idolatry that Soviet propaganda relentlessly constructed about his person.[6] More likely, Stalin's

    1. K. Vorochilov, *Staline et les forces armées de l'Urss* (Moscow, 1951), pp. 69, 81, 90–91, 221.
    2. *The Short Biography of Stalin* (Moscow, 1949). To assess the accuracy of the description, see the history of the debate that preceded the adoption of the constitution: Alberto Ponsi, *Partito unico e democrazia in Urss: La Costituzione sovietica del 1936* (Rome and Bari, 1977).
    3. *Bolshevik*, nos. 19–20, 1943, p. 56; *Pravda*, 8 and 9 March 1943; "Le XIX Congrès du Parti communiste de l'Union Soviétique," special issue of *Cahiers du communisme*, November 1952, p. 269.
    4. Stephen F. Cohen, "Bolshevism and Stalinism," in *Stalinism: Essays in Historical Interpretation*, ed. Robert Tucker (New York, 1977), p. 19.
    5. This episode was related to me by Giancarlo Pajetta, who had heard it personally from Nikita Khrushchev. Khrushchev gives a bowdlerized version in his so-called memoirs: *Khrushchev Remembers* (Boston, 1970), pp. 46–47.
    6. See what Khrushchev has to say on the subject in his "secret report," in ibid., pp. 605–7.

avoidance of the word "Stalinism" was a clever political ploy, something that Kaganovich, an implacable executor who had some organizational talent but was not known for his perspicacity, was not sharp enough to grasp.

"So far as I am concerned, I am only a disciple of Lenin and the aim of my life is to be a worthy one," Stalin had said as far back as 1931 in conversation with the German writer Emil Ludwig.[7] And this remains one of Stalin's most significant utterances because of the scrupulous care he took to portray himself as wise and capable before a presumptuous but not very sophisticated interviewer. "Lenin is our teacher," he repeated sixteen years later to an American visitor, "and we Soviet people are disciples of Lenin. We have never abandoned, nor will we ever abandon, Lenin's precepts."[8]

In practice his attitude toward the "teacher" was far less respectful than these declarations would lead one to believe. Many of Lenin's writings remained unpublished; others, though in print, were kept in restricted sections of libraries, accessible only to readers with special permits. It was all but impossible to publish memoirs or essays about Lenin, though it was not formally forbidden to do so.[9] In the carefully calculated calibration of mass propaganda, Lenin's name gradually slipped to second place behind Stalin's, and Stalin's profile was always superimposed over Lenin's in official iconography. Stalin, then, wanted to represent himself as Lenin's emulator rather than merely his follower. Stalin's brief authorized biography—checked, corrected, and polished in his own hand before being printed in millions of copies—stated: "Stalin is the worthy continuator of Lenin's work, or, as we say in the party, Stalin is the Lenin of today." And again: "In the people's art Stalin's name merges with Lenin's. 'We march with Stalin as we do with Lenin; we talk to Stalin as we talk to Lenin; he knows all our dreams and thoughts; he will take care of us as long as he lives.' So runs one of our loveliest Russian tales."[10] Passages of this sort were not only panegyrical adulation. They bore the hidden but rigid character of directives for all propaganda, written and oral.

And so an emulator, doubtless capable of keeping up with his predecessor, perhaps even of surpassing him in greatness, but also a

---

7. I. V. Stalin, *Sochineniia* (Moscow, 1947), 13:105.

8. I. V. Stalin, *Sochineniia* (Stanford, 1967), 3[16]:77.

9. *Spravochnik parti'inogo rabotnika* (Moscow, 1957), p. 364.

10. *Short Biography of Stalin.* For additions and corrections by Stalin himself, see Khrushchev, *Khrushchev Remembers*, pp. 605–6.

continuator and in this sense a disciple capable of continuing in the service of the same "cause"—"the cause," it was repeatedly pointed out, "of Lenin and Stalin." This image was of great importance for Stalin's authority. While hagiography never stinted on dithyrambic utterances exalting deeds directly tied to Stalin's name —five-year plans, collectivization, and above all victory over Nazi Germany—in the eyes of the Soviet people and of the international communist movement the constant identification of Stalin with Lenin, with Lenin's "teachings," with Lenin's "cause," nurtured the charisma of revolutionary legitimacy. It carried the symbolic significance of an avowed "loyalty" to the original ideals of the new state and of a no less vaunted consistency with a line of thought that ran through Lenin all the way back to Marx and Engels, the founders of "scientific socialism."[11]

To introduce the concept of Stalinism into such a design would have added no advantage and might have paved the way for a clash with that body of "principles" which Stalin himself had codified as "Leninism," thus fostering the suspicion already prevalent among his opponents (as Stalin knew only too well) of a break with the ideas, aims, and ambitions of the father of the revolution. During the dramatic confrontations of the 1920s, when Stalin was most in need of legitimacy, he had always taken care to present himself as a staunch defender of "Leninism." In 1924 he defined "Trotskyism" as a "specific ideological current" that was particularly hostile to "Leninism" and therefore had to be "buried"; and he used

---

11. Even in the official oleography, though the term "Stalinism" was always avoided, obvious euphemisms were freely used. In the message sent to Stalin by the Party Central Committee and the Soviet Council of Ministers on the occasion of his seventieth birthday, for example, we read: "Your classic works which develop Marxist theory, adapting it to the new epoch, to the epoch of imperialism and the proletarian revolutions, to the epoch of socialism's victory in our country, are the greatest patrimony humanity possesses; they are the encyclopedia of revolutionary Marxism": *Pravda*, 21 December 1949. Outside the USSR some writers managed to go even further. The Rumanian Gheorghe Gheorghiu-Dej exalted "the grandiose Leninist-Stalinist ideas" in *For a Stable Peace, for a Popular Democracy*, 21 December 1949. An editorial in the same newspaper, 6 January 1950, mentions "Comrade Stalin's doctrine" and its "victorious power." Expressions of this kind were so deeply rooted and so widely used that they even survived Khrushchev's critique of Stalin. The *Bol'shaia Sovetskaia Entsiklopediia* (1957), vol. 40, has under the entry "Stalin": "In his theoretical works, Stalin, while defending Leninism, developed Marxist-Leninist theory in an original way, adapting it to the building of socialism in the USSR; this had very great importance for the entire international workers' and communist movement."

this antithesis as one of his major calls to battle.[12] Only later did his opponents, especially those in the Trotsky camp, come to realize that it would have been a wiser move to speak of "Stalinism" as a phenomenon in its own right, if not as an original ideology. And they did thereafter make wide use of the term. Stalin was therefore well aware of the negative implications its official adoption could have. At the very least he deemed such a move superfluous.[13]

Though suppressed in Stalin's homeland, the term was widely applied first in international political discussions and later in the historians' debates after Stalin's death and especially after the famous indictment of his governing methods launched by Khrushchev in 1956 at the 20th Congress of the Communist Party of the Soviet Union. That notorious repudiation was so sensational that the term immediately became popular throughout the world. The sudden success of the term, however, did nothing to clarify its meaning. "Stalinism" was a pejorative term, but what it meant no one could say. Since the anti-Stalin critique coming from Moscow took the form of an indictment charging a series of abuses and misdeeds rather than an analysis of a sociopolitical phenomenon, it encouraged people to use the term quite loosely. At best it came to be substituted for "cult of personality," the Soviet leadership's term, to indicate that this was a more serious matter than Moscow was willing to acknowledge. But in the lexicon of the press and of political figures of the day, "Stalinism" retained a much more rudimentary sense, simply a pejorative label employed (particularly in leftist circles) to condemn oppressive ambitions, ideological intolerance, despotic tendencies, lack of scruples.

A partial exception to these vague usages is seen in the immediate use of the term "Stalinism" as a political weapon in the USSR and its satellites. It was banned from the official language, and therefore from the press; but in common speech such terms as "Stalinism," "Stalinists," "anti-Stalinism," and "anti-Stalinists"

---

12. Stalin, *Sochineniia* (Moscow), 6:347–57. "Trotskyism" is defined on p. 357.

13. Robert McNeal, "Trotsky and Stalinism," a paper read at the International Meeting for the Fortieth Anniversary of Leon Trotsky's death, Follonica, Italy, 1980. (Transcripts of the meeting can be found in *Pensiero ed azione di Lev Trockij* [Città di Castello, 1982], 2:376–87.) McNeal suggests that the word "Stalinism" was poison for Stalin "because it was invented by Trotsky and was first made popular by him."

came to stand for the trends behind the facade of unanimity, which set those who looked forward to a more consistent reawakening of public life against those who proposed to keep things substantially as they were. The Yugoslav communists, urgently demanding changes in the relationship between the Soviet Union and the countries then officially designated "people's democracies," used this terminology publicly.[14] But it was also widely used in private conversations, particularly among the intellectual circles of Moscow, Warsaw, Prague, and Budapest (as anyone who visited them in the 1950s and 1960s well knows); and from there it spread to communist movements in other parts of the world.[15] One scholar saw the use of these formulas as a simple manifestation at one historical moment of a perpetual confrontation between "reformism" and "conservatism" which presumably had been endemic throughout Soviet history.[16] And beginning with the second half of the 1960s, after the fall of Nikita Khrushchev, the most authoritative "de-Stalinizer" in Moscow, his supporters spoke of an emerging "neo-Stalinism" in the USSR.[17]

In historical analysis the term "Stalinism" was used cautiously at first.[18] Its multiple and unabashedly political implications sug-

14. The most famous example of such use is found in a speech by Tito at Pula on 11 November 1956: *Yugoslavia and the Soviet Union, 1939–1973: A Documentary Survey*, ed. Stephen Clissold (London, 1975), pp. 265–68. For similar usage elsewhere see Veljko Mićunović, *Moscow Diary*, trans. David Floyd (Garden City, N.Y., 1980), pp. 77, 161–62, 447. First published as *Moskovske Godine: 1956–1958* (Zagreb, 1977).

15. By way of example one can mention *Po Prostu*, a Polish youth weekly published in 1956–1957. A selection of articles from this publication can be found in K. A. Jelenski, *La realtà dell'ottobre polacco* (Milan, 1961), pp. 45, 47, 101–2. See also Aleksandr Solzhenitsyn, *The Oak and the Calf* (New York, 1979), p. 98; Jiri Pelikan, *S'ils me tuent* (Paris, 1975), p. 153; Antonin Liehm, *Trois générations: Entretiens sur le phénomène culturel tchécoslovaque* (Paris, 1970), pp. 13, 29.

16. Stephen F. Cohen, "The Friends and Foes of Change: Reformism and Conservatism in the Soviet Union," in *The Soviet Union since Stalin*, ed. Stephen F. Cohen, Alexander Rabinowitch, and Robert Sharlet (Bloomington, Ind., 1980), p. 13.

17. Alexander Rabinowitch, Introduction to ibid., p. 7; Roy Medvedev and Zhores Medvedev, *Khrushchev: The Years in Power* (New York, 1976), p. 183.

18. It is interesting to see how the term was used in the journal *Nuovi Argomenti*, no. 20 (May–June), 1956. This famous issue can be classified as one of the earliest attempts to upgrade analysis, if not actually to the level of history, then at least above the level of ad hoc political disputes. The issue is titled "Nine Questions about Stalinism." The word "Stalinism," however, appears in only one of the nine questions. Some of the people questioned—Lelio Basso, Carlo Cassola, Giuseppe Chiarante, Roberto Guiducci, Valdo Magnani, Alberto Moravia—picked up

gested prudence. Within the communist movement one finds real reluctance to use this expression, even downright opposition to it, in part for the reasons we have seen but mostly for tactical considerations.[19] Often the word was used between quotation marks, as if to indicate that it was borrowed from somewhere else and was not quite legitimate. Such caution was evident even among those who were beginning to criticize the "Stalin phenomenon" openly and who assumed that dissidence was rife in East European countries, that there was opposition to the governments that were anxious to preserve the core of the legacy they had inherited from Stalin.[20]

Despite such ups and downs, the importance of the historical reality hidden behind the disputes over semantics and the burden it continued to place not only on the Soviet Union but on the rest of the world as well rather quickly gave the Stalinist formula a legitimate place in the debates among historians.

At this point, however, the real problem of interpretation was barely beginning. In short, what did "Stalinism" actually mean?

---

the term in their answers and gave it various shades of emphasis and meaning; others—Arturo Carlo Jemolo, Gabriele Pepe, Ignazio Silone, Palmiro Togliatti—chose to avoid it altogether.

19. As early as 1956 Togliatti said: "We do not accept the term 'Stalinism' and its derivatives because it leads to the false conclusion that one is dealing with a system that was wrong a priori, rather than encouraging the search for those ills that infiltrated it later. This happened as a result of certain definite causes and within the framework of a positive economic and political building process, of correct and just activity in the field of international relations which led to decisive victories": *VIII congresso del Partito comunista italiano: Atti e risoluzioni* (Rome, 1957), p. 44. For this reason the term also does not appear in *Rinascita*, December 1961, even though that issue deals thoroughly with the Stalin theme in response to the renewed attack on Stalin at the 22d Party Congress in the Soviet Union.

20. Here are a few examples: " 'Stalinism,' a commonly used but equivocal term": Robert Havemann, *Un comunista tedesco: Considerazioni dall'isolamento sul passato e sul futuro*, ed. Manfred Wilke (Turin, 1980), p. 4; "The word 'Stalinism' should not be rejected, but in my opinion it has a few drawbacks. Historically speaking it is an invention of the bourgeoisie, a weapon serving its ideology and its politics, though it is commonly used in communist circles as a convenient and popular term": Jean Ellenstein, *Storia del fenomeno Staliniano* (Rome, 1975), p. 7. The discussion published in *Cahiers d'histoire de l'Institut Maurice Thorez*, October–November 1973, pp. 101–8, clearly reveals similar perplexities among French communist historians. Louis Althusser recognized that the term "designates a reality," but added that "it explains nothing," in spite of its "theoretical pretensions among bourgeois ideologists and many Trotskyists": *Essays in Self-criticism* (London, 1976), p. 81n. And finally, in an article in *Unità*, 21 December 1979, headed "Stalinism," the word is described as "an ambiguous and not very enlightening expression."

Did it refer to Stalin's personal autocratic power in the USSR, or perhaps to his governing methods as a whole? Or the massive terror he unleashed more than once as a means of control? Should one also include the concepts, the programs, the political will that came with the terror? And was Stalinism made up only of negatives? A historian wrote that it was, "to use a Soviet-style metaphor, two towering and inseparable mountains: a mountain of national accomplishments alongside a mountain of crimes."[21] In that case, how did its two aspects relate to each other? Even if we concede that the enormous influence Stalin exerted, the "vital" personal part he played, may justify the use of the term to bring all the elements together, are we then talking only about the man or about an entire form of government, a political regime, even a type of society that he had come to personify for one decisive moment in time? What connection is there between all these things and other phases of Russian and Soviet history before and after Stalin? But are we dealing with something that concerns the Soviet Union alone, or could this be a trend that reaches much farther in space and time? In sum, is it legitimate to think of Stalinism as a "distinct phenomenon with its own history, political dynamics, and social consequences," a "historical stage in the development of the Russian and other Communist revolutions and of Communism as a culture?"[22] As we shall see, the term reappeared with overwhelming force in Gorbachev's USSR when the debate over the recent past exploded once again, more passionate and more fervent than ever before.

Interpreting Stalinism, then, whatever one means by the term, implies an effort to interpret the entire Soviet experience within the framework of both Russian history and world events in our century. Before it could be interpreted, however, the Stalinist experience needed to be reconstructed on the concrete basis of facts, events, numbers, chronologies. Such a task has always been very difficult, and to some extent it still is. Only today are Soviet archives beginning to become accessible. In marked contrast to other areas of contemporary history, a major portion of the Soviet docu-

21. See Stephen F. Cohen, *Rethinking the Soviet Experience* (New York, 1985), p. 94.

22. Cohen, "Bolshevism and Stalinism," p. 4; Robert Tucker, "Stalinism as Revolution from Above," in his *Stalinism*, p. 77.

ment pool is still out of bounds.[23] Yet the more one learns about the Stalin phenomenon, the keener one's interest becomes, as the political-historical debate in the USSR today bears startling witness. And this is not the first time we have seen this interest awaken. After all, we owe the notable progress made in Soviet studies throughout the world in the 1960s and 1970s to the break in the clouds which threw the first light on primary sources that had been unavailable before the end of the 1950s. This breakthrough led to the publication of some documents and data and also made available the archival information cited in the monographs of a few Soviet researchers. No matter how tantalizing that brief spell of clear weather may have seemed notable progress in the exploration of Soviet history was made before the clouds rolled in again, and now even more noteworthy advances are becoming possible. Questions arose then, as they always do, and new ones present themselves now. Each time, one of the most significant results has been a refocusing of interest on the elements and general features of Stalinism. All these advances have come gradually, as the exploration of the past has probed deeper and interpretations have become increasingly commensurate with facts, less conditioned by preconceived ideological designs.

The difficulties, however, arise from more than the obstacles that to this day hinder the reconstruction of the past. Precisely because Stalinism, as both a regime and a tendency, is even now so tightly woven into the continually evolving plot of Soviet history, it cannot easily be circumscribed in time and space or considered as a thing complete in itself. Seen from this angle, Stalinism presents the scholar with problems that differ greatly from those encountered in the study of other historical phenomena, such as fas-

23. All the proceedings of the governing organs of the USSR from 1918 on, including those of the Central Committee of the Communist Party, are still mostly inaccessible to foreigners, and to a degree even to Soviet scholars. Among Stalin's speeches, at least three known to be extremely important have never been made public. I have in mind his address to the Central Committee in November 1929, dealing with collectivization; his speech on the eve of the war, 5 May 1941, before the graduating class of a military school; and his report to the Soviet hierarchy in December 1943 after his return from Teheran, on the Soviet Union's war aims. When Stalin's American biographer Robert C. Tucker asked Moscow only a few years ago for permission to see Stalin's personal library, he was told that the books containing marginalia were off limits. Today such rules are in the process of being revised.

cism or, to cite less controversial examples, Russian populism and European colonialism. Whereas at least the essential traits of these phenomena can be picked out from the mass of elements that went into their making, the research on Stalinism remains too closely linked to the dilemmas and choices of our own time. It cannot avoid the aftershocks of its own stinging contemporaneity.

No matter how one seeks to analyze Soviet society in recent years, it is difficult not to notice the many traits characteristic of the country under Stalin which survived the extensive criticism of the Stalin era in Khrushchev's time. It would also be difficult, however, simply to conclude that the system has continued unaltered. Important changes, recognized by the Soviets themselves as well as by foreign observers, have indeed taken place. Just how much vitality, then, has Stalinism demonstrated? If one can talk of Stalinism at all, how much of it has survived the man who gave it its name?

At this point the historical debate becomes entangled in disputes over what is happening now, over Soviet society as it is today, over its nature and peculiarities, its relations with other sociohistorical complexes of the past and the present. The influence of the Soviet Union's system and power in the world today is so routinely analyzed in the press that no lengthy discussion is necessary here. The USSR finds itself at the center of harsh political, ideological, diplomatic, and military strife in which all parts of the world have a stake, some more than others, but none a negligible one. Of course this situation should not be an obstacle to objective study conducted as far as possible along scientific lines; on the contrary, it should serve as a stimulus for precisely such an enterprise. But the task is not easy. The potential biases are too numerous, and whenever scholars have managed to shed them—or, more likely, thought they had shed them—any conclusions they reached, even if they told no one outside the small circle of specialists, would be dragged into political disputes or exploited for partisan advantage.

Besides, we are not dealing with the Soviet Union alone. Traits characteristic of the social and political system that came into being in the USSR under Stalin can be detected in other countries too. In some places they developed independently. Elsewhere they were imported by the Soviet armies, but even in these cases such traits were generally fueled by native drives. We encounter these political and social forms primarily in those countries governed for many years by communist parties, whether or not they were officially designated as such.[24] Nor should this surprise us, since the entire international communist movement (except for small fringe groups and minority factions) recognized Stalin as its leader for thirty years and saw the country he ruled as an example worthy of emulation, at least in many respects.

Even more important was the discovery of such characteristics in countries governed by parties or movements that clearly did not issue from the Comintern matrix—that is, from the original international family where communist parties were formed—though they had been induced to adopt some of communism's political theses, ideological stances, or organizational patterns. Since these countries generally had little or nothing to do with Stalin, they usually remained outside the political debates about Stalinism, or were barely touched by them. For this very reason, however, similarities between their social structures, political institutions, or historical happenings and those of more formally communist countries owe more to comparative investigation than to superficial analogies and can throw considerable light on the entire phenomenon. But once research is broadened to this extent, pitfalls proliferate—not only because this strategy can lead to arbitrary generalizations, but because the research itself then becomes the focus of all the passions and conflicts of interest generated by the numerous and diverse revolutionary processes of our time.

All of these considerations in no way imply a denigration of the serious studies that have been carried out. On the contrary, they underscore their merits. But even so, a warning is in order. As we examine these analyses of Stalinism, which inevitably cover a broad spectrum of problems past and present, we find it all but impossible to draw a clear line between historical and political interpretations. As a rule, the discussions have developed simultaneously on both levels. Many of the interpretations I shall examine stem from arguments put forth by the people who took a direct part in the battles that hatched and established Stalinism. Though the cultural debate fed on such sources, it did try to be independent of them, and often succeeded. But, for the reasons I have men-

24. Some of the parties in power were officially called the Polish United Workers' Party, the Hungarian Socialist Workers' Party, the Vietnam Workers' Party, the Korean Workers' Party, and the Mongolian Popular-Revolutionary Party, but they all claimed to be communist parties.

tioned, the investigations in turn influenced subsequent political clashes. One faction or another attempted to co-opt their findings, often vulgarizing them for easier consumption by the modern mass media. Though such a commingling of the historical and the political has obvious drawbacks, it also points to the fact that the problem of Stalinism is still very much alive and cannot be relegated to the archives.

I shall attempt to isolate and describe the main interpretive and analytical currents generated by some of the more legitimately historical investigations, bringing out the elements that most distinguished each of them from the others. Philosophical and sociological generalizations are not the aim of my inquiry: I mention them when they seem necessary, but only insofar as they are relevant to my main theme. Bear in mind, though, that in the course of their investigations these various schools of thought (if we can call them that), while preserving some of their distinctive characteristics, developed not inside airtight compartments but as part of a cognitive effort that unfolded across geographical, cultural, and political boundaries. Ideas, expressions, whole analytical trends nurtured within a given interpretive current can later be borrowed by writers with quite different outlooks. Such borrowings are sometimes made to fill gaps in an investigator's research; often for the simple convenience of adopting a more or less current terminology; in a few cases, finally, by a process of more reasoned assimilation. At any rate, osmosis is all but inevitable between lines of thought that develop in close proximity.

All of these considerations apply also to the basic distinction I feel obliged to make between the interpretations formed in the mainstream of Marxist culture and those developed largely outside of it. This distinction seems justified because historically Stalinism was born in the wake of Marxism and its Leninist evolution, though with considerable alterations (and this in itself is a moot point) in the original contours of both. Marxist culture has therefore suffered a backlash from the crises that affected Stalinism, from the criticism and denunciations leveled against it. This reaction led to an effort to analyze the phenomenon with the help of Marxism's own apparatus of social, political, and historical categories in a spirit of self-critical reflection.

The results have been quite interesting, and some of them have been widely circulated. Having said this much, one must quickly add that no dividing line exists between these investigations and those based on other cultural premises. We will find here not only the osmosis I mentioned earlier but (on some points, at least) a merging of Marxist interpretations with other lines of thought.

What finally emerges from this investigation is a sort of grand polyphonic debate in which the various sides level charges at one another. This debate is by no means over; indeed, it has become more vigorous since it was reopened so explosively in the USSR. An attempt to trace its development, then, seems that much more useful. It can serve as a first step toward putting in sharper focus the questions that remain open and the tasks that still face students of Stalinism and of everything connected with it, from the history of Soviet society all the way to the great revolutionary changes of our century.

2 Soviet Interpretation Up to Gorbachev

The Soviet interpretation that sees Stalinism as an unanticipated but coherent and substantially logical development of the Bolshevik revolution and the political course set by Lenin went virtually unchallenged for many years and is still very much in vogue today. In its most rigorous form it considers Stalinism never to have existed at all as a phenomenon in its own right.

The wide acceptance of this view rests on two versions, seemingly antithetical, certainly not fully compatible, but in fact much less contradictory than they may seem at first glance. Both of them see Soviet history as a linear evolution. Only the tone—apologetic in the first case, vituperative in the second—changes. The first approach represents the official Soviet attitude up until the advent of Gorbachev. The second, for all practical purposes almost exclusively Anglo-American, has dominated and occasionally monopolized Western historiography for many years.

Precedence belongs to the Soviet version, if only because it comes from the country most directly involved. As I have pointed out, it was an official version, exquisitely political, a true governing tool for the groups in power. And it was the only one allowed to circulate in the USSR, since no one was permitted to suggest a contradictory interpretation in the press or any other public forum.

It was the only one taught in schools, printed in books, spread by the mass media.

The origins of the official story are easily traceable. It goes back to Stalin's time, when the obsessive glorification of the personal imprint he gave to all Soviet precepts went hand in hand with an equally insistent claim of uninterrupted continuity and absolute faithfulness to the revolution (by then liturgically spelled with a capital *R*) and to Lenin personally. In the USSR this way of looking at things survived both Stalin himself and the harsh criticism his methods subsequently underwent for a number of years. There was a moment when it may have appeared to be shaken or compromised, but soon the storm abated and the waters grew calm again, at least on the shores of state ideology. This process merits closer scrutiny. It coincides with the adventures and misadventures that befell both the "cult of personality" formula adopted by Soviet officialdom to identify Stalinism and the line of interpretation implicit in that formula.

The rather esoteric expression "cult of personality" appeared in Moscow without any direct reference to Stalin a few months after his death, immediately after the arrest of Lavrentii Beria, his minister of police, when the new Soviet leadership felt the need to circulate the first critical comments about the period just past.[1] At first, and for some time to come, it drew little attention; it became popular only in 1956, when the 20th Congress of the Communist Party of the Soviet Union linked it explicitly with Stalin's government. Abroad, and privately in the USSR, the expression was accepted at the time as a cautious surrogate for other, possibly much harsher and more pertinent expressions; it was deliberately promoted to salvage the continuity of Soviet history and to circumscribe its most painful aspects as much as possible.[2] Actually, the situation was more complex, since the formula represented a sort of temporary balancing act invented by warring factions with conflicting views of Stalin and his methods. Some of the speeches dur-

---

1. *Pravda*, 5 June 1953; *Kommunist*, no. 11, 1953, pp. 25–26.
2. None of the participants in the discussion printed in *Nuovi Argomenti*, no. 20 (May–June), 1956, accepted the expression "cult of personality," and two of them (Lelio Basso and Carlo Cassola) explicitly criticized it. Outside the communist movement it was looked upon as a simple euphemism and never taken seriously. See Robert Tucker, ed., *Stalinism: Essays in Historical Interpretation* (New York, 1977), p. 18n.

ing the 20th Congress debate and the "secret report" delivered by Khrushchev at its conclusion suggested that the time had come to mend the prolonged and violent break with the original concepts of the Soviet state represented by the Stalin years.[3] But in that setting these were minority voices, however authoritative, and they did not make their way into the official documents of the assembly. And soon they were officially rejected.

Only a few months later, on 30 June 1956, the Central Committee of the party attempted to put an end to the conflicting views of the Stalinist past fostered by the Congress. It issued a *postanovleniie*, or deliberation, explaining what was to be understood by the term "cult of personality." This document later took on such importance that it requires careful examination. In measured terms designed to soften the Congress's more horrifying revelations, the *postanovleniie* recognized the "cult" as a negative phenomenon that had had "dire consequences," for it had produced not only "serious violations of Soviet legality" but also "mass repressions" in which "many honest people" had suffered. How, the document asked, could all this have happened? It offered two explanations, one objective, the other subjective: the "concrete historical conditions" in which the Soviet experience had unfolded and the "personal qualities" of Stalin.[4] An immediate consequence of these explanations was the perception that, historical circumstances being what they were, largely beyond the power of humans to alter, all the evil that had occurred could be ascribed only to the shortcomings of the one man who had exploited those circumstances.

This diagnosis was bolstered by the reasoning that followed it. The USSR, it was said, had become a "besieged fortress," a social-

3. Anastas Mikoyan claimed that a principle so basic to a proletarian party as "collective leadership" had been violated for about twenty years; that behind the formal homage to the leader of the revolution, Lenin's ideas had been completely neglected for the same length of time; and that the 20th Congress was "the most important" since Lenin's death because it put an end to this prolonged break in revolutionary continuity: *XX s'ezd Kommunisticheskoi partii Sovetskogo Soiuza: Stenograficheskii otchet* (Moscow, 1956), 1:302, 322, 328. Khrushchev, in his "secret report," published in *Khrushchev Remembers* (Boston, 1970), pp. 574–77, spoke about the assassination of Sergei Kirov in 1934 and the fate awaiting the delegates to the 17th Congress, held the same year. Khrushchev's language clearly implied subversive intent on Stalin's part against the postrevolutionary order.

4. "O preodolenii kul'ta lichnosti i ego posledstvii," in *Spravochnik parti'nogo rabotnika* (Moscow, 1957), pp. 321–38, 329, 325.

ist country alone, locked inside a ring of "capitalist encirclement," forced to transform its economy very quickly. The resulting internal tensions had forced the country to adopt "iron discipline, ever-increasing vigilance, [and] rigid centralization of control, which could not help but have negative repercussions on the development of some forms of democracy." Those were the circumstances that Stalin exploited. But it all had happened in the course of "the building of socialism in the USSR," a process that had remained unaltered from the revolution on. And the difficulties created by external conditions and the leader's shortcomings had been overcome under "the guidance of the party and of its Central Committee, which followed the general Leninist line with logical consistency." The result had been "the victory of socialism in our country," an achievement of "world-historical" import.[5]

Stalin had acted correctly for a long time. His adversaries, "Trotskyites, right-wing opportunists, bourgeois nationalists," were pictured not as people who had advocated that the revolution take a different course or that Lenin's ideas be developed in a different way but as "foes of Leninism," adversaries of its one and only correct development, people against whom a "merciless struggle" had been fully justified. Stalin had done his mischief only after his head had become swollen and he began to consider himself infallible. But even then he "had fought for the socialist cause," even if in doing so "he at times employed unworthy methods." And herein lay his personal "tragedy."[6]

In its crucial passage, the one most frequently quoted in official Soviet publications, the *postanovleniie* concluded:

> Despite all the harm Stalin's cult of personality did to the party and the people, it could not and did not change the nature of our social system. No cult of personality could change the nature of the socialist state, based on common ownership of the means of production, alliance of the working class with the peasants, and friendship of the peoples. Still, such a cult seriously impaired the development of socialist democracy and the growth of creative initiative in millions of individuals.
>
> To think that one person alone, even one as important as Stalin, could change our sociopolitical system is to fall into deep contradiction with the facts, with Marxism, with truth; it is to fall into ideal-

5. Ibid., pp. 326–27.
6. Ibid., pp. 326, 330.

ism. It would be to invest a single individual with immense and supernatural powers, such as the ability to modify the organization of a whole society, in this case a society where ultimate power lies with a multimillion mass of working people.

It is well known that the nature of a sociopolitical system is determined by its mode of production, by who owns its means of production, and by which social class controls political power. The whole world knows that after the October Revolution and the victory of socialism, the socialist mode of production was established in our country, and that for almost forty years political power has rested in the hands of the workers and peasants. For this reason the Soviet social system has grown stronger year by year and its productivity has increased. Not even our adversaries can ignore this fact.[7]

At the time of its publication the *postanovleniie* was a political document, subject to all the vicissitudes of a potential struggle between differing lines of thought.[8] As such, it might seem to be of little importance today. But clearly it can no longer be viewed so narrowly for its subsequent fate has changed its meaning considerably. There is no need to review here all the ups and downs of Khrushchev's judgments on the Stalin phenomenon. In his speeches and even more boldly in private conversation he ventured much further in his criticism of the past. Thus he spoke of a "cult of personality period," a separate phase in Soviet history—"harsh times for the party and the people when no one was safe from arbitrariness and repression."[9] But each time, whether out of personal conviction or, more likely, out of tactical expediency in domestic and international skirmishes, Khrushchev was obliged to fall back on the terms of the famous *postanovleniie*.[10]

During the Khrushchev years, then, as well as later, the *postanovleniie* became an inviolable text, an obligatory point of reference for all the successive editions of the *Party History Manual*, to

7. Ibid., p. 331.
8. For the circumstances in which this text saw the light of day, see Giuseppe Boffa, *Storia dell'Unione Sovietica* (Milan, 1976–1979), 2:506–20.
9. *XXII S'ezd Kommunisticheskoi partii Sovetskogo Soiuza: Stenograficheskii otchet* (Moscow, 1962), 1:105; 2:582, 587.
10. "They accuse us of being Stalinists," Khrushchev said in January 1957. "We have said repeatedly that, as we see it, the term 'Stalinist' (like Stalin himself) is inseparable from the great name of 'communist.' . . . Stalin's name is inseparable from Marxism-Leninism": Nikita Khrushchev, *Za prochnyi mir i mirnoie sosushchestvovaniie* (Moscow, 1958), pp. 12–13. Khrushchev echoed the fundamental concepts of the *postanovleniie* on several other occasions. See Nikita Khrushchev, *Velikoie prizvaniie literatury i iskusstva* (Moscow, 1963), pp. 30–31, 182–90.

which all of Soviet public education conformed. A canonical formula repeated in each edition proclaimed: "The party clearly explained the causes that had given rise to the cult of personality, its manifestations and consequences."[11] The idea was to emphasize the fact that the party, collective body that it was, had always operated correctly, with Stalin or without him. "The cult of personality could not shake the organizational, political, and theoretical foundations of the party, created and educated in the revolutionary spirit of the great Lenin. Even in the cult of personality situation the party acted as a living organism. . . . The policy pursued by the party was correct and it expressed the interests of the people."[12] A few historians attempted to escape from this cage, but without success. Each attempt was blocked by the iron constraints of the *postanovleniie*, henceforth the fundamental and definitive text of the dominant ideology.[13]

Curiously enough, such conduct led to a version of Soviet history even more simplistic than Stalin's own. Since his name was compromised a priori, official histories thought it useful to attenuate and virtually eliminate all references to Stalin's original contributions to that choral exercise known as the "building of socialism." In Stalin's day one had preferred for obvious reasons to glorify that originality and call it "a work of genius," always recognizing its fealty to the ideas of Lenin. The new course was intended to fix things by attributing to Lenin everything that Stalin had done.

While Stalin was in power, for example, it was said that the "program" of "socialist industrialization of the country" had been his. The collectivization of agriculture was described as "a new and

---

11. *Istoriia Kommunisticheskoi partii Sovetskogo Soiuza: Kratkii kurs* (Moscow, 1959), p. 644; 1962 ed., p. 659; 1969 ed., p. 577; English ed., *History of the Communist Party of the Soviet Union: Short Course* (Moscow, 1960), p. 670.

12. *Istoriia Kommunisticheskoi partii* (1962), p. 660; *History of the Communist Party*, p. 671.

13. *Istoriia Kommunisticheskoi partii Sovetskogo Soiuza v shesti tomakh: Kommunisticheskaia partiia nakanune i v gody Velikoi Otechestvennoi vo'iny, v period uprochneniia i razvitiia sotsialisticheskogo obshchestva* (Moscow, 1980), 5:455–56; "Krupnyi vopros istoricheskogo materializma," *Kommunist*, no. 18, B1979, p. 39; *Pravda*, 21 December 1969 and 21 December 1979. On the efforts made by historians, see especially *Vsesoiuznoie soveshchaniie o merakh uluchsheniia podgotovki nauchno-pedagogicheskikh kadrov po istoricheskim naukam* (Moscow, 1964). I wish to single out the contributions made by S. M. Dubrovskii, A. V. Snegov, V. S. Zaitsev, Viktor Danilov, and Efim Gorodetskii, among others.

grandiose task" decided upon by Stalin, a "new" and higher platform in revolutionary development, a "sharp . . . historical turnabout" rather than an "extension of old policies." Ultimately it
was claimed that Stalin had "created a complete and coherent doctrine for the socialist state," since Lenin had not had time to do
so.[14] Stripped of their adulatory emphasis, these statements were
not unfounded, though they tended to personalize crucial moments
of Soviet history beyond reason. At any rate, they were more justifiable than the ones that came to supplant them—that industrialization had been carried out "according to Lenin's precepts"; that collectivization was nothing but an application of Lenin's "cooperative
plan"; even that the Soviet state precisely matched the state Lenin
had planned.[15] The edifying image of an absolutely linear Soviet history, seen as a systematic and coherent implementation of a plan
designed in advance by Lenin for the "building of socialism,"
emerged so enhanced as to appear unquestionable. If the facts did not
support the image, the facts had to go.

This tendency was bound to be strengthened after the removal of
Khrushchev, Stalin's most persistent critic among Soviet leaders,
and in time the 1956 *postanovleniie*, though it remained a fixed
point of reference, would no longer do in its current form. It had to
be elaborated and made more explicit. The great anniversaries that
came round in due course served this purpose well. In 1967 the
fiftieth anniversary of the revolution and in 1970 the centenary of
Lenin's birth were celebrated with particular solemnity. On these
occasions the official version of history was condensed into a pair
of documents: a set of "theses" published in the name of the
party's Central Committee, and two speeches by Leonid Brezhnev

14. *The Short Biography of Stalin* (Moscow, 1949).
15. "50 let Velikoi Oktiabr'skoi Sotsialisticheskoi Revoliutsii: Tezisy Tsentral'nogo Komiteta Kpss," *Kommunist*, no. 10, 1967, p. 10; "K 100-letiiu so dnia
rozhdeniia Vladimira Il'icha Lenina: Tezisy Tsentral'nogo Komiteta Kommunisticheskoi partii Sovetskogo Soiuza," *Kommunist*, no. 1, 1970, pp. 13–15, 17–18;
Vladimir Il'ich Lenin: Biografiia (Moscow, 1960), pp. xi–xii. In this diligent revision
of history we once again find an alleged "science of victory" evoked, except that
this time it is attributed not to Stalin, as it was earlier, but to Lenin. See *Kommunist*, no. 18, 1979, p. 43. To be sure, Lenin was also credited with the accomplishments of other Bolshevik leaders, such as Trotsky, who meanwhile had been erased
from the pages of history. Brezhnev claimed, for example, that "Lenin directed the
defense of the Soviet Republic, and the formation of the Red Army": Leonid
Brezhnev, *On the Policy of the Soviet Union and the International Situation* (Garden City, N.Y., 1973), 2:17.

before the highest institutional bodies of the state. These texts were obviously invested with the celebratory tone of events designed as occasions for an apotheosis of the motherland's history. As such, all of them could be relegated to the archives along with other occasional utterances that call for no special mention. Yet they too survived for a long time as essential elements of an official interpretation of the problems that interest us here, and were quoted every time the authority of an unimpeachable source was called for. In short, the occasion for a celebration was deliberately chosen as a suitable cue to launch a more exacting ideological operation.

These documents always referred to the critique of the "cult of personality" as a party operation; it had been finished once and for all, and nothing further was needed. But some clarifications were nevertheless appended.

> The Communist Party of the Soviet Union has clearly condemned the cult of personality for its abuses of power, violations of socialist democratic principles, and revolutionary legality. The party has also condemned the subjectivism that ignores the laws of social development and the opinion of collective organs and replaces scientific guidelines with willful decisions. . . . The party has repulsed all efforts to turn its critique of the cult of personality and subjectivism against socialism and the people's interests, to belittle the building of socialism and its history, to discredit the revolution's achievements and revise the principles of Marxism-Leninism.[16]

This passage is so well coded that it needs deciphering. "Cult of personality" still means Stalin's way of doing things. "Subjectivism" is Khrushchev's behavior; his critique of Stalin, whenever it jumped the tracks of official sanction, was thus tacitly included among the excesses or "unjustified improvisations" of a person who did not heed the "opinion of collective organs."[17] As for the attempts to "belittle history," they included everything that diverged from the interpretation being canonized at that moment.

The entire Soviet experience from 1917 on was presented as a "triumph of Leninism," or of "Marxism-Leninism," as the application of a "Leninist plan for the building of socialism," described as "the model for a scientific, complex, and realistic approach to tasks

16. "K 100-letiyu," *Kommunist*, no. 1, 1970, p. 16.
17. Brezhnev, *On the Policy of the Soviet Union*, 2:41.

of world-historical importance."[18] The "total and final victory of socialism is the principal result" of this process.[19] According to Brezhnev:

> Everywhere and always, in times of stern trial and fierce battle, in times of joyous victories and grievous setbacks, our people have remained loyal to the Leninist banner, loyal to their party and to the cause of the revolution. On this momentous day, comrades, we can say that we have some achievements to report in honoring Lenin's memory. For the first time in the history of world civilization, socialism has scored a full and final victory, a developed socialist society has been built, and the conditions have been created for the successful construction of communism.[20]

To this pronouncement the "theses" on Lenin add:

> The Communist Party and the Soviet people, following Lenin's mandate, have come through a difficult and glorious voyage. The socialism whose inevitable victory was demonstrated by the founders of scientific socialism and whose building was begun under Lenin's guidance has become reality in the Soviet Union.[21]

Here we find spelled out for the first time the concept of "real socialism" which in years to come was to serve the Soviets as a systematic response to all critics unwilling to recognize the Soviet Union as the fulfillment of their own socialist ideals. As the quotations show, the concept implied two proud claims: (1) the only real socialism that exists is in the USSR and neighboring countries, and everything else is only wishful thinking; (2) it is also the only socialism that is in keeping with the doctrinal premises of Marx and of Lenin, the genuine socialism that has "shown the whole world the way towards resolution of the cardinal contradictions of our time."[22]

And the Stalin years? They had their drawbacks—that much was still admitted. But "despite their seriousness, those distortions never changed the nature of socialist society, never undermined socialism's precepts. The party and the people earnestly believed in the communist cause, worked with enthusiasm to realize Lenin's

18. Leonid Brezhnev, *Leninskim kursom* (Moscow, 1973), 2:83, and *On the Policy of the Soviet Union*, p. 22; "K 100-letiyu," *Kommunist*, no. 1, 1970, pp. 11–12.
19. "50 let," *Kommunist*, no. 10, 1967, p. 17.
20. Brezhnev, *On the Policy of the Soviet Union*, p. 26.
21. "K 100-letiyu," *Kommunist*, no. 1, 1970, p. 13.
22. "50 let," *Kommunist*, no. 10, 1967, pp. 18–19.

ideals, overcame difficulties, failures, and transitory errors."[23] In a nutshell, Brezhnev was suggesting that with the wisdom of hindsight one could say that some things might have been done better; but this was a new and difficult experience. In any case, the "errors" had no effect on the consistency of Soviet development. The state had always remained what it was when "The October Revolution created it."[24]

Upheavals, conflicts, successive crises disappear in this description, giving way to a sort of scientific demonstration of "Lenin's principles for the organization of the economy."[25] In fact, Lenin had had very little time and few means to conceive and formulate any such principles. "The New Economic Policy, industrialization, collectivization, the cultural revolution" are all presented not as conflicting episodes in a journey filled with controversy but as logically connected phases of an upward march, "the ABC of scientific communism." In the 1930s (that is, during the years when Stalinism emerged amid violent clashes with the peasantry and mass repressions against the Bolshevik party itself) "socialism became firmly established in every sphere of life in our country." With the 1936 Constitution (which in reality had hardly been approved before it was discarded) "the political superstructure was also brought into line with the economic base of socialism."[26]

With premises such as these, no one can wonder at the conclusion that Stalinism as a phenomenon in its own right had never existed. And this is precisely what was asserted in 1979.

> Anti-Soviet centers abroad . . . continue to speculate on the errors, true or presumed, and on the abuses of power that took place at one time under Stalin. Attempts are made to invent a so-called Stalinism as a particular system of theoretical and political concepts and of sociopolitical praxis. Under the pretext of criticizing Stalin and "Stalinism," nonsense is piled on top of calumny concerning the building of socialism; "arguments" are put forth to belittle the Soviet Union's decisive contribution to the victorious outcome of the Great Patriotic War; doubts are thrown on the victory of socialism and the successes achieved in the building of socialism in the USSR. . . . A few

23. Ibid., p. 17.
24. Brezhnev, *Leninskim kursom*, 2:84–85, 95.
25. "K 100-letiyu," *Kommunist*, no. 1, 1970, p. 18.
26. Brezhnev, *On the Policy of the Soviet Union*, pp. 23, 24; "50 let," *Kommunist*, no. 10, 1967, p. 12.

right-wing revisionists go so far in their slander as to deny that our party is communist and that the Soviet state is socialist. . . .

Stalin introduced nothing to the Marxist-Leninist doctrine that was not basically in accord with its fundamental theses. . . . This means that it is impossible to speak of any "Stalinism" as a current of thought either inherent in Marxist-Leninist doctrine or outside of it. The cult of personality arose as a consequence of well-known historical circumstances and of Stalin's own personal character; for this reason alone it cannot be viewed as a phenomenon that issued logically from communist ideology, which always inspired the party in everything it did, or even as in any way connected to it. . . .

A concrete analysis of the various stages of that difficult and complex period known as the building of socialism in the USSR and of the world-historical processes that coincided with it provides no basis for the hostile or naively ignorant fabrications that have Stalin's activity "distorting" society's development or drawing the party away from Marxism-Leninism toward a "Stalinism" that never existed. The attempt to isolate a "cult of personality period" as a "special" stage in the history of Soviet society is intended to cloud the scientifically objective image of the coming of the new regime.[27]

The straight line of Soviet history leading directly from the revolution to the establishment of the only "real socialism" was often disputed in the communist movement and in Marxist circles long before Gorbachev. Presently I shall analyze the main lines of interpretation this critique has produced. I must mention at once, however, the best known of these interpretations, if not the most intellectually rigorous, which was widely circulated in Maoist China. It seems that at some moment the Soviet Union had become the scene of a "capitalist restoration." This notion never went beyond purely political polemics and so was tossed about in all the factional skirmishes that were going on in China at the time, not to mention the power struggle between Moscow and Beijing. But what matters here is that, contrary to widespread belief on the extreme left in Europe in the 1960s and 1970s, the Chinese never used "Stalinism" as an argument. If indeed there had been a break in Soviet history, according to Maoist thinking, it came after Stalin's death, not before.

There is no need here to quote Mao and other Chinese writers on individual actions or statements by Stalin the "theoretician" or

27. *Kommunist*, no. 18, 1970, pp. 38–42.

Stalin the politician.[28] These opinions, mainly on specific aspects of Stalin's activity, never altered the Chinese communist leadership's overall appraisal of Soviet history as the first "historic manifestation of a dictatorship of the proletariat." This judgment, formulated rather early in general outline, was not substantially altered until the late 1970s—except, I repeat, for matters having to do with the post-Stalin era. Only on this more recent period did it differ substantially from the Soviet position.

But the Soviet and Chinese interpretations were never in complete accord even on the Stalin years, though the differences were a matter more of nuance than of substance. Under Mao the Chinese said repeatedly that Stalin had committed "grave errors," but the errors they were referring to were not always the ones the Soviets criticized under Khrushchev; and they attributed them not to Stalin alone but to "all those comrades who committed similar errors under his influence." In the Chinese version the phenomenon thus tended to lose that intensely personal character it acquired in the Soviet approach. The Chinese distinguished two "aspects" of Soviet history from the revolution to Stalin's death: a "primary" one, which was the "more important" of the two and had "a universal quality," and a "secondary" one. The first consisted of the "successful building of a socialist society"; it "transformed scientific socialism from theory and ideal into living reality," thus raising the "first paean of victory of Marxism-Leninism in human history." The second aspect consisted of the errors; it was contingent on the fact that "no system, however excellent, is in itself a guarantee against serious errors committed in the performance of our task," because everything in the world is judged by the way it is used.[29]

With more logic than the Soviets, the Maoist Chinese made no distinction between Stalin the man and some abstract "party" that supposedly always acted correctly, even under his rule. All in all, Stalin too had performed well. For them, in fact, Stalin was the

---

28. Mao Tsetung, "Concerning Economic Problems of Socialism in the USSR" and "Critique of Stalin's Economic Problems of Socialism in the USSR," in his *Critique of Soviet Economics* (New York and London, 1977), pp. 129–47. See also Mao Tsetung, *Discorsi inediti* (Milan, 1975) and *Rivoluzione e costruzione: Scritti e discorsi, 1949–1957* (Turin, 1979).

29. *More on the Historical Experience of the Dictatorship of the Proletariat* (Peking, 1957), pp. 21, 8, 10–11, 17.

man who "for almost thirty years after Lenin's death" had managed the building of socialism, had led the industrialization and collectivization drives, had achieved huge successes while always remaining "a great Marxist-Leninist." Therefore, in his case as in all others, what counted were his merits; the errors were of secondary importance.[30] It was he who had continued Lenin's work. His adversaries, the "Trotskyites, Zinov'ievites, Bukharinists and other bourgeois agents," had all been "enemies of Leninism."[31] In other words, the Chinese not only argued that the "errors" had "their origin in the socialist system"; they also rejected the idea that under Stalin the state, engaged as it was in shaping the economy, had "become a bureaucratic machine," and that bureaucratization had had unfortunate consequences.[32] They also chided Khrushchev for having spoken of the "cult of personality period" as a specific phase of Soviet history during which "the social system, ideology, and morality . . . had not been socialist."[33]

In 1956 the Chinese took a position they were not to abandon for a long time to come:

> When one examines the subject as a whole, even if one must speak of "Stalinism," this must mean first of all communism and Marxism-Leninism, which are its principal features; only secondarily does it contain a few extremely serious errors that must be fully corrected.[34]

But later things changed:

> After Stalin's death, Khrushchev's revisionist clique usurped the leadership of the party and the state, transformed the dictatorship of the proletariat into a dictatorship of the bourgeoisie, and began to restore capitalism in the Soviet Union, the first socialist country. This is the most important lesson in the history of the world proletariat.[35]

---

30. Ibid., pp. 20–21; "On the Question of Stalin," *Peking Review*, 20 September 1963, pp. 9–10.

31. *Peking Review*, 20 September 1963; "Reference Material for *A Great Historical Document*," *Notebooks of the Orient Editions*, no. 8, 1967, p. 12. This text, which dates back to the days of the "cultural revolution," declares also that these "enemies" had "insinuated themselves into the party." The same claim was made against those Chinese communist leaders whom the Maoist offensive was attempting to annihilate and who were rehabilitated with great fanfare after Mao's death.

32. *More on the Historical Experience*, p. 16.

33. *Peking Review*, 20 September 1963, p. 14.

34. *More on the Historical Experience*, pp. 20–21.

35. "Reference Material," p. 15.

This declaration seems to have been motivated solely by a desire to provide ideological ammunition in the no-holds-barred struggle that by then had begun between the communists of the two countries. In the process the invectives grew more and more savage on both sides. At times the Chinese leadership called the Soviet Union a "fascist dictatorship" that had swept "new tsars" to power.[36] The intent to defame and the political origins of such accusations were always clear, since they were never supported by any objective analysis of Soviet society that might have provided a basis in fact. The hiatus that the Chinese injected into Soviet history at the moment of Stalin's death, with no supporting evidence, appears to have had the same intent.

Only now and then in Mao's China was there an inclination to scrutinize Stalin's USSR for some antecedents to the subsequent capitalist "restoration." These antecedents were then sought in still another "error" committed by Stalin, who supposedly was unaware of the class struggle that went on "throughout the period of the dictatorship of the proletariat," thus permitting the resurgence of "bourgeois ideology."[37] But this assertion seems to betray little knowledge of Stalin, for in fact he often supported the idea of a continuing and even "intensifying" class struggle, and used it to justify his mass repressions.[38] The Chinese abandoned all these ideas, by the way, when they faced a similar problem and had to reassess their own past. Mao's passage from the scene goaded them to begin to rethink the history of the preceding decades, their own and others'.[39]

36. Lin Biao, "Report to the IX Congress of the Chinese Communist Party," 28 April 1969, and Zhou Enlai, "Report to the X Congress of the Chinese Communist Party," 3 September 1973, both reported by Hsinhua News Agency.

37. "Reference Material," pp. 13–14.

38. Class struggle was bound to intensify as society advanced toward socialism, or so went the "theory" Stalin created and repeatedly invoked to justify some of his government's most despotic measures. The first hints came in 1929, during his struggle against Bukharin and the "right." See I. V. Stalin, *Sochineniia* (Moscow, 1947), 12:32–33. Stalin developed it in its final form in 1933 (ibid., 13:207–12) and in 1937 during the mass repressions against the party (ibid. [Stanford, 1967], 1[14]:213–14). This theory was also invoked several times by the most authoritative organs of the press (*Pravda* among them) during the last weeks of his life, in that ominous and confusing month of February 1953. Finally, it became one of the best-defined targets of the anti-Stalin criticism from 1956 on. See *Khrushchev Remembers*, pp. 283–84; *Spravochnik partiinogo rabotnika* (1957), pp. 328–29.

39. For examples of these reflections on China's own cult of personality, see Shi

So much for the Chinese. Coming back to the Soviets and the
rest of the communist movement, I must point out that the "cult
of personality" formula, euphemistic though it was, had its interesting points, particularly if we consider its tempestuous political
origin. It focused attention on some of the elements of Stalinism:
the strong ideological charge, for example, which gave it an almost
religious aura; and the marked personal imprint Stalin the man left
on it, forcing Marxists to rethink the thorny question of "the role
of personality in history." On the other hand, the formula revealed
its inconsistency when it claimed to be the key to the interpretation of an entire historical phenomenon. On that score the Chinese
leadership was not alone among Marxist and other leftist circles in
challenging it. A sort of choral consensus against such an explanation of the past arose outside the USSR. The most reasoned critiques came from the Marxist culture, which felt deeply at odds
with an interpretation of that sort.

Palmiro Togliatti was among its first critics. It made no sense to
consider the "cult" a cause of historical processes that in his eyes
had defects of their own. To place all the blame on the "personal
shortcomings" of one man, and he the man whose superhuman
virtues had once been exalted, was to remain within the frame of
the "cult." "We have strayed from the good judgment that is characteristic of Marxism," Togliatti said. Thus one lost sight of the
real problem: to understand how and why those "errors" the Soviets themselves had once denounced in such somber tones could
have occurred. The solution dreamed up by the Soviet ideologues
consisted, as we have seen, in transforming Stalinism, or at least
all the phenomena that were coming to huddle under this umbrella
term, into one simple incident along a course that had always been
on the whole correct and in many respects even exemplary. Their
position was that "the facts under critical scrutiny had had a very
small impact on social life as a whole." And Togliatti commented:
"To say this, however, is not enough. One must also prove it." He
continued to believe that the "substance of the socialist regime
had not been lost" in the USSR. But he added: "A very deep breach
has come to light between the nature of a revolutionary regime,

---

Zhongquan and Yang Zenghe, "La pensée-maozedong vue par Zhou Enlai" and "La
pensée-maozedong: Evolution du terme au cours des 40 dernières années," *Beijing
Information*, no. 9 (2 March), 1981.

historically and socially well defined, and governing methods repugnant to that nature. This cannot be denied; it has to be admitted."[40]

In some respects a later critique by Louis Althusser was similar to Togliatti's; inasmuch as "it claimed to explain what in fact it did not explain," the cult of personality was a "pseudo-concept [that] could only mislead those it was supposed to instruct." It was

> a way of seeking the causes of grave events and of their forms in certain defects of the functioning of the legal superstructure . . . without looking into the whole of the State Apparatus constituting the Superstructure . . . and above all without getting to the root of the problem (one which was so serious and lasted so long): the contradictions of the construction of socialism and of its line, that is, without dealing with the existing forms of production relations, class relations and the class struggle.[41]

At this point Althusser countered the official Soviet explanation by introducing the concept of a "Stalinian deviation"—deviation from the revolutionary thought of Marx and Lenin, which was centered in the USSR and which presumably spread throughout the communist movement of the Third International in the 1930s. This deviation had gone in the direction of "economism" (enthusiasm for production forces outside of real production relations) cloaked in "humanism"—a marriage that is the essence, Althusser says, of all the social ideas of the bourgeoisie. The French philosopher then bowed to the spirit of the times in which he wrote, indicating that the only *real* critique of the "Stalinian deviation" was the one the Chinese carried into action in the "proletarian cultural revolution."[42] As we have seen, this position finds little support in the actual events of China's internal struggles and in the political thinking that accompanied them. Precious few Chinese, either under Mao or later, would have subscribed to it.

40. Palmiro Togliatti, *Problemi del movimento operaio internazionale, 1956–61* (Rome, 1962), pp. 162, 108.
41. Louis Althusser, *Essays in Self-criticism* (London, 1976), pp. 80–81, 85, 92.
42. Ibid., pp. 85, 92.

3 The Continuity Theory

The about-face executed by the Soviet world when it reversed the official history it had promoted for decades and declared that what had been pluses were now minuses, though the contents remained intact, only seems to be a paradox. The apologia and its reversal, contrary in their judgments but alike in their methods, are in fact linked by their strongly ideological approach. Instead of reconstructing the evolution of the Soviet Union by searching for its innermost dialectic, each promotes or implies wholesale acceptance or wholesale rejection of the Soviet experience from 1917 on. The ends are diametrically opposed, but the approaches are identical. It is not very surprising, then, to find the most systematic adversaries of the Soviet regime, inside and outside the country, interpreting the experience in a way that at many points coincides with the approach taken by the Moscow ideologues, though the coloring differs.

The similarities are especially apparent among the most radical of the intellectuals long known as Soviet dissenters, particularly among the émigrés. Consider the idea put forward by the most eminent of the émigrés, Aleksandr Solzhenitsyn:

We may justifiably wonder whether "Stalinism" is in fact a distinctive phenomenon. *Did it ever exist?* Stalin himself never tried to

establish any distinctive doctrine (and given his intellectual limitations he could never have created one), nor any distinctive political
system of his own. All Stalin's present-day admirers, champions and
professional mourners in our own country, as well as his followers in
China, adamantly insist that he was a faithful Leninist and never in
any matter of consequence diverged from Lenin. The author of these
lines, who in his day landed in jail precisely because of his hatred of
Stalin, whom he reproached with his departure from Lenin, must
now admit that he cannot find, point to, or prove any substantial
deviations. . . . "Stalinism" is a very convenient concept for those
"purified" Marxist circles of ours, who strive to differentiate themselves from the official line, though in reality the difference is negligible. (Roy Medvedev may be mentioned as a typical example of this
trend.) For the same purpose the concept of "Stalinism" is still more
important and necessary to Western Communist parties—they shift
onto it the whole bloody burden of the past to make their present
position easier. (In this category belong such Communist theorists as
G. Lukacs and I. Deutscher.) It is no less necessary to those broad
Left-liberal circles in the West which in Stalin's lifetime applauded
highly colored pictures of Soviet life, and after the Twentieth Congress found themselves looking most painfully silly.

But close study of our modern history shows that *there never was
any such thing as Stalinism* (either as a doctrine, or as a path of
national life, or as a state system), and official circles in our country,
as well as the Chinese leaders, have every right to insist on this.
Stalin was a very consistent and faithful—if also very untalented—
heir to the *spirit* of Lenin's teaching.[1]

Solzhenitsyn's personal evolution as he describes it here is common to several critics of the USSR, both within Soviet society and
in the communist movement: in their disenchantment they re-
thought their positions and values and extended their rejection of
Stalin to Lenin, and usually to Marx himself.[2] Of them all, Sol-

---

1. Aleksandr Solzhenitsyn, "Na vozvrate dyshaniia i soznaniia," in *Iz pod glyb:
Sbornik statei* (Paris, 1974), pp. 14–15; published in English as "As Breathing and
Consciousness Return," in *From under the Rubble*, trans. A. M. Brock et al. (Bos-
ton, 1975), pp. 10–12 (emphasis in original). See also Solzhenitsyn, *A World Split
Apart: Commencement Address Delivered at Harvard University on 8 June 1978*
(New York, 1978).

2. James Burnham, "Lenin's Heir," *Partisan Review*, Winter 1945, p. 70, where
we read that "under Stalin the communist revolution has been, not betrayed, but
fulfilled." For an extension of the critique of Marxism as a whole, see Leszek Kolakowski, "Marxist Roots of Stalinism," in *Stalinism: Essays in Historical Interpretation*, ed. Robert Tucker (New York, 1977), pp. 283–98, and "Marxism: A Sum-
ming-Up," *Survey* 23 (Summer 1977–1978): 165–71. Far from being a recent
phenomenon, this tendency can be found practically throughout the Soviet experi-

zhenitsyn has pushed his indictment the furthest. For him Marxism and communism and the "weakening . . . of the whole of Western civilization" stem from "a historical, psychological and moral crisis that affected the culture and world outlook which were conceived at the time of the Renaissance and attained the peak of their expression with the eighteenth-century Enlightenment."[3]

For a long time quite a different mechanism led Anglo-American historians to conclusions similar to Solzhenitsyn's, if less radical and more sophisticated. This vein of historical research achieved academic respectability mostly in the United States after World War II. The circumstances that surrounded its birth necessarily influenced its way of looking at things. First of all, those were the years of the Cold War, characterized in America by intense hostility toward the USSR; second, those were also the years of triumphant Stalinism in the Soviet Union, with all those dismal events that could easily seem to an outside observer to be the only noteworthy result of the country's entire revolutionary experience. Soviet studies in the United States, and to a lesser extent Great Britain as well, therefore began as a more or less conscious, more or less scientific weapon in a political struggle.[4] In fact, they owed a good part of their growth and of their technical and financial resources to precisely this circumstance.

Three other factors greatly influenced the tone of Soviet studies. In the first place, given the scarcity of home-bred specialists, their development depended largely on old Russian émigrés and a scattering of former communists. Second, at least in the early years, the pool of available documentation was sparse and tended to be biased even in the United States, where quite early on specialized

---

ence. Trotsky used it in his polemics as far back as the 1930s: *Biulleten' Oppozitsii*, nos. 58–59, pp. 6–7. On the general political and cultural attitudes of many former communists, we find useful opinions in Isaac Deutscher, "The Ex-Communist's Conscience," in his *Heretics and Renegades and Other Essays* (Indianapolis, 1969), pp. 9–22. See also Isaac Deutscher, *The Prophet Outcast: Trotsky, 1929–1940* (London, 1963), p. 467.

3. Aleksandr I. Solzhenitsyn, *Letter to the Soviet Leaders*, trans. Hilary Sternberg (New York, 1974), pp. 8–9. See also Solzhenitsyn, *A World Split Apart*.

4. The review *Soviet Studies* was an exception. It was started in the United Kingdom in June 1949 by Jack Miller and Rudolf Schlesinger under the auspices of the Department for the Study of the Social and Economic Institutions of the USSR, University of Glasgow.

centers got busy making indispensable source material available. The third factor was a general lack of interest in the inner workings and problems of the communist movement, which was seen (particularly during the McCarthy era) more as a malignant tumor to be excised than as a political phenomenon with its own historical legitimacy. Together these factors promoted uncritical acceptance of a whole series of value judgments set forth in Stalin-related studies. That body of work was criticized as a whole, but its assessments of many individual phases and phenomena in the Soviet experience were tacitly accepted. The pronounced ability of what can only be called Stalinist "culture" to influence American scholarship was later noticed, not without astonishment, by American scholars themselves.[5]

To point out these characteristics of that vast body of work is not to deny the value of what is best in it. On the contrary, many of those works had undeniable value as pioneer ventures at the time and are still of special interest today, though parts of them can be debated in light of our new knowledge. If we keep in mind the circumstances in which these works appeared, we can better understand how and why Westerners, too, came to see Soviet history as an uninterrupted continuum from the revolution on, through Lenin and Stalin and Stalin's successors. This line of thought enjoyed a monopoly for a long time and is still prevalent. Stalinism, it is claimed, along with the remnants of it that survive today, was implicit in bolshevism, or "Leninism," from the very beginning, and thus appears to be a logical or even inevitable consequence of its political agenda and its theoretical and organizational concepts. Essentially, then, Stalinism and Leninism are one and the same. This, at least, is the idea in a nutshell, despite any differences in nuance that may be recognizable between the two. In any case, Stalin and his way of governing turn out to be the only possible—indeed, the only legitimate—development of the October Revolution, which is seen as a sort of original sin from which everything else was fatally destined to follow.

We get glimpses of this view of Soviet history in excerpts from an academic debate that took place in 1954. Thomas Hammond, referring to the end of the nineteenth century: "The attitude ex-

---

5. Robert Tucker, Introduction and "Stalinism as Revolution from Above," in *Stalinism*, pp. xii, 77; Stephen F. Cohen, "Bolshevism and Stalinism," in ibid., p. 14.

pressed by Lenin in those days provides a good preview of the authoritarianism which was to carry over into the post-revolutionary period and impose its mark on so many areas of Soviet society. An examination of these Leninist attitudes should also show that although Soviet authoritarianism attained its most extreme form under Stalin, the foundation for it had been laid much earlier by Lenin." Adam Ulam: "Where was the original political force which propelled Stalin into such a commanding administrative position? The answer must be found, first, in the character and historical tendency of the Bolshevik party even before Lenin's death." Merle Fainsod sums up the discussion: "Both Hammond and Ulam tell us, and I gladly agree, that although Soviet totalitarianism attained its most extreme form under Stalin, the foundation for it was laid much earlier by Lenin."[6]

Hammond, Ulam, and Fainsod are among the most serious and authoritative of scholars. In other writings political bias is more evident, expressed in pamphleteering tones. At the beginning of the 1950s Waldemar Gurian too wrote that "despite all changes, the Soviet regime had maintained a fundamental continuity from Lenin to Stalin." He added: "The Leninist political religion had created and justified the totalitarian state . . . and this totalitarian state had developed from a means to an end in the present era." In sum: "Totalitarian control, beginning with the October revolution, was perfected and completed under Stalin."[7]

This approach was not limited to one time period or to one area of research, as we can see if we check works written by the same scholars at other times, and works by other scholars. Fainsod, for example, maintains in his major work that totalitarianism "was implicit in the doctrinal, organizational and tactical premises on which the structure of bolshevism was built"; and if we look at a later and more lapidary statement accepted by numerous other writers we find: "Basically, Soviet totalitarianism emerged full-blown during the great transformation of Soviet society."[8] Ulam,

6. Thomas Hammond, "Leninist Authoritarianism before the Revolution"; Adam Ulam, "Stalin and the Theory of Totalitarianism"; and Merle Fainsod, "Review," all in *Continuity and Change in Russian and Soviet Thought*, ed. Ernest J. Simmons (Cambridge, Mass., 1955), pp. 145, 160, 175.

7. Waldemar Gurian, *Bolshevism: An Introduction to Soviet Communism* (Notre Dame, Ind., 1952), pp. 3, 53, 72.

8. Merle Fainsod, *How Russia Is Ruled*, rev. ed. (Cambridge, Mass., 1963), pp.

for his part, asserts elsewhere that "[Lenin's] own psychology made inevitable the future and more brutal development under his successor." Even elements as typical of Stalin's Russia as the "cult of personality" and "mass terror and repression find partial explanation in the events and moods of Lenin's leadership of the Communist Party."[9]

But the level of near-dogmatism reached by such interpretations can best be seen in the words of numerous other writers; Anglo-American literature on the subject is full of such statements as Robert Daniels's: "Stalin's victory, in the last analysis, was not a personal one, but the triumph of a symbol, of the individual who embodied both the precepts of Leninism and the techniques of their enforcement."[10] Alfred Meyer: "Stalinism can and must be defined as a pattern of thought and action that flows directly from Leninism. . . . The kinds of decisions made by Stalin and the manner in which they were made and executed were prepared by Lenin."[11] John Reshetar finds that the differences between Leninism and Stalinism, "significant though they may be, are eclipsed by the Leninist heritage to Stalin. . . . Lenin provided the basic assumptions that, applied by Stalin and developed to their logical conclusion, culminated in the great purges."[12] Donald Treadgold blames the Bolsheviks in general and Stalin's opponents in particular for their inability to "bring themselves [either] to admit [or] to deny fully that the regime of Stalin and the casualties of the 'Second Revolution' were logical consequences of the single-party oligarchy . . . which was attempting to create socialism in a deeply anti-socialist country."[13] And finally for Zbigniew Brzezinski, who

---

31, 59. Fainsod's statement (the first edition of this work dates back to 1953) is picked up virtually verbatim by John Armstrong, *The Politics of Totalitarianism: The Communist Party of the Soviet Union from 1934 to the Present* (New York, 1961), pp. ix–x, and by Zbigniew Brzezinski, "Disfunctional Totalitarianism," in *Theory and Politics: Festschrift zum 70 Geburtstag für Carl Joachim Friedrich*, comp. Klaus von Beyme (The Hague, 1971), p. 377.

9. Adam Ulam, *The Bolsheviks: The Intellectual and Political History of the Triumph of Communism in Russia* (New York, 1973), p. 477.

10. Robert Daniels, *The Conscience of the Revolution: Communist Opposition in Soviet Russia* (Cambridge, Mass., 1960), p. 403.

11. Alfred Meyer, *Leninism* (Cambridge, Mass., 1957), pp. 282–83.

12. John Reshetar, Jr., *A Concise History of the Communist Party of the Soviet Union* (New York, 1964), pp. 217–19.

13. Donald Treadgold, *Twentieth Century Russia* (Chicago, 1972), p. 276.

had been a student of the USSR before he became famous as President Carter's chief foreign policy adviser, the transformation performed by Stalin had simply "helped to reinforce the totalitarian dynamics of the political system itself."[14]

The frequency with which the term "totalitarianism" recurs in these fragments requires a brief comment. In the quotations I have chosen it is practically a synonym for "Stalinism." The totalitarian interpretation of Soviet history and society is the most important contribution of the American school to the analysis of the problem that concerns us here. As such it has certain original characteristics that I cannot examine at this point. It deserves separate treatment and I shall address it in one of the chapters to come. Here I shall merely point out how quickly this school espoused the idea of an ironbound continuity in Soviet revolutionary development, thus contributing to the dominance of this idea in Anglo-American scholarship and, through its influence, in the West at large.[15]

American scholars themselves acknowledge this tendency and often are critical of it. At another scientific meeting in 1967, Hannah Arendt, a theoretician of totalitarianism, observed that everybody there "believed in an unbroken continuity of Soviet Russian history from 1917 until Stalin's death," and identified this conviction as "the mainstream of Western thought."[16] In *The American Historical Review* another writer complained that "the acceptance of the thesis that Lenin's actions and policies led directly to those of Stalin has caused many scholars in the West to assume that the problem of the historical roots of Stalinism has been solved and no longer requires serious analysis."[17] Robert Tucker is of the same opinion. He points out that Western historians waited quite a long time before they confronted the problem

14. Brzezinski, "Disfunctional Totalitarianism," p. 377.

15. See, for instance, Maximilian Rubel, "The Relationship of Bolshevism to Marxism," in *Revolutionary Russia*, ed. Richard Pipes (Cambridge, Mass., 1968), pp. 316–17.

16. Hannah Arendt, Comment on Adam Ulam, "The Uses of Revolution," in Pipes, *Revolutionary Russia*, p. 345. Concerning the ambivalence of the continuity theory, in the same essay Arendt wrote: "In other words, those who were more or less on the side of Lenin's revolution also justified Stalin, whereas those who were denouncing Stalin's rule were sure that Lenin was not only responsible for Stalin's totalitarianism but actually belonged in the same category, that Stalin was a necessary consequence of Lenin."

17. Robert Slusser, "A Soviet Historian Evaluates Stalin's Role in History," *American Historical Review* 77 (December 1972): 1393.

of Stalinism as a phenomenon in its own right.[18] The comfortable assumption that the origins of Stalinism were fully known explains why Western historians resisted the first and most interesting attempts by some Soviet dissenters to treat the Stalinist phenomenon separately and to challenge the idea that it flowed directly from the revolution and from Lenin.[19]

Neglect of the problem of Stalinism was not the only consequence of the continuity theory. It also conditioned and partly determined opinions on all phases of Soviet history. War communism, for example, is seen as nothing but an attempt—premature, perhaps, but logical and intentional—to carry out the Bolsheviks' programs and achieve their aims, an "effort to put utopian dreams into practice."[20] In other words, a sort of Stalinism in advance. In the light of available documentation, such an assessment seems much too simplistic. The final harsh conflict between Stalin and Lenin in 1922–1923 is reduced to a marginal episode caused mainly by Lenin's terminal illness.[21] The NEP suffers most from this way of seeing things. It becomes merely an atypical moment in the Soviet experience, a clever way to *reculer pour mieux sauter*, a "tactical maneuver" while one waited for better times, for conditions favorable to a resumption of the old program. It is strange that in all these instances we find substantial conformity with the old Stalinist history, despite the vast amount of proof to the contrary accumulated since then.[22] Even a careful student of Soviet

18. Tucker, "Stalinism as Revolution from Above," p. 77. See also Cohen, "Bolshevism and Stalinism," p. 24.

19. Roy A. Medvedev, *Let History Judge: The Origins and Consequences of Stalinism* (New York, 1971). For the reservations with which this work was received, see the reviews by Leonard Schapiro in *Sunday Times*, 26 March 1972, and by Merle Fainsod in *Book Week*, 2 January 1972.

20. Treadgold, *Twentieth Century Russia*, p. 165; Fainsod, *How Russia Is Ruled*, p. 93; Gurian, *Bolshevism*, p. 43; Reshetar, *Concise History*, pp. 178–79.

21. Adam Ulam, *Stalin: The Man and His Era* (New York, 1973), pp. 215–20; Treadgold, *Twentieth Century Russia*, p. 214. Treadgold also revives the legend, borrowed directly from Stalin, that "Stalin never embroiled himself in a conflict with [Lenin] either on principles or tactics."

22. Treadgold, *Twentieth Century Russia*, pp. 196, 199. Treadgold goes so far as to write: "It is difficult to find a parallel for a regime or a party which held power for ten years, biding its time, until it felt strong enough to fulfill its original program" (p. 258). This view of the first period of Soviet history, up to the early 1930s, does not match reality. Its only support comes from the version promoted by the Soviet historiography of the Stalin era, which had this to say about the NEP: "War Communism was an attempt to launch a frontal assault against the fortress of capitalist elements in the cities and the countryside. In that offensive the party had moved so

agriculture considers collectivization to be an "inevitable consequence" of the Bolshevik victory in 1917.[23]

And finally, Stalinism itself is seen as something well defined
from the beginning and substantially unchanged later, rather than
as a phenomenon with an evolution and a history of its own. The
1930s, the era of its final victory, are seen as the climax of the
revolutionary adventure, the time when the Bolshevik system—
not just the Stalinist system—became mature and "full-blown."
This way of looking at a historical process must inevitably focus
on some of its aspects and neglect others: on government rather
than on society, on initiatives promoted by the leadership rather
than on the country's response, on official ideology perceived as
rigidly doctrinaire (even when it was not) rather than on the evolution of dominant ideas and their real influence on public life.[24]

Such a pronounced flattening of Soviet history generated a crisis
within this school of thought and aroused criticism against it. As
we shall see, an ever-growing number of works written from a variety of perspectives posed explicit challenges to the school's premises and conclusions.

The relationship between continuity and break, between conti-

---

far forward that it risked losing contact with its base. Now Lenin proposed to turn
back a little, to retreat temporarily, to switch from an assault on the fortress to a
more lengthy siege, so as to be able to attack again after regaining strength": *History of the Communist Party of the Soviet Union: Short Course* (New York, 1939),
p. 257. This interpretation of Lenin's thought, which falls far short of what Lenin
actually proposed, has not been entirely abandoned in later official versions. Along
with Lenin's own writings of that time, see Esfir' Genkina, *Gosudarstvennaia de-
iatel'nost' Lenina, 1921–23* (Moscow, 1969). Stalin was very much aware of having
profoundly altered Lenin's NEP policies. To counteract the sense of alarm his actions aroused, he felt it necessary to say as far back as June 1930, that the NEP,
which he had actually abandoned between 1928 and 1929, was still in effect, though
in a different form: I. V. Stalin, *Sochineniia* (Moscow, 1947), 12:306–8. For a
more detailed analysis of the demise of the NEP, see Giuseppe Boffa, *Storia
dell'Unione Sovietica* (Milan, 1976–1979), 1:378–79.

23. Naum Yasny, *The Socialized Agriculture of the USSR* (Stanford, 1945), p. 18.
Yasny was an émigré with a Menshevik past. This circumstance may serve as a
reminder of the influence the Menshevik émigrés had abroad. From the start they
criticized precisely those aspects of the Soviet regime which Stalin was later to
develop and push to their limit. The Menshevik point of view doubtless encouraged
people to see Lenin as a "premise and precondition for Stalin." The phrase is Vit-
torio Strada's in his introduction to Iulii Martov, *Bolscevismo mondiale: La prima
critica marxista del leninismo al potere* (Turin, 1980), p. ix.

24. See Gurian, *Bolshevism*, pp. 21–23. For Gurian, everything in Bolshevik ideology that is not "cynical power politics" must be "utopia."

nuity and change in the course of grand historical events, is well known to scholars as a most complex and controversial problem; it is a delicate one also because it is among the most sensitive to ideological choices. The relationship between bolshevism and Stalinism—or, as some prefer to say, between Lenin and Stalin, though the personalization is often inexact—certainly is one of the most important questions raised by the revolution and by later developments in the USSR. The problem is not new; because it has appeared in other revolutionary situations, past and present, and it has often provoked passionate debate. Though the subject matter and the players vary, the form does not. The example from the past that most readily comes to mind is the French revolution from 1789 to Napoleon's empire and the Restoration. In the present, the most obvious example is the Chinese revolution and the debates (among the Chinese and others) about its future fate. It is therefore all the more astonishing to note the uniformity of the answers supplied by Soviets and non-Soviets alike in their interpretations of the USSR and its history.

To justify the conclusion they reach, one of its keenest critics has observed, people invoke an ironclad determinism of the kind that many of them would regard with great skepticism if it were applied to other historical phenomena. Proof lies in the very terminology they usually employ: "logical," "inevitable," "fatal," "inexorable."[25] Even when they grant that Stalinism did indeed exist, people immediately point out that "germs" or "seeds" of it were already present in its historical antecedents—in the prerevolutionary and revolutionary Bolshevik experience and in Lenin's thought and actions. But this sort of argument, the critic will say, is hardly unique. The same thing can in fact be said of any historical phenomenon, since they all do have antecedents.[26] "Seeds" and "germs" of Stalinism can be found not only in bolshevism but also in populism, in the tsarist autocracy, in Western European progressive democratic thought, and in World War I, but no one claims that Stalinism must therefore be an inevitable consequence of any of them.

Elements of continuity between the Russian revolution and Stalinism are undeniable. This conclusion is so obvious that no one

25. Cohen, "Bolshevism and Stalinism," p. 14.
26. Ibid., pp. 11–12.

can want to question it, and therefore it is also likely to be very incomplete or very superficial. The problem is not to discard the idea but to see whether alongside these elements of continuity there may have been elements of discontinuity, and whether at some moment the latter may have gotten the upper hand and turned out to have more lasting consequences.

The weakest point in the theory of linear continuity in the Soviet experience lies in its inability to account for crucial events connected with the rise and evolution of the Stalinist phenomenon. At best it manages to single out one of their causes (perhaps not even the most important one) while neglecting everything else. I am not referring only to the dramatic clashes, including the one between the ailing Lenin and the rising Stalin, which split the old Russian bolshevism in the 1920s. The continuity school usually downgrades these clashes to personal "power struggles." But there were also changes of course, now correctly assessed by several scholars as crucial for Stalinism, such as Stalin's "revolution from above" from 1929 to 1932, including collectivization and the first five-year plan, and the Great Terror of 1936–1938, with its mass repressions unleashed primarily against the Bolshevik party.[27] After decades of undisputed dominance, the continuity school found itself in difficulty when an increasing abundance of documentation enabled historical research to advance our knowledge of those events.

Repercussions can now be noticed even among the school's supporters. With the slight simplification permissible in such cases, one can even hold that the better historians they are, the more tempted they are to discard or even contradict their underlying assumptions once they come face to face with certain developments in Soviet history. We find evidence of this change in many of the writers I have quoted. Although he considers Stalin to be an "incarnation of Lenin," Daniels is forced to wonder why and how, under the circumstances, "the forces of communist dissent managed to survive as long as they did in the USSR."[28] Meyer, another supporter of the theory, admits that "many non-Stalinist or anti-Stalinist

27. The expression "revolution from above" is of Stalinist origin and was codified in the official historiography. See *History of the Communist Party*, p. 305. The other expression is Robert Conquest's in *The Great Terror: Stalin's Purge of the Thirties* (London, 1968).

28. Daniels, *Conscience of the Revolution*, p. 398.

interpretations are derived from that same Leninism." And he also admits that Stalinism itself had not always been uniformly consistent, "because the Stalin of 1925 was very different . . . from the Stalin of 1935."[29] Having asserted that "Stalin took the half-truths and half-myths of [Lenin's] dogma and turned them into palpable reality in the lives of millions," Ulam finds that "in spirit Soviet Russia of today is still much more Stalin's than Lenin's," suggesting that the two men differ not only in character (as many are willing to acknowledge) but also in "vision"—in their ideas in general.[30] Treadgold assures us that "Russia's second revolution (1929) was infinitely more far-reaching in its scope than the revolution of 1917."[31] But then how can he insist that one was the inevitable continuation of the other? And finally Fainsod also manages to show that "revolutionary heredity" is only one of Stalinism's elements, and admits that there are others that need to be considered.[32]

But the crisis suffered by the continuity theory has been demonstrated more directly. Even some Anglo-American historians raised their voices against it. A whole series of scholars whose names I have already mentioned or soon will mention—Robert Tucker, Moshe Lewin, Stephen Cohen, A. F. K. Organski, Alexander Erlich, Alexander Rabinowitch, Jerry Hough, and others—have voiced opinions that explicitly or implicitly reject the continuity thesis. These writers concentrate mainly on "turning points" and "breaks" in the postrevolutionary history of the USSR; they focus on "alternatives" that repeatedly presented themselves, even if we look no further than the Bolsheviks. They therefore look at the various "potentialities" of bolshevism and at the harsh conflicts these potentialities occasioned.[33] Quite often these writers have

29. Meyer, *Leninism*, p. 282.
30. Ulam, *Stalin*, pp. 740–41.
31. Treadgold, *Twentieth Century Russia*, pp. 272–74.
32. Fainsod, *How Russia Is Ruled*, pp. 116–17.
33. The pioneer of this line of thought was Robert C. Tucker, with his book *The Soviet Political Mind: Studies in Stalinism and Post-Stalin Change* (New York, 1963). We must also note Tucker's *Stalin as Revolutionary, 1879–1929: A Study in History and Personality* (New York, 1973). Other works of interest include three by Moshe Lewin: *Lenin's Last Struggle* (New York, 1968), *Russian Peasants and Soviet Power: A Study of Collectivization* (Evanston, Ill., 1968), and *Political Undercurrents in Soviet Economic Debates: From Bukharin to the Modern Reformers* (Princeton, 1974); Alexander Erlich, *The Soviet Industrialization Debate, 1924–28*

specifically disproved the assumptions implicit in the linear conception of the Soviet experience, whether pre-Stalinist, Stalinist, or post-Stalinist.[34]

But the real stumbling block for the continuity theory lies in what happened in the mid-1930s, when the massive wave of repression dealt a sledgehammer blow to the whole of Soviet society. Many Soviet writers tend to refer to that phenomenon simply as "the year '37"—its most nightmarish moment.[35] But in reality this "moment" lasted much longer—from mid-1936 to the fall of 1938. For a long time foreign scholars and other observers found it difficult to grasp the full proportions of the Great Terror because their attention was all but monopolized by the spectacular Moscow trials. The actual beheading of the country that took place between 1936 and 1938 became apparent only after more thorough studies were done in the 1960s. A historian who otherwise favors the continuity theory felt obliged to summarize all that had happened then as "Stalin's victory over the party."[36] In other words, the victim was the very party that had made the revolution and had emerged victorious from that revolution. "A whole river of blood," Trotsky remarked at the time, "runs between bolshevism and Stalinism."[37] The entire Bolshevik leadership was swept away. Why? If Stalin indeed *was* bolshevism, its "incarnation," its "inevitable" outcome, then what need did he have to defeat bolshevism, get rid of it to open the way for what many scholars see as quite a different sort of party, certainly much different from anything bolshevism had been before?[38]

It is curious how many historians and other people who excori-

---

(Cambridge, Mass., 1960); and Stephen F. Cohen, *Bukharin and the Bolshevik Revolution: A Political Biography, 1888–1938* (New York, 1973).

34. In addition to the essays by Tucker and Cohen in Tucker's *Stalinism*, see also Moshe Lewin, "The Social Background of Stalinism," in ibid., pp. 114–17.

35. Two writers who have used this expression though they differ markedly from each other are Ilyia Ehrenburg and Aleksandr Solzhenitsyn. See Ehrenburg, *Eve of War: 1933–1941* (London, 1963), p. 100; Ehrenburg, *Post-War Years: 1945–1954* (Cleveland, 1967), pp. 13, 42; and Solzhenitsyn, *The Gulag Archipelago*, 2 vols. (New York, 1974, 1978), 1:25, 68.

36. Leonard Schapiro, *The Communist Party of the Soviet Union* (London, 1960), pp. 399, 416–17. For Schapiro's contribution to the continuity theory, see *The Origin of the Communist Autocracy: Political Opposition in the Soviet State. First Phase, 1917–22* (London, 1977), pp. 360–61.

37. *Biulleten' Oppozitsii*, nos. 58–59, p. 11. See also ibid., nos. 54–55, p. 3.

38. Tucker, *Soviet Political Mind*, pp. 55–56, 179. For a reconstruction and evaluation of this period, see Boffa, *Storia dell'Unione Sovietica*, 1:575–96.

ate Stalinism accord only secondary importance to this political operation that represents Stalinism's crowning moment, the action that gave Stalin unchallengeable domination of the Soviet scene. At best they see it as an episode, monstrous perhaps, but just one of many in Soviet history.[39] Bear in mind that a historian cannot simply pass a moral judgment condemning violence, especially such wholesale violence. This may be a highminded reaction but it is no way to reconstruct history. The task here is to understand why the phenomenon reached such orgiastic proportions, why it occurred just when it did, how it was aimed to strike a particular target, what effect it had on Soviet society, and for how long. By seeing the postrevolutionary development of the USSR as one coherent process, the continuity theory precludes an answer to these questions.

To understand that there was a connection between the Great Terror and Stalinism's other decisive moment, the "revolution from above," was in itself a sign of progress.[40] But now we have to establish just what that connection was. And this task becomes even more essential when we realize that the repression began when the two fundamental operations of the "revolution from above"—industrialization and collectivization—seemed already to be crowned with success. For a long time we lacked a satisfactory explanation. All we had were conjectures, later demolished by facts, such as the belief that the repression was triggered by fear of the approaching war or, even less plausibly, by Stalin's sudden "insanity."[41]

39. Solzhenitsyn, *Gulag Archipelago*, 1:70; Gurian, *Bolshevism*, pp. 71–73; Brzezinski tends to agree, although he calls the mass purge and the mass terror unprecedented both in their pervasiveness and in the actual toll taken. See Zbigniew Brzezinski, *The Permanent Purge: Politics in Soviet Totalitarianism* (Cambridge, Mass., 1956), pp. 98–115, 169–70.

40. Schapiro, *Communist Party*, p. 430.

41. The first theory (the approach of the war) may be found in Ulam, *Stalin*, p. 477, and in Isaac Deutscher, *Stalin: A Political Biography* (New York, 1961), pp. 376–78. Most scholars have treated the madness theory with skepticism and above all as politically and historically irrelevant. See Medvedev, *Let History Judge*, pp. 305–13. All the same, it continues to enjoy some popularity. Even a historian as serious as Emmanuel Le Roy Ladurie, in his review (otherwise quite favorable) of Giuseppe Boffa and Gilles Martinet, *Dialogo sullo stalinismo* (Rome and Bari, 1976), chides me, "a communist," for "having difficulty grasping the fact that the USSR was governed by a semimadman during the critical decade of 1930–1940." A French translation of the book appeared in 1977 and the review can be found in *Nouvel Observateur*, 21 November 1977. One may wonder whether Le Roy Ladurie, a non-

The historian who has paid most attention to "the year '37" wrote that the repression "amounted to a revolution as complete as, though more disguised than, any previous changes in Russia." I myself have spoken elsewhere about the obvious similarity to a coup d'état.[42] Others have called it a "counterrevolution"[43]—an ambiguous term because it usually implies a simple restoration of the prerevolutionary order. Some people therefore felt obliged to specify a "cultural counterrevolution" or a "bureaucratic-statist counterrevolution."[44] These terms are useful because they indicate that the 1937 "coup" was directed against individuals, ideas, institutions, and political concepts that had been integral parts of the 1917 Bolshevik revolution, its basic elements. One may then also say, with the principal critic of the continuity theory, that Stalinism was "centered on a revolution that wrecked a revolution in the earlier one's name."[45] The terminology leaves much to be desired. Confused and imprecise, it reveals persistently inadequate scholarship and a weakness in the conceptual apparatus used to approach the problem. But even with these limitations it comes closer to an understanding of the historical events than the linear interpretation of the Soviet experience ever could.

---

communist, has equal difficulty grasping the fact that later, during the war, that semimadman managed to mastermind Soviet diplomacy (among other things) and grappled so successfully, according to the participants themselves, with such men as Franklin D. Roosevelt, Winston Churchill, and Charles de Gaulle. The relative and historically determined value of the concept of madness is, as we know, a motif French culture has enriched with original contributions in recent years. So much, then, for its usefulness as an answer to the questions that concern us here.

42. Conquest, *Great Terror*, p. 251; Boffa, *Storia dell'Unione Sovietica*, 1:596.
43. Roy Medvedev uses the term in *L'Unione Sovietica alle soglie del 2000*, ed. Livio Zanotti (Milan, 1980), p. 63. Another example can be found in Alain Meyer, "La société stalinienne de 1934 à 1941: Essai de bilan," in *Feux croisés sur le stalinisme* (Paris, 1980), p. 38.
44. The first expression is Alec Nove's in *Stalinism and After* (London, 1975), p. 63, the second Predrag Vranicki's in *Marksizam i socijalizam* (Zagreb, 1979), p. 77.
45. Robert Tucker, "Stalin the Last Bolshevik," *New York Times*, 21 December 1979.

4 Russia's Revenge

The continuity problem was bound to confront scholars—continuity not only between Stalinism and the revolution but also between postrevolutionary Soviet history, in which Stalinism plays such a dominant role, and all the preceding centuries of Russian history. In view of the proliferation of Russian themes in Stalin's government, the society he ruled, and his official ideology, it is reasonable to wonder whether the revolution constituted a true break with the past, as its makers intended, or whether its aftermath may have been shaped by more ancient factors. Couldn't these forces, having dominated Russian history for centuries, have continued to exert decisive influence even after 1917?

The view that Stalinism can be traced back in a straight line not to the revolution but to much earlier times has been popular for quite a while, particularly in political circles. Accordingly, under Stalin old Russia is supposed to have quickly overcome the effects of that brief and basically unsuccessful episode of 1917. This theory was most eloquently summarized by de Gaulle in his sketch of Stalin in his memoirs. Stalin had used the revolution and its instruments simply to fulfill his desire for domination and power. And he had succeeded.

Thenceforth, with all Russia in his hands, alone, Stalin regarded his country as more mysterious, mightier, and more durable than any theory, any regime. He loved it, in his way. Russia herself accepted him as a tsar during a terrible epoch and tolerated Bolshevism to turn it to her own advantage, as a weapon. To unite the Slavs, to overcome the Germans, to expand in Asia, to gain access to open seas—these were the dreams of Mother Russia, these were the despot's goals.[1]

As literature of this sort so often does, de Gaulle's prose tells us more about the literary and political propensities of the author than about the phénomenon it so colorfully describes. Stripped of stylistic ornamentation, however, this judgment has been expressed time and again, especially since the 1930s, by many other observers of the Soviet scene, including a few scholars. It was particularly current among diplomats, the military, journalists—all people whose professions propelled them to produce instantly marketable political overviews of the Stalinist and post-Stalinist USSR. They, like de Gaulle, were especially interested in manufacturing conclusions about Moscow's foreign policy.[2] Often they were the same people who liked to quote at length from *La Russie en 1839*, in which Baron Astolphe de Custine described the empire of Nicholas I 150 years earlier, to show how well those observations still fitted some aspects of Soviet customs and public life in recent decades.[3]

Because this interpretation has been so popular among people ready to leap to conclusions, it has spawned a rather simplistic or plebeian version that, as a serious scholar has summarized it, sees Stalinism as "an inevitable outcome in harmony with Russian his-

1. Charles de Gaulle, *The War Memoirs: Salvation, 1944–46* (New York, 1960), pp. 68–69.
2. I wish to single out the opinion of Eduard Beneš, former president of Czechoslovakia, as quoted by the U.S. ambassador to the Soviet Union, in Averell Harriman and Elie Abel, *Special Envoy to Churchill and Stalin, 1941–1946* (New York, 1975), p. 287; also the opinion of another U.S. ambassador to Moscow, Charles Bohlen, numbered among the foremost experts on Russian history, as quoted in Veljko Mićunović, *Moscow Diary*, trans. David Floyd (Garden City, N.Y., 1980), pp. 49–50; and Joseph Davies, *Mission to Moscow* (New York and London, 1942), pp. 280, 465, 509–10.
3. Astolphe, Marquis de Custine, *La Russie en 1839* (Paris, 1843). An abridged version of this vast four-volume work is available in English with an introduction by George Kennan and a foreword by Daniel J. Boorstin: *Empire of the Czar: A Journey through Eternal Russia* (New York, 1989).

torical destinies."[4] This thesis, another whose principal or sole yardstick is the development or underdevelopment of liberal, democratic-parliamentary forms of government, asserts basically that Russia has always been governed by authoritarian, bureaucratic, despotic methods, and that with Stalin it simply returned to its age-old fate, since other effective forms of leadership were alien to its culture. In this framework the revolution was nothing but an episode of unrest, the same as others in the past (the most notorious being the protracted *smuta* that disrupted the country in the sixteenth and seventeenth centuries, and from which the Romanov dynasty eventually emerged). The revolution's aftermath was thus reduced to a simple change in ruling personnel within the ongoing continuity of Russian history. Given its simplistic terms, this interpretation never found many supporters among scholars, if only because of the rather cavalier and condescending way it treated Russian history past and present. But this objection did nothing to hinder its spread.

The theory of Russia's revenge for the revolution does, however, have a loftier version and a better cultural genealogy. This second version is supported by facts. The weight of the Russian national factor, national element, or national aspirations in Stalinist and post-Stalinist history is by now so well known, established, and documented that no scholar may ignore it, whatever his or her general persuasion. From "socialism in one country" to the themes of the "Great Patriotic [*Otechestvennaia*] War" and the explosion of nationalistic chauvinism orchestrated from above in the late 1940s—here we have one of the most important themes of Stalin's rule and of the legacy he left behind.[5] This was a theme that actually had some influence even outside the Soviet Union, for it encouraged the communist movement in other countries to sink its roots deeper into its own national history, thus fostering those national idiosyncrasies that were bound to appear, especially after Stalin's death.[6] Stalin, for his part, not only did not reject refer-

4. Moshe Lewin, "The Social Background of Stalinism," in *Stalinism: Essays in Historical Interpretation*, ed. Robert Tucker (New York, 1977), p. 115.

5. For a more detailed analysis of this theme, see Giuseppe Boffa, "Componente nazionale e componente socialista nella rivoluzione russa e nell'esperienza sovietica," in *Momenti e problemi nella storia dell'Urss* (Rome, 1978).

6. See Giuseppe Boffa, "L'internazionalismo del Pci," *Critica Marxista* 1 (1981): 6–8.

ences to ancient antecedents in Russian history, he encouraged
them by exalting the figures of great tsars and famous military
commanders of old as inspirations. As early as 1928, on the eve of
that "offensive on all fronts" from which the image of his political
regime and of Soviet society were to emerge, he modeled himself
on Peter the Great.[7]

If the search for constants in Russia's march through history is
to provide a key to the present, one must look further back than
1928. Just as the theory of Bolshevik continuity betrays the influence of Menshevik thought, so in this vision of the Soviet experience we also see a connection with the Russian political-cultural
debate of the early twentieth century. It can be said to have originated with the liberal historian Pavel Miliukov, leader of the Kadet
party and foreign minister in the first provisional government in
1917. Miliukov proved to be a better scholar than politician. He
saw his country's history as a protracted conflict between socially
disruptive tendencies and a typically Russian "statism" that fostered hypertrophy of its own functions, its own centralizing and
organizing role, but at the same time was eager to get to work
conditioning society as the main creative force in the historical
process.[8]

"A certain lack of cohesion and bonding of the elements that
make up the social apparatus" has always been a Russian characteristic. Statism—largely a foreign import, according to Miliukov—had arrived late in Russia. The people were too poor to bear
the cost of a modern state over their immense territory. They accepted the state only so far as it could be useful; otherwise they
continued to "feel independent of the central power." Miliukov
saw a series of consequences flowing from this situation: the huge
rural population was by its nature essentially anarchic; all important changes were introduced from above; every new leadership

---

7. I. V. Stalin, *Sochineniia* (Moscow, 1947), 11:248–49. One must note, however, that though in many ways he encouraged the glorification of Peter the Great,
Stalin was also very careful to emphasize the differences between the persona of the
famous tsar and the image of himself he wished to project. Peter was a man with
vastly different programs "at the service" of vastly different social forces. See the
interview with Emil Ludwig in ibid., 13:104–5.

8. Pavel Miliukov, *Ocherki po istorii russkoi kul'tury* (St. Petersburg, 1896–
1901), esp. 1:138, 220–25.

could count on passive submissiveness so long as it did not squeeze the "simple folk" too much. The same factors also explained the "maximalism" of the Russian intelligentsia, born in the service of the court and therefore prone to "abstract thinking," alienated from the people even as it searched for an autonomous role of its own. In applying these criteria to the revolution, Miliukov saw the policies of the Bolsheviks, especially after the civil war, as a resurgence of "Russian statism" over the anarchic and maximalist tendencies that prevailed at the time of the great upheaval.[9]

For Miliukov these ruminations were mainly an exercise in the reading of history; they never moved him to relinquish his opposition to the Soviet regime, except during the war against Nazism. In the 1920s, however, they became a political and ideological platform for many intellectuals and specialists who had opposed the new regime but now, with greater or lesser conviction, aligned themselves with it. This movement became known as *smenovekhovstvo*, after the title of a pamphlet published in 1921 by a group of émigrés.[10] The six authors, all of them once active in the Kadet party, were strongly influenced by Miliukov's ideas; so were all the other liberals in the Russian intelligentsia. Thus it is not surprising to find them echoing some of his themes, though they expressed them more briefly and drew different practical conclusions from them. In the end they gave their allegiance to the reality represented by the Bolshevik government precisely because that government had put an end to the long period of revolutionary "maximalist anarchy" and become the voice of a new Russian statism. As N. V. Ustrialov, one of the pamphlet's authors, put it: "When the red flag flew over the Winter Palace, the question was whether the flag had taken over the palace or vice versa."[11] Another writer, who later rose to prominence in Stalin's Russia, saw the Bolsheviks as the saviors not only of Russian statism but "of Russia one and indivisible," of its borders, of its "spirit as a great

---

9. Pavel Miliukov, *Rossiia na perelome* (Paris, 1927), pp. 29–37, 132–33.

10. *Smena vekh: Sbornik statei* (Prague, 1921). The six essays in this work are: Iu. V. Kliuchnikov, "Smena vekh"; N. V. Ustrialov, "Patriotika"; S. Luk'ianov, "Revoliutsiia i vlast'"; A. V. Bobrishchev-Pushkin, "Novaia vera"; S. S. Chakhotin, "V Kanossu!"; and Iu. M. Potekhin, "Fizika i metafizika russkoi revoliutsii."

11. Ustrialov, "Patriotika," p. 58.

power [*velikoderzhavnost'*]."[12] What they were creating was not socialism but a "New Russia," a "Great Russia."[13]

In the 1920s such ideas were much better known than the names of the people who publicized them; their influence spread farther than the *smenovekhovtsy's* brief celebrity could have led one to predict—far enough to penetrate the Bolshevik ranks. The communists in power debated these issues several times at their congresses, wavering between relief at the appearance of new converts to their cause and fear of the possible consequences. Lenin saw here one of those classic cases in which the superior culture of the vanquished manages to overwhelm the victors.[14] Infiltration of the Bolshevik leadership by Great Russian chauvinism became one of the two fundamental sticking points in his final harsh conflict with Stalin (the other was an arbitrary use of power).[15] When Bukharin accused Stalin of wanting to move toward an old-fashioned "military-feudal exploitation" of the peasant masses in 1928, Stalin accused Bukharin of being a slanderer who borrowed ideas from Miliukov's arsenal.[16]

In reality, although Stalin was deeply involved in the resurgence of statism from the beginning, the nationalist element of his policy, in ideology as well as in practice, became fully apparent only as time went on, especially in the 1930s. His attack on the Pokrovskii school of thought was a clear manifestation of his nationalism. Mikhail Pokrovskii was considered to be the foremost Russian Marxist historian, yet Stalin abruptly accused him of defaming past national history because Pokrovskii was intensely hostile to nationalism of any stripe.[17]

12. Aleksei Tolstoi, *Sobraniie sochinenii v 10 tomakh* (Moscow, 1961), 10:34–39. It is interesting to note that this text appeared in the early 1960s, albeit in a publication closely resembling an *opera omnia*.

13. Nikolai Bukharin, *Put' k sotsializmu v Rossii* (New York, 1967), p. 177.

14. *Odinnadtsatyi s'ezd RKP(b): Stenograficheskii otchet* (Moscow, 1961), pp. 27–30.

15. Giuseppe Boffa, *Storia dell'Unione Sovietica* (Milan, 1976–1979), 1:205–9, 240–43.

16. *Kommunisticheskaia partiia Sovetskogo Soiuza v rezoliutsiiakh i resheniiakh s'ezdov, konferentsii i plenumov Tsentral'nogo Komiteta* (Moscow, 1970), 4:186.

17. S. M. Dubrovskii, "Akademik N. M. Pokrovskii i ego rol' v razvitii sovetskoi istoricheskoi nauki," *Voprosy istorii*, no. 3, 1962, pp. 28–30. For an echo of the old Stalinist critiques, see the discussion of this text in ibid., p. 39. See also "O metodologicheskikh voprosakh istoricheskoi nauki," in ibid., no. 3, 1961, pp. 26–

The vision of a fundamental continuity in the Russian world, unaffected by the revolution, was common among the émigré professors who were among the pioneers of Western scholarship on the USSR. Though Miliukov was no longer teaching, he was still the best known of the group. But others—Georgii Vernadskii, Mikhail Karpovich, Nikolai Timashev—though less original thinkers than Miliukov, gained influence in academic circles.[18]

The member of this diaspora who most systematically expressed the concept of a Russia emerging from its convulsions stronger than ever was the Christian philosopher Nikolai Berdiaev. In the mid-1930s Berdiaev concluded that the revolution, "universal in its principles, like any great revolution, [and] carried out under the flag of internationalism," was becoming increasingly "nationalized." He saw bolshevism as the "the third appearance of Russian autocratic imperialism; its first appearance being the Muscovite Tsardom and its second the Petrine Empire . . . a synthesis between Ivan the Terrible and Marx, with the worst coming from Ivan and not from Marx." Berdiaev was also among those who believed that "Russian *étatism* always had Russian anarchism as its obverse." He saw the Third International as a "Russian national idea," a "transformation of Russian messianism." He explained that "bolshevism entered into Russian life as a power which was militarized in the highest degree, but the old Russian state also had always been militarized. . . . The people [had been] held together by a unity of religious faith; so also a new single faith had to be expressed for the masses in elementary symbols. Marxism in its Russian form was wholly suitable for this." In the USSR of the 1930s one heard insistent references to "socialist patriotism." But "the socialist fatherland is still the same Russia, and in Russia perhaps popular patriotism is coming into being for the first time." Objectively one could "consider the process taking place [as] one of integration, the assembling of the Russian people under the standard of communism." In short, in Berdiaev's opinion

---

27; *Vsesoiuznoie soveshchaniie o merakh uluchsheniia podgotovki nauchno-peda-gogicheskikh kadrov po istoricheskim naukam* (Moscow, 1964), p. 17; Rudolf Schlesinger, "Recent Soviet Historiography," *Soviet Studies*, April 1950, pp. 297–301.

18. See esp. Nicholas Timashev, *The Great Retreat: The Growth and Decline of Communism in Russia* (New York, 1946). Mikhail Karpovich contributed greatly to the spread of Miliukov's ideas by editing an abbreviated English version of his most famous work, *Ocherki po istorii russkoi kul'tury*.

communism in the period of Stalin may be taken as a continuation of Peter the Great's work. The Soviet government is not only the government of the Communist party which professes to realize social justice; it is also a state and has the objective nature of every state; it is interested in the preservation of the state and its power, in its economic development.[19]

Yet despite the many clues available, astonishingly neither Berdiaev nor others of his persuasion followed their line of thought to the obvious conclusion that the advent of Russian statism represented a dramatic revision and mangling of bolshevism. The resurrection of deeply traditional Russian motifs ought to have implied a break with the revolutionary experience rather than a continuation of it, since there was nothing specifically Russian about that experience in its early stages. Had their theory been more consistent, they would have recognized Stalinism as a true dramatic about-face from the original bolshevism. But such consistency was beyond them, and by straining mightily they contrived to place the birth of the revolution's Russification at the start of the Soviet experience. Therefore they, too, saw a basic linearity in Soviet history from 1917 on. Thus their thesis lost some of its bite but became more palatable to those who preferred other interpretations, including Bolshevik continuity.

The Russian motif was so salient in Stalin's time that many scholars simply listed it as an element of Stalinism and never bothered to consider what significance it might have for the history of the revolution. They did what many other historians had done and saw Stalinism as an unavoidable product of bolshevism. Comparisons of Stalin with Peter the Great or Ivan the Terrible are also common in their works. Fainsod listed the "traditional nationalism of tsarism" among the "legacies" that Stalinism tried to "exploit." Daniels saw that "communist Russia sooner or later returned to many of the traits of the tsarist past." Brzezinski pointed

---

19. Nicholas Berdiaev, *The Origins of Russian Communism* (London, 1948), pp. 114–47. The first edition of this work was published in French in 1936 and its original Russian text appeared only later: Nikolai Berdiaev, *Istoki i smysl russkogo kommunizma* (Paris, 1955). Berdiaev returned to these ideas and developed them in *Russkaia ideia: Osnovnyie problemy russkoi mysli XIX-go veka i nachala XX-go veka* (Paris, 1946), published in English as *The Russian Idea* (New York and London, 1948).

out a "definite perpetuation in autocratic pattern" among the tsarist and Soviet executives.[20]

But even a writer sensitive to the complexities of the problem
and aware of the "tremendous transforming power of the forces
unleashed by the October Revolution," and therefore not given to
explaining too many things by analogy with Ivan or Peter, wrote as
far back as 1954 that "the conservative colors of the old Russian
regime have long since begun to show through the fading revolutionary red of Soviet Marxist communism."[21] Partisans of other
schools of thought also picked up the idea of Stalinism as a typical
product of Russian history. Even Alex Nove, to whom we owe
some original insights, has thought it "useful" to see Stalin as "a
Russian leader, heir to a Russian tradition and meeting Russian
needs in ways that had deep Russian roots."[22]

20. Merle Fainsod, *How Russia Is Ruled* (Cambridge, Mass., 1963), p. 116; Robert
Daniels, *The Conscience of the Revolution: Communist Opposition in Soviet
Russia* (Cambridge, Mass., 1960), p. 405; Zbigniew Brzezinski, *Ideology and Power
in Soviet Politics* (New York, 1962), p. 40. Brzezinski also finds in the Soviet experience the survival of a "Russian autocratic culture" (pp. 39–50), and he points out
the similarities between Stalin and R. P. Pobedonostsev, the ultrareactionary defender of autocracy, orthodoxy, and nationalism, procurator of the Holy Synod, and
until 1905 the gray eminence for the last tsars. (p. 43). Earlier Berdiaev had even
more boldly compared Lenin with Pobedonostsev: *Origins of Russian Communism*,
pp. 155–57.
21. Ernest Simmons, ed., *Continuity and Change in Russian and Soviet Thought*
(Cambridge, Mass., 1955), Introduction, pp. 4–5.
22. Alec Nove, *Stalinism and After* (London, 1975), p. 11. An East European
scholar, the Hungarian Mihaly Vajda, also favors the thesis that Russian motifs are
more prevalent than the more rigorously revolutionary ones in the Soviet experience. He contributes several original insights. His "methodological" proposal runs
as follows: "In my view the characteristics of bureaucratic totalitarian socialism
should be analyzed in relation to the form of Russian civilization." Then, having
cautioned the reader that his declaration has nothing to do with any presumed "ser-
vility" in the Russian people, Vajda continues: "What was lacking in Russia is the
need and capacity for a democratic decision-making process. . . . If we want to
understand the tragedy of the Russian revolution, then it is essential to keep in
mind that what it produced was in principle an institutional structure aimed at
eliminating the defects of bourgeois democracy and at changing individuals who
had never had a chance to appropriate those forms of behavior which are the prereq-
uisite of even 'simple' democracies." Vajda points out that "the whole civilizing
process in the West took a specific direction, a further consequence of which in the
twentieth century was the participation of the working class in the decision-making
process, [whereas] . . . the unity of Russia, the Russian central power, came into
being in an entirely different way." See Mihaly Vajda, *The State and Socialism:
Political Essays* (London, 1981), pp. 115–19.

Still, the principal shortcoming of the Russian revenge theory is the failure of most of its supporters to recognize the scope of the conflict aroused by the reemergence of archaic national themes in the framework of a revolution that differed so radically from the one its creators envisioned. They had seen it as a complete break with the past and everything it represented, and as inspired by a spirit of internationalism or ecumenism. The Russian revenge theory became vulnerable to still another criticism expressed by the English historian E. H. Carr—that by itself continuity can never explain the historical process, least of all the periods of history's greatest upheavals. Carr wrote:

> Revolution automatically raises the familiar issue of continuity and change in history. It is a commonplace that no continuous situation, however static, is exempt from change and that no change, however revolutionary, wholly breaks the continuity. But two observations are in point here. The first is that conservatives tend to dwell on the element of continuity. . . . Radicals, on the other hand, insist on the element of sudden and fundamental change. . . . The second observation is that the elements of continuity in any revolution are in the nature of things, those pertaining to a particular country, and the elements of wider or universal application are those of change.[23]

In the ongoing efforts to clarify the relationship of Stalinism, bolshevism, and Russian history, then, the most interesting developments have come relatively late, from scholars who are sensitive to suggestions of a Russian revenge but are still aware of the limitations implicit in the line of thought initiated by Miliukov. Their most outstanding representative is Robert Tucker, the Princeton historian who has pointed most persistently and accurately to the wrenching conflicts triggered by the emergence of Russian nationalism in the course of the revolution. He saw Stalinism as a phenomenon that not only "does not issue directly from Leninism" but cannot be reduced to simple nationalism; a phenomenon revolutionary in its own way, but not in the usual sense of the word.

Tucker generalizes the "revolution from above" which Stalin limited to the task of agrarian collectivization.[24] He assesses Stalin-

---

23. E. H. Carr, *The October Revolution: Before and After* (New York, 1969), p. 1.
24. Robert Tucker, "Stalinism as Revolution From Above," in his *Stalinism*, p. 77. The characterization of collectivization approved by Stalin runs as follows: "It was among one of the profoundest revolutionary transformations, a leap from society's old qualitative state to a new qualitative state, equivalent in its consequences

ism as a "revolutionary phenomenon" in which the legacies of both old Russia and bolshevism, particularly in its war communism phase, played important parts; but for him it also has a character of its own. Stalinism, which first appeared in the late 1920s and encompassed the whole of the following decade, represents a new phase in the Russian revolutionary process. This "second phase" had even more profound and lasting consequences than the first. It contrasted sharply not only with the Soviet society that Lenin envisioned in the last years of his life (when he formulated the New Economic Policy) but with the "revolutionary process of destruction of the old order and makeshift creation of the new that had marked the earlier 1917–1921 stage." This "change of character is to be understood," Tucker says, "in terms of a reversion to a revolutionary process seen earlier in Russian history." Basically he maintains that "Stalinism as revolution from above was a state-building process, the construction of a powerful, highly centralized, bureaucratic, military-industrial Soviet Russian state" capable of bringing about radical changes in society. In this sense it had a "pre-history in the political culture of Russian tsarism; it existed as a pattern in the Russian past and hence *could* be seen . . . as both a precedent and a legitimization." Stalin's was a revolution from above just as Peter's had been a revolution from above, "the culminating phase of tsarism as a dynamic political superstructure."[25]

Since the state is the principal player in such revolutions, Tucker sees a repetition of the tsarist "pattern" not only in this general overview but in details as well. Industrialization "from above" followed a line traced in the past from Peter to Count Sergei Witte, the minister of finance who presided over the great industrial expansion at the end of the nineteenth century. In the same way, Tucker sees Stalin's agrarian collectivization as a far cry from Lenin's cooperative projects; it was almost an "accelerated repetition of the serf system," or at least of some of its essential elements. Obligatory work on the collective farms reprised the *cor-*

---

to the revolution of October 1917. The originality of this revolution lay in the fact that it was carried out *from above*, through the initiative of the power of the state and with the direct assistance *from below* of millions of peasants struggling against the yoke of the Kulaks and for the free life of the Kolkhoz": *History of the Communist Party* (Moscow, 1939), p. 385.

25. Tucker, "Stalinism as Revolution from Above," pp. 90–98.

vée system. The tsarist governments controlled migration by requiring an identification document—a passport—for any move within the country, and denied passports to peasants; collective farm workers were no more free to move than they. State functionaries were no more rigidly ranked under the tsars than they were under Stalin. The fundamental analogy with the past lies for Tucker in the "binding of all classes of the population, from the lowest serf to the highest noble, in compulsory service to the state." In this sense he sees Stalin's revolution from above developing in two stages: the first, between 1929 and 1932, was intended to put workers and peasants in the service of the state; the second imposed the same burden on the intellectuals (this is how one might explain the year '37), and especially on the intellectuals who made up the Bolshevik party.[26]

Tucker understands Stalinism—or, as he prefers to call it, "Russian national bolshevism"[27]—as a "state-dominated system of society . . . formed in [Stalin's] revolution from above"; Marxism was "the doctrine that sanctified such a system as socialist." The result was a "radical reversal" to policies and solutions that went back to "Russia's distant past" and conflicted with what had been bolshevism's "mainstream." This reversal provoked a reaction, and Stalin eventually cut it short by methods that also had long precedents in the history of tsarism: the methods of Ivan the Terrible. Finally, Tucker feels that although the policies of the 1930s had some "distinctly reactionary and counterrevolutionary accents," Stalin was "the last Bolshevik"—"an extreme Russian nationalist" but still a revolutionary—who favored a return to the past "in a way fatally destructive to the bolshevism that had seen Lenin as its leader."[28]

Similar, though not identical, to Tucker's analysis is the one proposed by Moshe Lewin, who focused more sharply on the social shifts in the country during Stalin's years. According to Lewin, the revolution and the civil war left the young Soviet state stripped of that essentially proletarian social base which ought to have been there but had meanwhile been destroyed and dispersed. Stalinism therefore represented more than the building of a state: "Once

26. Ibid., pp. 96–100.
27. Robert C. Tucker, "Communism and Russia," *Foreign Affairs*, Summer 1980, pp. 1178, 1183.
28. Robert C. Tucker, "Stalin, the Last Bolshevik," *New York Times*, 21 December 1979.

more, in a pattern not unfamiliar in Russian history, a ruling layer was created by the state, trained, indoctrinated, and paid by it—exactly as the early tsars, some centuries earlier, created the gentry (*dvorianstvo*) and enserfed the peasantry for them as a prize for their service to the state." But the peasant masses, leveled by the revolution and locked in their archaic world, had preserved if not increased their "suspicious, even hostile, attitude towards state officialdom and state coercion." From this point of view the peasant was particularly "anarchical." Lewin therefore agrees that after the revolution Miliukov's old "dualism" between state and society reappeared, and that Stalin confronted and resolved it à la Peter the Great, by that war against the peasant masses called collectivization. In the end the statization of the peasants and their stormy urbanization had what Lewin calls "a contaminating effect" on the state, in the sense that it not only promoted a return to tsarist models but encouraged the offering of surrogates for the peasants' traditional religious customs and the revival of other old ways of behaving that were familiar and therefore more comprehensible to them.[29] The changes introduced by Stalin's state were of course radical. But here Lewin ventures an aphorism: "The quicker you break and change, the more of the old you re-create."[30]

For Lewin, Stalinism was basically a Leviathan state, "the state as the main tool and as an aim in itself, the highest principle in fact of his socialism." He sees Stalin as a "system founder and its ideologist [who] did the job of adapting the previous ideological framework to the reality of this new system." Lewin leans toward an interesting, if still simplistic, explanation of the massive repressions in the late 1930s—an Ivan-the-Terrible answer to an excess of autonomy for the state bureaucracy and a transformation of Stalin himself (as earlier of the tsars) from "autocrat" to "chief bureaucrat," overconditioned by his own state apparatus. But this explanation does not altogether satisfy Lewin. To give it more substance, he adds "resistance" to Stalinism by the old Bolsheviks, aroused by the ascendency the police were gaining under Stalin,

---

29. Lewin, "Social Background of Stalinism," pp. 120, 124–28. See also Moshe Lewin, "Bucharin e lo stato-leviatano," in *Bucharin tra rivoluzione e riforme* (Rome, 1982), pp. 145–64. For the role and importance of the peasant in Stalinist and Soviet society, see Nicholas Vakar, *The Taproot of Soviet Society* (New York, 1961).

30. Lewin, "Social Background of Stalinism," p. 126.

even over the party. This was the resistance that was crushed in 1937.[31]

Tucker's and Lewin's ideas have been attacked by those who, like Solzhenitsyn and unlike Berdiaev, see them as insulting to Russia and are convinced that all evils in the USSR stem from communism, none from national history.[32] So stated, the objection adds little to our understanding of history, and Tucker curtly rejects it. In fact the major weakness of Tucker's and Lewin's interpretations lies elsewhere. No matter how numerous its ties with Russia's past (and certainly it does have many), Stalinism is still a modern phenomenon, well rooted in our century. It is to these writers' credit that they relocate Stalinism within a centuries-old national evolution, rather than try to explain it as originating exclusively in the events of 1917 (or, as others have done, by citing single episodes of the Russian revolutionary movement, such as Lenin's *What Is to Be Done?* with its concept of a vanguard party). But an emphasis on the revival of past models, though extremely useful to historical analysis, can obscure what is new and contemporary in Stalinism by highlighting its most archaic aspects.[33] These analysts are partially aware of this danger. Lewin warns that Stalinism "was not a replica of the past but a new, original creation, a hybrid of Marxism and tsarism."[34] Tucker has defined the Soviet regime as a "revolutionary mass-movement regime under single-party auspices."[35] Were these characteristics totally lost dur-

31. Ibid., pp. 128–36.

32. Aleksandr Solzhenitsyn, "Misconceptions about Russia Are a Threat to America," *Foreign Affairs*, Spring 1980, pp. 802–5. Here Solzhenitsyn repeats that "Stalinism" never existed; it was a concept "invented in 1956 by the intellectuals of the European left." For Robert Tucker's answer, see his "Communism and Russia." It is significant that the only merit Solzhenitsyn is willing to concede Stalin is that during the war Stalin used the "old Russian national flag": Aleksandr Solzhenitsyn, *Pis'mo vozhdiiam Sovetskogo Soyuza* (Paris, 1974), pp. 15–16. Solzhenitsyn also suggests that "if Russia for centuries was used to live under autocratic systems and suffered total collapse under the democratic system that lasted eight months in 1917, perhaps . . . we should recognize that the evolution of our country from one form of authoritarianism to another would be the most natural, the smoothest, the least painful path of development for it to follow": *From under the Rubble*, trans. A. M. Brock et al. (Boston, 1975), p. 24.

33. Robert Tucker, "Some Questions in the Scholarly Agenda," in his *Stalinism*, pp. 322–23.

34. Lewin, "Social Background of Stalinism," p. 136. Tucker also uses the term "neo-tsarist Marxism": "Stalinism as Revolution from Above," p. 103.

35. Robert C. Tucker, *The Soviet Political Mind: Studies in Stalinism and Post-Stalin Change* (New York, 1963), p. 7.

ing the 1930s, in the years of (to use Tucker's formula) "Stalinism as revolution from above"?

Though Russia's revenge is certainly a significant contribution to an understanding of Stalinism, even its most sophisticated versions do not seem to be exhaustive, let alone unique. This explanation threatens to obscure what was new in the conflicts that accompanied the victory of the "revolution from above" even as it calls attention (and here lies the greatest merit of such writers as Tucker and Lewin) to the significance of those conflicts and to the gap that separates the way they were resolved from the original Bolshevik idea.

5 The Totalitarian School

Few interpretations of Soviet history have enjoyed such success, at least with the mass media, as the totalitarian theory. Its terminology is still used in writings of all kinds—theoretical essays and historical reconstructions, parliamentary speeches and newspaper accounts. Its basic formulas have become commonplaces. But though its popularity is obvious, its ideas are not. They have always been murky and vague, often taking for granted explanations that are not supplied. These two characteristics—diffusion and confusion—are the result of the political rather than scientific function this interpretation has long served and still serves today.[1]

The adjective "totalitarian" had appeared as early as the 1920s, but it did not gain currency until the 1930s, in connection with the simultaneous growth of Nazism in Germany and of Stalinism in the USSR. From that time on it can be found in writings of all sorts. But it was used sporadically and in a variety of meanings. Some writers, mostly Americans, used it to point to real or as-

1. For an analysis of this function, see Lee K. Adler and Thomas G. Paterson, "Red Fascism: The Merger of Nazi Germany and Soviet Russia in the American Image of Totalitarianism, 1930s–1950s," *American Historical Review*, April 1970; Herbert J. Spiro and Benjamin R. Barber, "Counter-ideological Uses of 'Totalitarianism,'" *Politics and Society* 1 (November 1970). The first essay is more descriptive, the second more argumentative.

sumed similarities between the two regimes and to distinguish such regimes from liberal democracy.[2] But writers of quite another sort, such as Trotsky and Bukharin, also used the term occasionally. For them it described mainly Germany and Fascist Italy; if they applied it to the USSR at all, it was only to evoke the menace of the total subversion of those principles that had triumphed with the revolution.[3]

Propaganda aimed against the Axis powers made some use of this word during World War II; but it attained its greatest popularity in the late 1940s as the antifascist coalition broke up and the harsh conflict between the United States and the USSR began. Struggle against "totalitarianism" became the great ideological rallying cry in the United States and in the bloc it led, just as struggle against "imperialism" was the ideological banner of the USSR and its sympathizers. President Harry Truman declared in 1947: "There isn't any difference in totalitarian states. I don't care what you call them—you call them Nazi, communist or fascist—they are all the same."[4] Communism and the regime of the victorious Soviet Union were thus equated with the fascist movement and the regime of defeated Germany to justify a rapid reversal of alliances. In both cases, whatever was defined as totalitarianism became absolute evil; it was "slavery," and no nation that represented "freedom" could reach any understanding with it. It constituted one of the two terms in that seemingly irreducible equation known as the Cold War. The entire school of thought that adopted this idea never managed to free itself of its original imprint.

Yet there was no lack of effort to transform this belligerent attitude into a modern current of thought and to invest it with the respectability of a political theory, key to the interpretation of con-

2. Nicholas Berdiaev, *The Origins of Russian Communism* (London, 1948), p. 143; Adler and Paterson, "Red Fascism," pp. 1048–51.

3. For Trotsky, see *Biulleten' Oppozitsii*, nos. 68–69, pp. 2, 4; no. 70, p. 16; nos. 79–80, p. 6. For Bukharin, see "Filosofiia kul'turnogo filistera," *Izvestiia*, 8 and 10 December 1935. Though the terminology differs, Bukharin here already argues with Berdiaev about the future problems of "totalitarianism." See also Stephen F. Cohen, *Bukharin and the Bolshevik Revolution: A Political Biography, 1888–1935* (New York, 1973), pp. 361–62.

4. *Public Papers of the Presidents of the United States: Harry S Truman. Containing the Public Messages, Speeches, and Statements of the President, January 1 to December 31, 1947* (Washington, D.C., 1963), p. 238.

temporary history. The effort mobilized considerable intellectual energy. Its early promoters in the United States were a few scholars of German descent, more philosophers and sociologists than historians. Their origin made them better judges of Hitler's Germany than of Stalin's Russia. Only later were they joined by historians, many of them specialists in Soviet history. Most of the historians merely made use of the functional body of ideas already assembled without scrutinizing them or elaborating on them. As we have seen, they brought nothing really original to the study of Soviet history because they unhesitatingly absorbed the sterile idea of its continuity.

All the same, the totalitarian school requires scrutiny because of the influence it exerted and still exerts, and because it expressed some promising and somewhat innovative points, particularly at the beginning. The main idea always centered on the basic similarity between Nazi Germany and the Soviet Union, between fascist and communist regimes, despite some analysts' efforts to distinguish at least between the ideologies that had given rise to the two experiences.[5] As a whole, writers of this school

> saw the totalitarian system as a novel twentieth-century form of ideologically motivated, thoroughly bureaucratized, terroristic total tyranny which was everywhere identical in substance though it varied somewhat in externals, and which found classic manifestation in two countries: Nazi Germany under Hitler and communist Russia under Stalin.[6]

Even in such a questionable view—and many people did question it—the most fertile and promising themes are found in the effort to single out the "unique" characteristics of these phenomena, the essence that made them different from other dictatorial and despotic manifestations in the past—so different that one could see in them something that had "never before existed."[7] The first systematic work in this direction was *The Origins of Total-*

5. Raymond Aron, *Démocratie et totalitarisme* (Paris, 1965), pp. 292–95; Hans Kohn, *Fascism and Communism: A Comparative Study in Revolutions and Dictatorships. Essays in Contemporary History* (Cambridge, Mass., 1939), pp. 182–83; Hans Buchheim, *Totalitarian Rule: Its Nature and Characteristics* (Middletown, Conn., 1968), p. 19.

6. Robert Tucker, ed., *Stalinism: Essays in Historical Interpretation* (New York, 1977), xii–xiii.

7. Carl J. Friedrich and Zbigniew K. Brzezinski, *Totalitarian Dictatorship and Autocracy* (Cambridge, Mass., 1956), p. 10.

itarianism, by the German-American philosopher Hannah Arendt.
This book concentrates so closely on the German experience that
Arendt bases her analysis almost exclusively on the rise of anti-
Semitism. In Arendt's work one can find insights of notable interest alongside arguments of marginal value, such as her statement
that "neither National Socialism nor Bolshevism has ever proclaimed a new form of government"—an obvious inaccuracy so far
as bolshevism is concerned, or even Stalinism.[8]

Arendt saw imperialism as the seedbed for the process that produced totalitarian societies and the crisis that launched World War
I on that fateful day in August 1914. To Arendt that war accelerated, if it did not actually start, another process that seemed to her
decisive in the genesis of totalitarianism: the entrance of the
masses into the political arena; military mobilization encouraged a
vast number of people to become involved in public life, entire
sectors of populations that "never before had appeared on the political scene." The crisis of the "classist society," the "breakdown of
the class system," came, according to Arendt, when the smaller,
more active and aware social groups became bound together by
common interests and could express their opposition through allegiance to certain parties and programs. Arendt speaks with aristo-
cratic contempt of those masses of newcomers, that *Lumpenprole-
tariat*, and sternly rebukes the intellectual elite who succumbed to
"the fun of watching how those who had been excluded unjustly
in the past forced their way into [civilization]." This elite, says
Arendt, provided the second foundation for the successful establishment of totalitarian regimes.[9]

This sort of thing need not detain us; it is typical of Arendt's
work but it does not cancel out the interest of her more stimulating propositions. One that deserves probing is her discovery of a
connection between the so-called mass societies and the political
phenomena encompassed by the term "totalitarianism." The connection has attracted the attention of other researchers of this
school.[10] But for political and ideological reasons of which Arendt

8. Hannah Arendt, *The Origins of Totalitarianism* (New York, 1973), p. 326.
9. Ibid., pp. 267, 312, 308–15 (esp. 315), 332. For the entire analysis, see pp. 227–
66.
10. "All modern societies involve mass manipulation, especially since the
masses have now become economically and politically important. Whether it is an
election or merely a matter of consumption, the crucial factor is the behavior of the

herself soon became aware, as we shall see, its most promising possibilities were never explored in connection with Soviet history.

A second direction taken by exponents of the totalitarian school
was an attempt to identify the characteristic features of these new
societies, to construct a typology for them—in sum, to observe
them so closely that eventually one could identify a unique and
new type of "community" clearly different from the tyrannies and
autocracies of the past, though related to them. Two Americans in
particular dedicated themselves to this task: Carl Friedrich, also of
German descent, and a younger man, Zbigniew Brzezinski. The
two have occasionally worked together, and that is where their difficulties began. They were unable to agree on a set of distinctive
features common to totalitarianism. Friedrich listed five: an official ideology, a single mass party, an almost total monopoly on
armaments based on modern technology, a similar monopoly on
mass communications, and, finally, police terror.[11] When he and
Brzezinski wrote together, they added a sixth: a centrally planned
economy. Later they added two more: expansionism in foreign policy and administrative control over justice.[12]

Later still, writing independently, Brzezinski criticized these
lists—especially Friedrich's—as "by no means exclusively totalitarian" (an obviously correct observation, if we exclude the "modern" component of the technology in question). In his opinion the
lists become exclusively totalitarian only if they are combined
"with the total social impact stemming from the inherently dynamic revolutionary spirit," or, in other words, with the "institu-
tionalized revolutionary zeal" that for Brzezinski was the "essence" of totalitarianism.[13] These differences of opinion make it

---

activated mass." A whole series of factors (industry, education, nationalism) "have
contributed to the politicizing of the masses and have made the politics of mass
consciousness a feature of our age. Practically all contemporary leaders have to appeal to popular sentiments and organize various forms of mass action in order to
wield power effectively." The author sees here also the reason for the "profound
difference" between totalitarianism and "old-fashioned dictatorships": Zbigniew
Brzezinski, *Ideology and Power in Soviet Politics* (New York, 1962), pp. 65–67.

11. Carl Friedrich, "The Unique Character of Totalitarian Society," in *Totalitarianism: Proceedings of a Conference Held at the American Academy of Arts
and Sciences* (Cambridge, Mass., 1954), pp. 52–53.

12. Friedrich and Brzezinski, *Totalitarian Dictatorship and Autocracy*, pp. 21–
22n.

13. Brzezinski, *Ideology and Power*, pp. 19–20.

easy to deduce that Friedrich was thinking mainly of Nazism, Brzezinski of the Soviet experience. When one compares Friedrich's and Brzezinski's works, what the two phenomena have in common becomes lost. The differences and contradictions become even more pronounced when one looks at similar efforts by other writers at other points in time.[14]

Thus the definitions become tentative and increasingly confused. Here is how Brzezinski defines totalitarianism when he attempts to summarize it:

> Totalitarianism is a system in which technologically advanced instruments of political power are wielded without restraint by centralized leadership of an elite movement, for the purpose of effecting a total social revolution, including the conditioning of man, on the basis of certain arbitrary ideological assumptions proclaimed by the leadership in an atmosphere of coerced unanimity of the entire population.[15]

But such a definition—in which, by the way, some of the traits mentioned earlier become lost—is no better than any other. Critics of the totalitarian school, rather numerous today, have collected quite a few of them, all different if not downright contradictory.[16] It is therefore astonishing to find historians (we can forgive the politi-

---

14. Leonard Schapiro, for example, lists five "contours" and two "instruments" of totalitarianism. The contours: (1) the Leader; (2) the subjugation of the legal order; (3) control over private morality; (4) continuous mobilization; (5) legitimacy based on mass support. The instruments: (1) ideology; (2) the party: *Totalitarianism* (New York and London, 1972), p. 20. For details, see ibid., pp. 28–63. Leszek Kolakowski thinks that an "almost perfect" form of totalitarianism (and for him Stalinism is one) requires "state ownership of the means of production," which clearly did not exist in the Fascist and Nazi regimes: "Marxist Roots of Stalinism," in Tucker, *Stalinism*, p. 284. Mihaly Vajda, an East European writer who subscribes to this idea, says: "As soon as society as a whole becomes one single productive unit . . . there exist two possibilities: either all parts are rationally adapted to each other (by the mediation of all individuals with each other), or a central power (authority) is required, i.e. a form of domination which is usually totalitarian." And "The holders of power in every society try to impose their own aims, their own will on the whole of society. And any attempt to exchange their aims for others is naturally considered to be disruptive": *The State and Socialism: Political Essays* (London, 1981), pp. 116, 119.

15. Brzezinski, *Ideology and Power*, pp. 19–20.

16. See the lists compiled by Frederic Fleron, Jr., in "Soviet Area Studies and the Social Studies: Some Methodological Problems in Communist Studies," *Soviet Studies* 19, no. 3 (1968): 327; Benjamin R. Barber, "Conceptual Foundations of Totalitarianism," in *Totalitarianism in Perspective: Three Views*, ed. Carl J. Friedrich (London, 1969), pp. 8–10.

cians) who have used the term "totalitarianism" as if its meaning were agreed upon and no clarification were required. But the main weakness of the term when it is applied to Soviet history lies elsewhere—in the low yield of original findings, which can be attributed to the superficial attention paid to the concrete evolution of Soviet society, or of other societies assumed to be in its sphere.

This is a most curious case. To describe Soviet reality the way he wanted it to be, Stalin coined, or had somebody coin, the term "monolithic," which may be—in fact sometimes was—linked to "totalitarian."[17] From the beginning of his rise to power Stalin also spelled out, cautiously at first, then more and more systematically, a whole series of ideas on the Soviet state, socialist society, and methods for ruling the masses: the party as a military-ideological entity; the equation of party and state; the state as a system of "transmission belts" for "directives" from above; the need for an official ideology; the total centralization of the economy; and so on.[18] These ideas were original in the sense that it would be difficult to find them anywhere in Lenin's thought or in Bolshevik thought in general; and they, too, could be called "totalitarian," if one could manage to pin down the meaning of the word. The supporters of the totalitarian interpretation might have been interested at this point in examining the impact of these ideas on revolutionary Russia and the obstacles they had to overcome.

But nothing of the kind happened. In their historical analysis, as we saw earlier, they accepted the continuity theory from the outset; they did not even face the problem of Stalinism realistically as a separate phenomenon. On the whole, these analysts used "Stalinism" reluctantly or not at all; they usually preferred "totalitarianism"—that is, something no different from other phases of the Bolshevik or Soviet experience, or from communism in general, not even from such phenomena as Nazism and Fascism.[19] Stalinism was seen at best as a variant, the "communist" variant, particularly significant, "full blown," perhaps even the most typical variant of an ill-defined totalitarian society.

17. Erik Hoffmann, "Changing Soviet Perspectives on Leadership and Administration," in *The Soviet Union since Stalin*, ed. Stephen F. Cohen, Alexander Rabinowitch, and Robert Sharlet (Bloomington, Ind., 1980), p. 71.
18. For a more detailed analysis of Stalin's ideas on this issue, see Giuseppe Boffa, *Storia dell'Unione Sovietica* (Milan, 1976–1979), 1:296–305, and Introduction to *Per conoscere Stalin* (Milan, 1979), pp. 11–13, 28–30.
19. Tucker, *Stalinism*, p. xiii.

If this way of looking at things created difficulties in explaining the pre-Stalin phases of Soviet history, it brought no less serious ones for subsequent periods. After Stalin, in fact, such characteristics as police terror, the cult of the leader, and the bloody purges—all generally considered essential to a totalitarian society—disappeared or were greatly reduced.[20] Contrary to what the partisans of the totalitarian school had believed, the Soviet Union, not to mention other "communist" countries, was revealed to be capable of evolution and subject to conflicts that had their roots in its earlier history.[21] Though this fact once again called many of its basic beliefs into question, the school as a whole saw no reason to abandon the "totalitarian" explanation so adaptable to various modern societies, the Soviet foremost among them, with Stalin or before him or after him.

The way to solve those problems, it seems, lay more in semantic dodges than in legitimate answers. Brzezinski, for example, having emphasized that Stalinism, for all its radical transformations of society, did nothing more than help "to reinforce the totalitarian dynamics of the political system itself," then tried to tack on some subtle distinctions: "This was the stage of the totalitarian revolution within society, not to be confused with the earlier totalitarian seizure of power within the totalitarian system." Then, dealing with the post-Stalin era, he introduced the concept of "disfunctional totalitarianism," meaning—if I understand him correctly—a totalitarianism that no longer agreed with certain needs of society. According to Brzezinski, in the history of a totalitarian system such as the Soviet,

---

20. "Terror . . . is the very essence of [the totalitarian] form of government": Arendt, *Origins of Totalitarianism*, p. 344. "The purge is thus inherent in the totalitarian system. . . . The purge is not only a unique manifestation arising out of the very nature of the totalitarian system but also a distinctive technique of totalitarian government. . . . Terror is the most universal characteristic of totalitarianism. . . . Totalitarianism needs the purge. . . . The need for the purge will not diminish with the growing stability of the totalitarian regime": Zbigniew Brzezinski, *The Permanent Purge: Politics in Soviet Totalitarianism* (Cambridge, Mass., 1956), pp. 23, 25, 27, 168, 170.

21. "The totalitarian regime does not shed its police-state characteristics; it dies when power is wrenched from its hands": Merle Fainsod, *How Russia Is Ruled* (Cambridge, Mass., 1953), p. 500. This statement has been deleted in the 1963 edition. Friedrich and Brzezinski, in the 1966 edition of *Totalitarian Dictatorship and Autocracy*, p. 375, admit that "the notion . . . that the totalitarian regimes will become more and more total (an opinion we expressed in the First Edition [p. 300]). . . , is no longer defensible."

it is useful to distinguish between the following phases: (1) the formation of the totalitarian party; (2) the seizure of political power; (3)
the organizational consolidation of power by the ruling totalitarian
party; (4) the totalitarian revolution of society; (5) the appearance of
a totalitarian political and social system; and (6) the waning of totalitarian momentum and the gradual separation of society from the
political system.[22]

Conceptual acrobatics of this sort leave particular historical
events in such countries as Italy, Germany, the USSR, and China
(also often seen as "totalitarian") barely recognizable.[23]

So far as Soviet history is concerned, it should be noted that
Hannah Arendt is a partial exception among exponents of the totalitarian school because she has attempted a less simplistic approach
to these problems. She distanced herself somewhat from the continuity theory. She introduced a distinction between Lenin's "revolutionary dictatorship" and Stalin's "totalitarian regime"; she identified "totalitarianism" only with "the communism of the thirties," not with any of its earlier phases; she recognized that "there
existed an obvious alternative to Stalin's seizure of power . . . and
this was the pursuance of the NEP policy as it has been initiated by
Lenin"; and she commented: "This alternative is usually overlooked in the literature because of the understandable, but historically untenable, conviction of a more or less smooth development
from Lenin to Stalin." In the post-Stalin years Arendt chooses to
see "an authentic, though never unequivocal, process of detotali-

---

22. Zbigniew Brzezinski, *Theory and Politics: Festschrift zum 70 Geburtstag für
Carl Joachim Friedrich* (The Hague, 1971), pp. 377–78. Ulam speaks of "a sane
pattern of totalitarianism": Adam B. Ulam, "The Russian Political System," in *Patterns of Government: The Major Political Systems of Europe*, ed. Samuel H. Beer
and Adam Ulam (New York, 1962), p. 646. It should be pointed out that Brzezinski's
ideas differ greatly from those of other writers of this school. Arendt, for instance,
writes that "where totalitarian rule has not been prepared by a totalitarian movement (and this, in contradistinction to Nazi Germany, was the case in Russia) the
movement has to be organized afterward": *Origins of Totalitarianism*, p. 323.
23. "I should guess that if we knew enough of the psychology of research we
would find those who wish to retain 'totalitarianism' in studying communism because of its negative connotations. This may be one of the reasons why the definition of 'totalitarianism' is constantly revised so that as the Soviet Union changes
(e.g. away from the overt use of terror) the concept can still be used to denote that
system. Various acrobatics are performed with the concept (e.g. 'mature totalitarianism') so that we can continue to pin a 'boo' label on a 'boo' system of government": Fleron, "Soviet Area Studies," p. 339.

tarization."[24] An interesting statement, though the lack of precision in all of the totalitarian school's terminology certainly does nothing to help us evaluate its meaning.

But these efforts also bore no fruit. Arendt, it must be noted, is not a historian. And the obstacles that an antitotalitarian ideology creates for scientific researchers are present in her case as well. She has admitted as much herself:

> It does not facilitate matters in either theory or practice that we have inherited from the cold-war period an official "counter-ideology," anti-communism, which also tends to become global in aspiration and tempts us into constructing a fiction of our own, so that we refuse on principle to distinguish the various communist one-party dictatorships, with which we are confronted in reality, from authentic totalitarian government.[25]

In trouble whenever it tried to explain the events of Soviet history, the totalitarian theory has met with a curious fate. On the one hand, its terminology has spread so prodigiously that it is now applied to a wide variety of phenomena and tendencies, thanks to the perpetual carelessness of politicians and the mass media. On the other hand, the choices it offers seem less and less adequate to many scholars who deal with the history of the countries whose way of life this theory was supposed to settle once and for all.

Consider the idea of "totalitarian democracy," introduced in the 1950s by an Israeli scholar, Jacob Talmon. The idea was absolutely inconceivable to the more rigid exponents of the school, who saw it as a contradiction in terms. Talmon drew a sharp distinction between "right-wing and left-wing totalitarian regimes," and declared that one could speak of "democracy" only in connection with the latter. Regimes of this sort, an "integral part of the Western tradition," represented one of the "two currents of democratic thought." The "totalitarian democratic" orientation is distinguished from its "liberal democratic" counterpart not by its denial of the "value of freedom" which the other supports, but by its "messianic" designs. It strives to realize a "preordained, harmonious and perfect state of affairs" through political action that embraces the "entire sphere of human existence," whereas the liberal

---

24. Arendt, *Origins of Totalitarianism*, pp. xxxi–xxxii, xxv.
25. Ibid., p. xxvii.

orientation hopes that by trial and error it can find its way to "greater harmony," and does not set itself overly ambitious goals.[26] Both stem from the "common root of eighteenth-century ideas." The totalitarian orientation supposedly can be traced to Rousseau and was first manifested during the French revolution, in the Jacobins and above all in the Babeuf conspiracy. Naturally, in Talmon's eyes, this legacy was destined (and here he joined the totalitarian school) to lead straight to "implacable tyranny," "servitude," "enormous hypocrisy," and "deception," since it attempted to reconcile contradictory instincts of "human nature."[27]

The elasticity of these concepts and the muddle of their definitions permitted the term "totalitarian democracy" to stretch far enough to cover a broad spectrum of historical, social, and political phenomena, robbing each of them of its individuality. Attempts by such writers as Brzezinski and Ulam to apply the term to the USSR led others to doubt the analogies with Nazism which were the very essence of the totalitarian doctrine. At times "totalitarianism" came to be identified simply with one-party regimes or dictatorships in possession of modern technology. Thus the totalitarian tag was applied not only to the USSR and other countries with a communist orientation (China, Yugoslavia, East European nations) but also to the new states of the so-called Third World. This tagging process tended to be subject to the position each country occupied in the international arena at the moment.

Basically, "totalitarian" came to be simply an insult, a pejorative term useful in identifying movements, governments, and countries to be blacklisted. Hence the vast confusion even among scholars. A French historian called Robespierre's regime "totalitarian."[28] Herbert Marcuse found that all of contemporary society everywhere tends to be "totalitarian," regardless of its political orientation: "Not only a specific form of government or party rule makes for totalitarianism, but also a specific system of production and distribution which may well be compatible with a 'pluralism' of parties,

26. Jacob L. Talmon, *The Origins of Totalitarian Democracy* (London, 1955), pp. 1–8.

27. Ibid., pp. 249–55.

28. Joseph Calmette, *Trilogie de l'histoire de France: Les révolutions* (Paris, 1952), p. 183.

newspapers, 'countervailing powers,' etc."[29] During the Six-Day War in the Middle East one well-known American liberal weekly condemned en masse all "totalitarian movements—whether communist, fascist or Arab socialist."[30]

Given such vagueness, we can well understand many scholars' reluctance to adopt any part of the totalitarian theory. The same reluctance is seen today among those who focus mainly on Italian Fascism and German Nazism.[31] But a trenchant critique of the entire totalitarian school was to develop especially among those who concentrated on Soviet history, on other countries with communist orientations, and on the various revolutionary regimes that have appeared throughout the modern world.

After a period of unchallenged supremacy, the totalitarian point of view ran into heavy opposition in the United States, the country where it had first become established and from which it had then spread abroad. The principal focus of the critics was the school's strong ideological imprint. An early adversary, Frederic Fleron, wrote in one of the most systematic essays on the subject: "The study of Communism has been so pervaded with the values prevalent in the United States, that we have not an objective and accurate body of knowledge of communism but rather an ideologically distorted image. Not only our theories, but the concepts we employ—e.g. 'totalitarianism'—are value-laden."[32] These observations, Fleron makes clear, apply particularly to studies of the USSR.

The political-ideological character of the totalitarian school, say its critics, has smothered or distorted anything of interest its investigations might have produced. The distinction it introduced (but never explained in any detail) between "totalitarian" and traditional dictatorships, for example, was often only a device to justify

---

29. Herbert Marcuse, *One-Dimensional Man: Studies in the Ideology of Advanced Industrial Society* (Boston, 1966), p. 3.

30. *New Republic*, 17 June 1967, p. 1.

31. Renzo De Felice, *Interpretations of Fascism*, trans. Brenda Huff Everett (Cambridge, Mass., and London, 1977), pp. 60–67; first published as *Le interpretazioni del fascismo* (Bari, 1969). See also De Felice's statement in *Stalin: L'uomo, la nazione, il partito*, ed. Robert McNeal (Milan, 1980), p. 15. On Nazism see Wolfgang Sauer, "National Socialism: Totalitarianism or Fascism?" *American Historical Review*, December 1967, pp. 404–24.

32. Fleron, "Soviet Area Studies," p. 339.

an alliance with tyrannical but conservative regimes in the struggle against communist or neutralist regimes organized by a single party and involved in political choices associated with socialism.[33] The supporters of the totalitarian theory usually replied that the criticism itself was "politically and ideologically motivated."[34] And in fact the debate that raged around these themes in the United States during the 1960s did in part reflect sharp divisions in the country, particularly on matters of foreign policy. But that was a fate that a theory so politically charged could hardy have avoided.

It would not be correct, however, to see the debate as exclusively political. It had quite a different significance for historians. So far as the USSR was concerned, the totalitarian theory meshed perfectly with the theory of a fated inevitability in Bolshevik history, so those who criticized the one were also criticizing the other. It was one of these critics who spoke of the "unfortunate effect" of the totalitarian explanation on historiography.[35] So far the disagreement seems not at all surprising and adds little or nothing to what we have already seen. But the circle of critics of the totalitarian interpretation is much wider. Several scholars who cannot easily be associated with any particular school—E. H. Carr, Isaac Deutscher, R. W. Davies, Rudolf Schlesinger, David Dallin, Alexander Rabinowitch, and many others I will have occasion to mention later—have scrupulously avoided using the totalitarian terminology, preferring to organize their findings in less nebulous categories. Others still, such as Frederic Fleron, analyzed and rejected it. Even proponents of the continuity theory, such as Alfred Meyer, have questioned the usefulness of the conceptual apparatus inspired by "totalitarianism": "To be sure, all those who use it

33. The term's "utility for propaganda purposes has tended to obscure whatever utility it may have had for systematic analysis and comparison of political entities": Herbert J. Spiro, "Totalitarianism," in *International Encyclopedia of the Social Sciences*, ed. David L. Sills (New York, 1968), 16:112. Spiro and Barber voice the same opinion in "Counter-ideological Uses of 'Totalitarianism,'" pp. 14–15. The purely diplomatic distinction between "totalitarian" and simply "authoritarian" dictatorships, the first term being pejorative, was still used by the Reagan administration to justify some of its foreign policy initiatives. See the *New York Times* editorial "Semantics and Human Rights," reprinted in *International Herald Tribune*, 25 May 1981, p. 6.

34. Brzezinski, *Theory and Politics*, p. 376n. This footnote simply refers the reader to Friedrich, *Totalitarianism in Perspective*, p. 132.

35. Stephen F. Cohen, "Bolshevism and Stalinism," in Tucker, *Stalinism*, pp. 7–8.

might agree on a very broad and vague definition, but terms that are too vague become useless."[36] Many younger historians agree, along with numerous representatives of other social sciences, though all of them are openly critical of Soviet tenets and their history.[37]

The very usefulness of the totalitarian concept has thus been denied, at least so far as historical, political, and sociological analysis is concerned. Naturally some continue to defend it, asserting that the term, for all its vagueness, is still handy, just like "democracy" and all its derivations, which after all are also quite vague and, today, ideologically charged.[38] Others, finally, while aligning themselves with the critics of the whole "totalitarian" vocabulary, have come out in favor of preserving, if not the term itself, then at least the concept or intuition it so ineptly tried to express. Generally, however, they have sought some substitute that, even if it stood little chance of catching on, would have fewer shortcomings or would be less subject to confusion. Thus in respect to the USSR one spoke of a "mono-organizational society," a "mono-hierarchical polity," a "monocratic system." In all these expressions one hears an echo, whether intentional or not, of Stalin's famous "monolithism."[39]

One suggestion deserves special mention because it seems more structured than any of the others, at least for an interpretation of Stalinism and Soviet history. It comes from the Australian historian T. H. Rigby, who has analyzed the USSR as a "mono-organizational" society. He explains his meaning this way:

36. Alfred G. Meyer, *The Soviet Political System: An Interpretation* (New York, 1965), p. 471.

37. The list could be lengthened considerably, but I will limit myself to Michael Curtis's essay in Friedrich, *Totalitarianism in Perspective*, and all eighteen contributors to Cohen et al., *Soviet Union since Stalin*, who unanimously distance themselves from the totalitarian school.

38. Maurice Cranston, "Should We Cease to Speak of Totalitarianism?" *Survey* 23 (Summer 1977).

39. T. H. Rigby, "Stalinism and the Mono-organizational Society," in Tucker, *Stalinism*, pp. 53–76, and "Politics in the Mono-organizational Society," in *Authoritarian Politics in Communist Europe: Uniformity and Diversity in One-Party States*, ed. Andrew C. Janos (Berkeley, 1976); Roy D. Laird, *The Soviet Paradigm: An Experiment in Creating a Mono-hierarchical Polity* (New York, 1971), p. 92; Zdenek Strmiska, "Social System and Structural Contradiction in Soviet-type Societies" (Paris, 1980), pp. 1, 195–96 (mimeo). This paper is part of the research project "Experiences of the Prague Spring, 1968," directed by Zdenek Mlynar.

It is a society in which, despite significant traditional and marked "survivals," most activities are directly managed by innumerable organizations or bureaucracies, all of which are linked up in a single organizational system. In its operation this system displays a distinctive blend of mechanistic and organic aspects, and the party, which combines a bureaucracy superordinated over all other bodies with a membership permeating all segments of the system, plays a crucial role in its coordination. The range and combination of functions performed by this mono-organizational system have engendered an ideology comprehensive in scope and monopolistic in its claims, a highly salient system of coercive social controls dominated by its political security and vetting-inquisitorial aspects, and a lively crypto-politics within and between its bureaucratic structures, on whose outcome the conflicting ambitions and interests of individuals and groups primarily depend.[40]

So much for the sociological definition. How can it be reconciled with history? Rigby concedes that it fits the USSR of the 1920s very poorly. This type of society, he argues, became "crystallized" only during "Stalin's dictatorship." Yet it cannot be confused with Stalinism either, because the description he provides lacks important features of Stalin's rule, such as personal power, the cult of the dictator, the use of terror. According to Rigby, Stalinism was that type of society with Stalin's tyranny thrown in; a complete description requires both elements. Stalinism was a "tyranny exercised under the conditions of a mono-organizational society, or, as I would prefer it, the mono-organizational society as run by a tyrant."[41]

But since the two phenomena coincided in time, how were they connected? Though Rigby finds potential elements of a "mono-organizational society" before Stalin and even in prerevolutionary Russia, he admits that their realization encountered "substantial obstacles." To overcome them one needed "deliberate acts of human will, acts, moreover, that called for great determination and political skill, and a strong initial power base." Stalin provided all these things. In a combination of "mono-organizational society" and "personal dictatorship," which for Rigby constitute Stalinism, each element was the condition for the other, in the sense that neither could have become established without the other. It becomes quite obvious to Rigby that after Stalin the "mono-organiza-

40. Rigby, "Stalinism and the Mono-organizational Society," pp. 59–60.
41. Ibid., p. 60.

tional society," by then firmly rooted, could and did survive without the personal dictatorship.[42] This interpretation, if one sets aside any reservations aroused by the terminology, offers ideas of unquestionable interest, but fails to overcome a few key stumbling blocks. It does not tell us, for instance, how thoroughly Stalin's original ideas had programmed the features of the so-called monoorganizational society, or which problems those ideas were attempting to solve, or the specific obstacles that had to be overcome before such a society could be created. Yet surely these are questions that the historian cannot ignore.

So even a vision as analytical as Rigby's can be traced back to the totalitarian school, or at least to the set of problems it attempted to confront. Still, we have come a long way from that school's simplifications—such a long way that we can in good conscience deny that we are dealing with two analogous interpretations. One might even say that when scholars who have been influenced by the totalitarian school have managed to answer questions concerning typical problems of Soviet history in truly interesting ways, it has always been after they abandoned the stance assumed by the totalitarian school. Here lies its cultural limitation, and it is hard to see how it might be overcome. This circumstance does not doom its political fortunes, however, for political success is always rooted in the harshest conflicts of the world we live in.[43]

42. Ibid., pp. 64–70, 75–76.
43. For understandable reasons the "totalitarian" terminology was commonly used by the political opposition in East European countries, including the USSR, as we can gather from Vaclav Racek's letter in *New Statesman*, 24 April 1981, pp. 6–7. Today this terminology is routinely used in those countries to describe the former monopoly of power held by the communists.

6 The Development Revolution

To emphasize the differences between the German and the Soviet experiences, a student of Germany and Nazism and critic of the totalitarian theory even in his own field of interest wrote in 1967: "Neither V. I. Lenin nor Joseph Stalin wished to turn the clock back; they not merely wished to move ahead, but they wished to jump ahead. The Bolshevik revolution had many elements of a development revolution not unlike those now under way in the underdeveloped countries."[1] Here Wolfgang Sauer aligned himself with a new school that was then emerging in the field of contemporary history, and of Soviet history in particular.

This school was attempting a new approach to Soviet studies, quite different from those that had dominated the field up to that time. It had first appeared at the end of the 1950s and it gained increasing authority over the following decade. A variety of factors contributed to its birth and its development, some of them only tenuously linked to Soviet history. By far the most important of them was the anticolonial movement, an irresistible force that by that time had taken the world by storm. Its success, first apparent at the end of the 1940s, had gradually become a dominant theme in

1. Wolfgang Sauer, "National Socialism: Totalitarianism or Fascism?" *American Historical Review*, December 1967, pp. 418–19.

international politics. In Asia, in Africa, in Latin America, following different paths, violent and nonviolent, a whole string of countries long subjected to foreign domination acquired their own autonomous identities as states. Others were searching for ways to consolidate the often fictitious independence they had had in the past. But they all faced tragic problems created by the enormous disparities in wealth and welfare that separated their largely primitive economies from those of the industrialized countries of Western Europe and America that had been their masters in years gone by. Consequently, their newfound independence remained conditional and weak. The development of these immense backward areas was emerging as one of the world's most dramatic problems and was attracting the attention of scholars in a variety of fields.

But though this factor was decisive, it was not the only one involved. The shock of the pioneering Soviet space achievements that so astonishingly caught the West by surprise was added to the picture in 1957 and 1958. It pleased many Western Europeans and Americans, scholars among them, to believe that a "socialist" economy—that is, an economy based on public ownership of the major means of production—could not function.[2] And now the Soviet experience was proving to them all that even though the Soviet economy was plagued by serious imbalances (and what economy is ever immune to setbacks?), it had managed to move forward. If nothing else, it had been able to ensure Russia's industrial development. The Soviet leadership, as susceptible as anyone else to the spirit of the times, was tempted to emphasize this theme above all others in the country's history. Soviet propaganda concentrated mainly on extolling the quickening rhythms of economic growth, and this proved to be a clarion call that leaders of the new states, then coming to grips with their own developmental problems, could not ignore, eager as they were to find avenues of understanding and collaboration with the Soviet Union.[3] Some

2. Among the writers who argued against such a belief was A. F. K. Organski, *The Stages of Political Development* (New York, 1965), pp. 120–21.

3. All of Khrushchev's speeches in this period were heavily weighted in this direction. One can find numerous examples in the eight-volume collection of his speeches: Nikita S. Khrushchev, *Stroitel'stvo kommunizma v SSSR i razvitiie sel'skogo khoziaistva* (Moscow, 1962–1964). See also the closing remarks in his introductory report in *XX s'ezd Kommunisticheskoi partii Sovetskogo Soiuza: Stenograficheskii otchet* (Moscow, 1956), 1:118–19.

countries (including the largest of them, China) had already started
to move in a direction similar to the one taken by the USSR. When
the obscenities of the Stalin era were denounced at the Moscow
congresses, the reactions were far milder in these countries than in
Europe and America, where public opinion had been aroused ever
since the beginning of the workers' movement.[4]

The theme of backwardness—or better, of an initial backwardness that had been defeated and left behind—first appeared in Soviet studies in 1958.[5] It provided new perspectives from which to
view events in the Soviet Union. Economists, sociologists, economic historians were the first to become interested. Their concern (and this is an important detail) became manifest simultaneously in Western (at that time still mainly Anglo-Saxon)
academic activities and within the communist cultures of Western
countries, where the need for independent reflection on Soviet affairs was just beginning to be felt.[6] At first not even this new orientation added much to the serious analysis of the various phases of
Soviet history. Apparently the results already achieved seemed sufficient and valid, and the traditional terminology—totalitarian on
one side and communist on the other—stayed more or less the
same. But the new way of looking at problems was beginning to
alter their nature appreciably. Political and ideological preoccupa-
tions did not vanish overnight, but they did change, and in any
case became less obsessive.

The new way of looking at things focused on the country's
"modernization," which one writer defined as "the process of
change from an agrarian to an industrial way of life that has resulted from a dramatic increase in man's knowledge of and control
over his environment in recent centuries." Challenges to this sort
of assertion were not to create a sensation until ten or fifteen years
later; at the time, the process was still considered "a desirable if

4. "They often regard those political issues which are the objects of the sovi-
etologists' past and present attention as quite incidental": Alex Inkeles, *Social
Change in Soviet Russia* (Cambridge, Mass., 1968), p. 425. Similar observations
have been reported in Giuseppe Boffa, "1956: Alcune premesse dell'eurocomu-
nismo," *Studi Storici*, no. 4, 1976, p. 211.

5. Cyril E. Black, ed., *The Transformation of Russian Society: Aspects of Social
Change since 1861* (Cambridge, Mass., 1960), a collection of the principal papers
presented at a meeting in New York, 25–27 April 1958. At that time the new lines
of research still mingled with more traditional themes.

6. For an example see *Nuovi Argomenti*, no. 20 (May–June), 1956.

not inevitable change," though it had been "in many ways a vastly destructive process."[7] The first comparisons made were between this change as it occurred in the USSR and as it had been experienced by Western Europe and America. For the first time people began to notice not only the differences, always seen as radical and absolute, but also the similarities, which up to that point had been virtually unsuspected. And there was more. Industrialization in Russia could not be treated as a process that had begun only after the revolution; in 1917 the country had already had islands of modern industrial development, though they were submerged in a sea of economic and political backwardness. Even the powerful industrial surge under Stalin began to be considered not as something unheard of but as part of an evolution that had started much earlier. These initial studies placed its beginnings in 1861, the year of the great tsarist reforms and the end of the serf system.

Alexander Gerschenkron, economist and economic historian, moved in this direction more swiftly than others. According to him, the Soviet government could be "properly described as the product of the country's economic backwardness." When he spoke of the "Soviet government" he was thinking of what others called or were about to call Stalinism, because only Stalin's government had seen that the public would accept industrialization as "a function which could not be discharged in its absence," and so for the most part would acquiesce, despite the "violent struggle" it provoked. But for Gerschenkron this too was part of the backwardness drama, because he continued to believe that in the "natural course of events" industrialization would take a more "western," bourgeois or capitalist form.[8]

According to Gerschenkron, Stalin's actions represented only one phase of Russian industrialization. His analysis showed that Russia had already experienced two "great spurts of industrialization." The first, in the last decade of the nineteenth century, had been engineered by Finance Minister Sergei Witte, and therefore

7. Cyril E. Black, "The Modernization of Russian Society," in Black, *Transformation of Russian Society*, p. 661.

8. Alexander Gerschenkron, *Economic Backwardness in Historical Perspective* (Cambridge, Mass., 1962), pp. 28–29, 139. This text had appeared earlier under the title "Problems and Patterns of Russian Economic Development," in Black, *Transformation of Russian Society*. It was one of the principal reports heard at the 1958 meeting in New York.

was strongly conditioned by state policy and nurtured by heavy
financial exploitation of the peasantry. The second, between the
1905 revolution and 1914, had been less subject to state control
and was oriented toward the "western model." This second phase,
Gerschenkron assures us with a strong propensity for hypothetical
history, would most certainly have achieved its goals had the war
and revolution not intervened. Gerschenkron and his followers saw
the "formidable political changes" brought by those two events,
along with the civil war and the NEP, as an unfortunate interruption of the industrialization process. The NEP in particular "was
unlikely to lead to a period of rapid industrialization."[9]

Gerschenkron, like so many others, drew an analogy between
Stalin and Peter the Great, between collectivization and the serf
system. But his view was quite different from the idea of "Russia's
revenge." If the disruptions experienced by the USSR in the 1920s
were similar to those encountered in earlier phases of the industrialization process, Stalin's answer turned out to be something
else again, because Stalin "re-enacted . . . a pattern of economic
development which seemed to have been relegated to the role of a
historical museum piece"—a pattern based wholly on the despotic
will of the state, resembling Peter's way of doing things much
more than Witte's. But the "anachronistic" character of this enterprise did not "prevent it from attaining a very high measure of
success. . . . By holding down forcibly the consumption of the population," Stalin's government "succeeded in channeling capital and
human resources into capital formation, thus assuring the rapid
growth of the only segment of the economy in which it was interested." The indexes of industrial growth rose much higher than in
either of the earlier phases. Collectivization had been "the initial
stage in a new great spurt of industrialization, the greatest and the
longest in the history of the country's industrial development."[10]

Whether or not anyone at this point mentioned socialism was for
Gerschenkron a matter of arbitrary choice and quite irrelevant.[11]
The mere fact that he ignored this aspect of the question, however,
was itself a notable novelty in American (and not only American)

9. Ibid., pp. 136–38, 148. See also Black, "Modernization of Russian Society," p.
665.
10. Gerschenkron, *Economic Backwardness*, pp. 146–51.
11. Ibid., p. 150.

historiography of that era. A careful examination of his overview cannot fail to show that no matter how stimulating it may appear, it suffers from hasty simplification. And yet his point of view was already being shared by others.

The historian Theodore Von Laue asserted that in its effort "to remake all of Russian society according to the needs of industrialization," the Soviet government "applied for the first time the full logic of the Witte system." Von Laue also believed that there could be no "other choice" and that the same direction would eventually be taken by the entire underdeveloped world.[12] A third scholar, Cyril Black, saw Soviet industrialization as a mere variant of a broader industrialization process unfolding throughout the world. It had links with the prerevolutionary experience and some of its aspects "could hardly have been avoided by any regime," but it also had a "modernization formula that is in many respects quite distinct from European precedents." This process goes back to 1928, a date Black considers to be more important than 1917. In his view, therefore, "Stalin rather than Lenin should appear as the initiator of the Soviet phase of Russian modernization."[13] And finally Walt Rostow, another intellectual who, like Brzezinski, was later to achieve celebrity but who also suffered a stinging personal defeat in the political arena, simplified things even further by declaring that from the technical-economic point of view, at least, Soviet modernization had not taken a substantially different path from the earlier phases and that Stalin should be seen simply as "Witte's successor."[14]

The first attempts to size up the problem appear to have been quite schematic. But the new approach, like all valid lines of research, was to lead to some interesting results. In the 1960s Alec Nove, one of the keenest English students of the Soviet economy, introduced the concept of the "necessity" of Stalin. Nove was among those who were seeking new ways to conceptualize the de-

---

12. Theodore Von Laue, "The State and the Economy," in Black, *Transformation of Russian Society*, pp. 223–25. See also the comment by Merle Fainsod in ibid., pp. 231–32.

13. Black, "Modernization of Russian Society," pp. 669, 675–78.

14. Walt Rostow, *The Stages of Economic Growth* (Cambridge, Mass., 1960), pp. 66, 93–105. On the political vicissitudes of Walt Rostow, national security adviser to Presidents Kennedy and Johnson, see David Halberstam, *The Best and the Brightest* (New York, 1972).

velopment in which an ever-growing number of countries were then caught up. "What may be called Stalinism," as he put it then, seemed to him to be a product of industrialization or, better, a "necessary" consequence of the decision to proceed rapidly with the development of heavy industry—a decision the Bolsheviks could not help but make precisely because they were Bolsheviks and thought like Bolsheviks. It was, in sum, the product of an objective and deep necessity. To be sure, Stalin's government had engaged in excesses that were not "situation-determined"—"excessive excesses," as Nove called them. But this was not what counted. "In 1928 any practicable Bolshevik program would have been harsh and unpopular," so "social coercion" was needed to implement it. Certain "scarcely avoidable" consequences followed: a semimilitarized party, a single dictator.[15]

In the course of his fruitful historical labors Nove amply developed these ideas. Stalin's economy was for him the equivalent of a "war economy."[16] Later he would write:

> To understand what Stalinism was all about, it is necessary to dwell on the problem of the twenties. To see him merely as a power-hungry despot is to see only one aspect of the truth. There was the problem of *industrialization*, begun under the tsars and disrupted by war and revolution. New and large investments were necessary to carry Russia forward, beyond reconstructing the industries which already existed in 1913. How were the necessary resources to be obtained? There were now no landlords, no large capitalists. Foreign capital was unlikely to be forthcoming. . . . Accumulation and sacrifice would be at the expense of the people, and the bulk of the people were peasants.[17]

Thus, putting aside the "excessive excesses" imposed by the man's despotic will, Nove saw Stalin's entire policy, including its repercussions for the state, the party, and the culture, as a global strategy of industrialization, very costly in human and social terms, but very effective.[18]

This school of thought, however, was also evolving in another direction. In the USSR and among its East European allies the de-

15. Alec Nove, *Economic Rationality and Soviet Politics: Was Stalin Really Necessary?* (London, 1964), pp. 25–27, 31–32.

16. Ibid., pp. 53–56. This expression had already been used by the Polish economist Oskar Lange; see ibid., p. 71.

17. Alec Nove, *Stalinism and After* (London, 1975), p. 29.

18. Ibid., pp. 72–75; and, for a broader analysis, pp. 41–63.

bate over how the economy should be organized had meanwhile revived interest in the discussions of economic ideas that had taken place in the USSR during the NEP.[19] This awakening had repercussions in the West, where people began to pay closer attention to those remote confrontations between ideas and programs. Nove himself would write later that the modern "economics of development" originated in those very disputes.[20] In Great Britain, E. H. Carr was publishing the pertinent volumes of his monumental history of Soviet Russia's first twelve years. Although this vast and detailed work certainly cannot be placed exclusively in the development school category, it does pay close attention to the Soviet government's economic policies and the controversies they triggered. But as far back as 1960 the American historian and economist Alexander Erlich had published an eminently innovative study on the same idea. Erlich focused on what he called the "debate on industrialization" in the USSR of the 1920s, and he was the first to do so. The usual pattern was to see the conflicts of that period merely as a "struggle for power" or "for succession" after Lenin. Erlich broke that pattern, and other researchers soon followed his lead.[21]

Erlich carefully reconstructed the old Soviet debate, and though he did not analyze it, he treated it with the utmost respect. But he did not stop there. In his concluding pages he also showed that, starting in 1928–1929, all the outcomes of those intense discussions had been set aside and swept away by Stalin's industrialization policy, and that the choices made by Stalin and his followers had been determined as much by political concerns and projects as by economic considerations. Erlich argued that this was not the only path that could have been chosen, and that no one could take it for granted that alternative paths to development advocated by other participants in the debate would necessarily have yielded less substantial results. Finally, Erlich showed that the alternatives so

19. For this phenomenon, see Moshe Lewin, *Political Undercurrents in Soviet Economic Debates* (Princeton, 1974), pts. 1 and 3.

20. "Soviet economists can be said to have virtually invented development economics, anticipating many arguments that were first heard in the West when development and growth became fashionable, i.e. after the second World War": Nove, *Stalinism and After*, p. 33.

21. See, for instance, Nicolas Spulber, *Soviet Strategy for Economic Growth* (Bloomington, Ind., 1964), and his edited volume *Foundations of Soviet Strategy for Economic Growth: Selected Soviet Essays, 1924–1930* (Bloomington, Ind., 1964).

forcefully rejected by Stalin and his faction at the end of the 1920s cropped up again, though on a "higher level," in the ensuing evolution of the USSR, or in the experience of other countries that had set out on the same road.[22] With these ideas, which he was to develop in later works, Erlich considerably broadened the whole question of the development revolution in the USSR and opened the door to controversies that engage scholars to this day.[23]

The most important lesson to emerge from the new studies was that if the Stalin phenomenon cannot be seen exclusively as a politics of industrialization, it certainly did fit the aspirations and necessities of overcoming underdevelopment. It should therefore not be considered solely within the framework of the Russian revolution, of the October insurrection, of its goals and ideals, whether or not they are seen as justified. The whole history of the Stalin phenomenon had become interwoven with early forms of other significant currents in the modern world. The old arguments between Bolsheviks and Mensheviks to determine whether Russia was or was not ready for socialism, a quarrel that had already been reprised so often in the historical journals, now appeared in a new light—as Lenin's last writings and some phases of the subsequent Bolshevik debate seem to have anticipated.[24]

A hint of the shock felt in more traditional historiographic quarters is seen in the evolution of the thinking of a sociologist such as Alex Inkeles. For quite a while Inkeles had tried to explore Soviet society with the tools used by sociology in the United States, in accordance with the tenets of the "totalitarian" approach. But in the mid-1960s he declared them to be totally inadequate:

> I suggest that for analysis of the recent past and the contemporary scene in the USSR we need a model different from that developed to deal with totalitarianism. . . . I think we can best refer to it as the "development model." This model either deals with certain problems common to all developing societies, or tries to treat the distinctive problems of a particular society, but always from the perspective of development. It is a quite different perspective from one which

22. Alexander Erlich, *The Soviet Industrialization Debate, 1924–28* (Cambridge, Mass., 1960), pp. 164–187.

23. Alexander Erlich, "Stalinism and Marxian Growth Models," in *Stalinism: Essays in Historical Interpretation*, ed. Robert Tucker (New York, 1977), pp. 137–54.

24. For an analysis of this problem, see Giuseppe Boffa, "Dall'imperialismo alla lotta contro il fascismo," in *Bucharin tra rivoluzione e riforme*, ed. Moshe Lewin (Rome, 1982), pp. 59–75.

sees society mainly in terms of power and politics. I personally feel that we have seriously neglected looking at the Soviet Union in these terms. . . . The Soviet Union was the first nation which confronted us with the kind of preoccupation with *growth* that characterizes the developing nations. Its history foreshadowed the kinds of solutions that have been typically adopted to meet the distinctive problems facing developing countries, though it must be acknowledged that often the problems which are distinctive are so because the leaders have made them so.[25]

On the other hand, in summing up Soviet achievements on the occasion of the fiftieth anniversary of the October Revolution, Inkeles did not stop with emphasizing the enormous strides made in production or with relating Soviet development, as others were doing, to its huge human and material costs; he also respectfully acknowledged the great organizational and institutional effort made to build a "basically modern national state" sufficiently versatile to serve the ends set for it. In this case, according to Inkeles, the price paid turned out to be the abandonment of the revolution's ideals and original promises.[26]

The thesis that Stalinism was a mere historical variant of industrialization politics won a growing number of adherents. One of them, A. F. K. Organski, another sociologist, introduced a new and interesting distinction when he suggested that Stalinism was a phenomenon in its own right, not to be confused with communism. To Organski the politics of industrialization was a necessary but ephemeral phase of modern economic and social development.

As it is an error to confuse nineteenth-century bourgeois politics with twentieth-century mass democracy, so it would be misleading to equate Stalinist politics with the politics of Khrushchev and his successors or to attribute the obvious differences to matters of temperament and personality. Stalinism, like bourgeois politics, represents a form of the politics of industrialization. . . . For this reason I prefer to use the term *Stalinist* rather than the more general *communist* to describe the period of industrialization in Russian politics. The term can also be applied to the present regime in communist China.[27]

Of course Organski also saw the differences between what he called "bourgeois regimes" and Stalinism. But he was much more

25. Inkeles, *Social Change*, pp. 422–23.
26. Ibid., pp. 41–61.
27. Organski, *Stages of Political Development*, p. 94.

interested in what they had in common. He was perhaps the first
to emphasize the similarities so insistently. Both sorts of regime
had stimulated an increase in productivity, the accumulation of
capital, migration from the countryside to the cities; both were
repressive and curtailed consumer goods, often by methods not easily distinguishable, despite the more direct role played by the state
in the USSR. "During the Stalinist era, low consumption was simply the other, less attractive side of the coin marked 'heavy capital
investment.'" The industrialization process was perhaps carried
out "more rapidly and probably more painfully" under Stalin than
in Western countries. "Repression permeated the Stalinist system
from top to bottom." But there was no shortage of results. Organski saw even collectivization as basically a success. It was a "brutal
success in getting Russian peasants off the land and remolding
them into an industrial labor force. . . . [It] broke up forever the old
peasant society . . . [and] uprooted Russia's vast, backward peasantry." Here Organski was drawing a parallel with the eighteenth-
century English enclosures. Through repression Stalinism succeeded in imposing and spreading "new values," always the most
difficult task of any industrialization policy. It made any "popular
control" impossible, but it developed the "popular participation"
that also is "an essential ingredient of a modern nation."[28]

Organski was also willing to risk an interpretation of the mass
repressions against the Communist party that became known as
"the year '37." If Stalinism could not be identified with communism, neither could it be identified with historical bolshevism. All
revolutions bring to power a new elite. Once power has been se-
cured with the help of the masses, Organski says, the new elite re-

28. Ibid., pp. 97–120. Under the influence of this analysis, analogies were also
drawn between the Soviet Union and Victorian England. "Perceptive sociologists
have noted how, with industrialization and the new class society, the Soviet Union
began to acquire official mores, ethics and aesthetics that were sometimes more
reminiscent of Victorian England than post-October Russia": Adam Ulam, "Stalin
and the Theory of Totalitarianism," in *Continuity and Change in Russian and
Soviet Thought*, ed. Ernest Simmons (Cambridge, Mass., 1955), p. 169. The same
analogy was noted by Alberto Moravia in his editorial "Riflettendo sui processi di
Mosca: Ma Stalin è morto . . .," *Corriere della Sera*, 14 July 1978: "One might say
with some justification that Stalinism was the terrible and bloody Victorian era of
the Soviet Union." For another intelligent comparison of Victorian England and the
USSR, this time carefully specifying the lengths to which such analogies can legitimately go, see E. H. Carr, *The October Revolution: Before and After* (New York,
1969), pp. 87–88.

fuses to admit them into the governing process. But industrialization was not the work of the original Bolsheviks; that task fell to
a "second group," which he calls the "bureaucrats of politics and
economics." The bureaucrats gained the upper hand over the Bolsheviks—the "intellectuals"—and eventually exterminated them:

> The bitterness of the struggle cannot be ascribed completely to the
> personality of the leaders of the dispute or to the immediate circum-
> stances of the quarrel. Stalin's ruthlessness was important in the
> elimination of the old guard, but the conflict was more profound.
> The seeds of the conflict were planted deep in the revolution and in
> the party of the men who made it. It was conflict between men who
> fight authority and those who exercise it.[29]

At this point, rather than follow the individual contributions of
the various exponents of the school, I think it would be more useful to offer what can be seen as a synthesis of its ideas by a student
of the Soviet political system, Jerry Hough. His basic idea is that
"the Soviet Union has been a developing nation throughout its history." If one considers the basic indicators commonly used to
measure underdevelopment, he argues, then the figures we find in
the Soviet Union in 1926 are quite comparable to those of such
countries as Mexico, Egypt, and even Uganda in the 1970s. There
was an embryonic "industrial base," but steel production was well
below that of India today. There was also a very backward agricultural sector. Hough says:

> There have been regimes of all different types in the Third World in
> this century, and the vast majority of them have been very unstable
> over any fifty-year period, especially while undergoing industrializa-
> tion. They have been very susceptible to military dictatorship, but
> then the military dictatorships themselves have had the greatest dif-
> ficulty developing long-term legitimacy. From this perspective one of
> the most striking facts about not only the Soviet Union but also the
> other Communist regimes that have come to power more or less by
> their own forces (China, Vietnam, Cuba, and to some extent Yugo-
> slavia) is the degree of their stability. . . . To a considerable extent
> the stability of these regimes can be explained by their use of force,
> but other dictatorships have been repressive and yet have found their
> military and security forces dissolving in a crisis. There must be rea-
> sons that the force has remained effective for so long, and there must

29. Organski, *Stages of Political Development*, p. 100.

be something wrong with any analysis that insists that the Soviet
regime has never developed "the most elemental legitimacy."[30]

So far as Hough is concerned, all this stability can be traced to
the October Revolution. Like other contemporary historians, he re-
fuses to call that revolution a "coup," since it was supported by
critical masses of the population.[31] Nor was this legitimacy lost
later on—essentially for three reasons, all related to industrialization: the great social mobility it made possible; the spread of a
"dogmatic Marxism" that provided simple and attractive solutions
to many problems, which at least in the future would justify present suffering and which combined Western ideas with uniquely
Russian ones; and finally the identification with the "nationalist
cause."[32] In connection with the first point, Hough makes an observation that closely concerns the idea of Stalinism:

> We have focused our attention so exclusively on the horrors of col-
> lectivization and on peasant resistance that we have failed to ask a
> critical question. How did Stalin pull it off? In the 20th Century,
> dissatisfied peasantry have frequently provided the manpower and
> the haven for large-scale guerrilla action. . . . Why didn't this type of
> guerrilla [activity] happen during collectivization when the provoca-
> tion to the peasantry was so much greater? Well, it did, but within a
> year or two the regime was essentially able to contain it. Basically, I
> think that the explanation for the regime's success lies in the mass
> of jobs created in the simultaneous industrialization drive and the
> opportunity for peasant upward mobility that they provided. The tal-
> ented, the young, and the ambitious among the peasantry—and
> these are precisely the type of people who first form the heart of any
> successful guerrilla action—had a real choice, and the vast majority
> selected the certainty of advancement in the city over the uncertain-
> ties of warfare in the countryside.[33]

I have described the ideas and development of this school in detail mainly because their original innovative approach is still relatively unfamiliar, certainly less current than others in the ongoing

---

30. Testimony by Jerry Hough in U.S. House of Representatives, Committee on
International Relations, *The Soviet Union: Internal Dynamics of Foreign Policy,
Present and Future: Hearings before the Subcommittee on Europe and the Middle
East* (Washington, D.C., 1978), p. 265 (hereafter *Hearings*).
31. Ibid. Among works that refute the coup d'état theory are Alexander Ra-
binowitch, *The Bolsheviks Come to Power: The Revolution of 1917 in Petrograd*
(New York, 1976); Dietrich Geyer, "The Bolshevik Insurrection in Petrograd," in
Revolutionary Russia, ed. Richard Pipes (Cambridge, Mass., 1968).
32. *Hearings*, pp. 265–67.
33. Ibid., p. 266.

historical and political debates. Their contribution to historical analysis is limited but important. It consists mainly of a few insights into hitherto neglected aspects and motivations of events in the postrevolutionary USSR. Thus the development school highlighted the turnabout of 1928–1929 as the beginning of a new era, and at least some of its exponents intuited the significance of Stalinism as a phenomenon in its own right. One can even say that it dealt mostly, if not exclusively, with Stalinism, often to the neglect of Lenin, the revolution, and the revolution's place in the Bolshevik tradition. Moreover, it was perhaps the first to glimpse the elements of strength in the Stalin phenomenon and therefore its place in postrevolutionary Soviet history, without ignoring its horrors and tragedies. It is characterized primarily, then, by its effort to draw attention to this point in an argument, sometimes even overstating the case to emphasize its importance. Indeed, it would not be difficult to find several inaccuracies in the passages I have quoted.[34] Finally, though it concentrated on various setbacks in Soviet life, it did set their course in a broader world framework, well beyond a mere clash between capitalism and socialism or the communist movement seen simply as a child of revolutionary thinking and of workers' struggles in the West.

Not even this theory, however, can be accepted as a thorough interpretation of Soviet history. The insights it provides are largely one-sided and so are open to criticism. And criticism was quick in coming. It was noted, for example, that Stalinism had consisted of more than "modernization"—there had been real "archaization" as well.[35] Alexander Erlich, one of the major contributors to this new line of research, noted that the debate over industrialization in the 1920s basically stayed within the outlines of what he calls "Marxian growth models"; but he also noted that these models were then summarily discarded in 1929, less because of the demands of in-

---

34. I shall limit myself to two examples in Jerry Hough's testimony. Though the terms in which he speaks of the Soviet regime's "stability" may be generally accepted, it is debatable whether such a description can be applied to the USSR of the 1930s, convulsed as it was in the second half of the decade. It also seems odd to compare the USSR with such countries as Egypt and Uganda today, at least if we think of them in terms of development levels as they were in the world fifty or sixty years ago. These partial objections, however, do not diminish the overall interest of Hough's thesis. For other critical observations, see what Jeremy Azrael has to say on the subject in *Hearings*, pp. 272–73.

35. Robert Tucker, "Stalinism as Revolution from Above," in his *Stalinism*, p. 98.

dustrialization than because of a preoccupation with building an immensely powerful state.[36] Though one finds exceptions, on the whole this school tended to view Stalinism, if not as ordained by the goal of development, then certainly as "necessary" and imposed largely by circumstances; and it dismissed as irrelevant any and all imaginable alternatives.

But this is, and probably is destined to remain, one of the most controversial points. It is precisely here that the argument began as to whether other industrialization policies advocated in the 1920s might have yielded at least comparable results, perhaps better ones, at much lower cost.[37] This question is certainly hypothetical and historically unanswerable, but it has its interest. That it cannot be simply dismissed with a gesture of annoyance is demonstrated by the fact that other countries, having moved in directions that can be described as Stalinist, have then felt the need to seek other approaches, and in their search have shown renewed interest in those Soviet debates of the 1920s.[38]

The desire to find an unquestionably basic element of Stalinism and the entire Soviet experience is praiseworthy, but the development school did not look closely enough, at least from the point of view of historical reconstruction, to see whether the element it identified either blended or clashed with other, no less important factors in that history. Its enterprise thus risks being seen as the extrapolation of a single factor from a much more complex whole. In any case, it throws no light on crucial questions that the past vicissitudes of the USSR continue to pose for historians and politicians. The unquestionable value of these inquiries notwithstanding, this is their principal limitation.

36. Erlich, "Stalinism and Marxian Growth Models," pp. 144–54.

37. Two writers who criticize the idea that Stalinism was an effective—perhaps the most effective—solution to industrialization are James R. Millar, "Mass Collectivization and the Contribution of Soviet Agriculture to the First Five-Year Plan: A Review Article," *Slavic Review*, December 1974, pp. 764–65; and Jerzy F. Kartz, "From Stalin to Brezhnev: Soviet Agricultural Policy in Historical Perspective," in *The Soviet Rural Community*, ed. James R. Millar (Urbana, Ill., 1971). For an analysis of Soviet objections to this thesis in the 1950s and 1960s, see Lewin, *Political Undercurrents*, pp. 134–57. Tucker summarizes all of these reservations in "Stalinism as Revolution from Above," pp. 87–89.

38. The most significant example is seen in contemporary China, at least up to the events of the spring of 1989. It must be added, however, that the true character of those events, at least from the historian's point of view, is still badly in need of clarification.

7 The Thermidor School

The idea of Stalinism as a historical phenomenon in its own right first developed within Marxist thought; its origin can hardly be disputed, since practically no one else paid any attenton to it for a number of years.[1] Trotsky initiated it, and he is still, many years after his death, its most original spokesman. It is only fair, then, to focus on Trotsky as we begin to examine the interpretive currents that developed within Marxism.

Trotsky's interpretation was based on certain similarities between the Russian and French revolutions. Its originality, however, lies elsewhere. Similarities and comparisons between the two revolutions had appeared as early as 1917. The Bolsheviks saw themselves as Jacobins in their resolute determination to put a radical stamp on the democratic aspects of their revolution.[2] Later the comparison was often revived in the course of political disputes, sometimes to justify Stalin's actions in the 1930s.[3]

---

1. Robert McNeal, "Trotskyist Interpretations of Stalinism," in *Stalinism: Essays in Historical Interpretation*, ed. Robert Tucker, p. 32; Robert Tucker, "Stalinism as Revolution from Above," in ibid., p. 78.

2. V. I. Lenin, *Collected Works* (Moscow, 1965), 33:51–54.

3. "I approved unreservedly, in fact enthusiastically, the vigor and toughness employed by Stalin against those who were identified as enemies of socialism and agents of imperialism. Facing the capitulation of the Western democracies, Stalin

Quite soon, however, the comparison acquired a precocious re-spectability of its own among historians. In 1920, in fact, it was picked up and validated by one of the best-known historians of the French revolution, Albert Mathiez.[4] More recently, one of the most interesting contributions to the analysis of Stalinism has come to us from Italy. Giuliano Procacci sees this phenomenon as a succes-sive stratification of authoritarian elements—military, bureaucra-tic, pedagogical, technocratic—overlying the original "Jacobin model."[5]

Yet the Bolsheviks, Lenin and Trotsky first among them, were immediately accused by their adversaries of the exact opposite of Jacobinism: the anti-Jacobin reaction, the Thermidor. Such accusa-tions mounted in 1921, especially when "war communism" gave way to the NEP. They came from the most disparate sources. We can find them (though not always with the same pejorative impli-cations) in the works of writers as diverse as the socialists Iulii Martov and Karl Kautsky, the *Smenovekhovets* Nikolai Ustrialov, and the liberal Pavel Miliukov.[6] The same critics also mentioned the "Bonapartism" of the Soviet leadership. But, as we know, an unfounded suspicion of "Bonapartism" plagued Trotsky in his own Bolshevik circles because of his role as head of the Red Army, and even contributed to his defeat in the mid-1920s. All these compari-sons belong more in the realm of political debate than of historical analysis, and the people who thought them so compelling soon found it difficult to explain, at least in Marxist terms, what exactly

returned to the Jacobin lesson that taught terror and implacable violence in defense of socialism's native land": Giorgio Amendola, *Lettere a Milano: Ricordi e docu-menti, 1939–1945* (Rome, 1973), pp. 17–18. See also Lelio Basso in *Nuovi Argo-menti*, no. 20 (May–June), 1956, pp. 4–5, 7.

4. "History never repeats itself. But the similarities between the two great crises of 1893 and 1917, which our analysis has demonstrated, are neither superficial nor accidental. The Russian revolutionaries imitated their French prototypes con-sciously and deliberately. They are animated by the same spirit": Albert Mathiez, *Le bolchévisme et le jacobinisme* (Paris, 1920), p. 24.

5. Giuliano Procacci, *Il partito nell'Unione Sovietica, 1917–1945* (Rome and Bari, 1974).

6. *Smena vekh: Sbornik Statei* (Prague, 1921), p. 69; Pavel Miliukov, *Emigra-tsiia na pereput'ie* (Paris, 1926), p. 75. For a Soviet response to Kautskii and Martov, see *Correspondance Internationale*, no. 131, 1926, pp. 1631–33. An American histo-rian follows the same line when he speaks of "a Thermidorian reaction in 1921 and a Bonapartist dictatorship after 1929": Robert Daniels, *The Conscience of the Revo-lution: Communist Opposition in Soviet Russia* (Cambridge, Mass., 1960), p. 404.

these phenomena labeled "Thermidor" and "Bonapartism" meant for Soviet society in terms of shifts in class power structure and their political consequences.

The accusations of a "Thermidorian degeneration" in the regime became quite heated, particularly in 1926 and 1927, at the time of the struggle between the Stalinist majority and the opposition led by Trotsky and Grigorii Zinov'iev. This was one of the things that most poisoned the dispute.[7] The opposition described the Soviet Thermidor as an imminent alliance between the bureaucratic party and state apparatus and the urban and rural bourgeoisie (nepmen and kulaks), who enjoyed a certain freedom of action under the NEP. Today we know that this prediction was grossly inaccurate, because under Stalin's leadership Soviet policy immediately took quite a different turn, if not a directly contrary course. Trotsky, to be sure, later maintained that he had not agreed with this analysis at the time, and admitted that the Thermidor analogy had "helped to cloud rather than clarify the issue." For several years he preferred to talk of "Thermidor tendencies" and "Bonapartist traits" in the Soviet regime.[8] All the same, in exile in the mid-1930s he himself revived the analogy when he attempted a more thorough analysis of the evolution of Soviet society under Stalin's leadership in a series of articles and in one of his best-known books, *The Revolution Betrayed*. The title boosted the fortunes of the book considerably but it gave an oversimplified impression of its contents.

If we are to understand this rethinking that was to bring so much criticism down on Trotsky's head, we must keep in mind some of its essential characteristics. This was a passionate intellectual exercise; it had nothing to do with academic objectivity. Trotsky had a pugnatious political will, and as he went charging into dispute after furious dispute, he maintained direct contact with the most dramatic events of Soviet and world history throughout the fateful decade of the 1930s. Thus his thoughts never had a chance to become a polished theory. They reveal mental processes in perpetual evolution, sometimes self-contradictory, constantly tested by a swift succession of largely unforeseeable events. Bear in mind that

7. *XXII s'ezd VKP(b): Stenograficheskii otchet* (Moscow, 1961), 1:703–4; *Correspondance Internationale*, no. 131, 1926, pp. 1631–33; no. 6, 1927, p. 92; no. 110, 1927, p. 1558.
8. *Biulleten' Oppozitsii*, no. 43, p. 3; nos. 17–18, pp. 29–31.

the tragic climax of Stalin's repressions against the Bolshevik party came at the very time Trotsky was recording his thoughts. This fragmentary and unfinished aspect of the work could be seen as its major drawback, and indeed that was how many people did see it.[9] Actually it constitutes one of the work's most singular merits, for it demonstrates a scrupulous refusal to leap to conclusions or to permit intellect to be smothered by passion.

Trotsky carried out this difficult interpretive task under a motto chosen from Spinoza: "Don't weep, don't laugh, but understand."[10] And to understand was not always easy. In fact, it was almost never easy. Trotsky therefore did not escape serious errors in political judgment in this period, or indeed in earlier periods. These errors have been pointed out many times.[11] I shall not rehash them here because they do not seem to diminish the interest of Trotsky's overall reflections on Soviet history and society; and that is what counts so far as my analysis is concerned.

Trotsky's often inexact analogies, as one scholar has rightly observed, seemed more polemical than analytical, and Trotsky himself later warned against using them too freely.[12] Having said this much, one must also recognize that Trotsky's thoughts were in many respects original, even more notably so in view of the time they were formulated. Their worth becomes more apparent if we contrast them with the official Stalinist explanations, or with the modest average level of scholarship dealing with the USSR at that time. Trotsky was the first to reject publicly the idea of continuity between bolshevism and Stalinism; clearly, anyone who might have reached similar conclusions inside the USSR was in no position to voice them. "The tendencies of the present government," Trotsky wrote in 1938, "are directly opposed to the program of bolshevism."[13] He was not unaware of the historical link between the two phenomena. "Naturally, Stalinism 'sprang' from bolshevism, but dialectically, not logically; not as its revolutionary confirmation but as its Thermidorian negation. And that's not the same

9. McNeal, "Trotskyist Interpretations," pp. 30–31.

10. *Biulleten' Oppozitsii,* nos. 58–59, p. 5.

11. I have pointed them out myself in my *Storia dell'Unione Sovietica* (Milan, 1976–1979), 1:179–80, 250–52, 494.

12. McNeal, "Trotskyist Interpretations," p. 35; *Biulleten' Oppozitsii,* no. 43, p. 11.

13. *Biulleten' Oppozitsii,* nos. 66–67, p. 19.

thing."[14] This insight still stands as the major contribution to historiographic research to emerge from the entire Trotskyite school.

Trotsky's thought attained its greatest originality in his effort to understand how the break between bolshevism and Stalinism had occurred. His prose is full of fierce denunciations, but he did not stop with invective. He tried to pinpoint the nature of the phenomena he was dealing with, even when they contradicted his own predictions, by analyzing the specific evolution of postrevolutionary Soviet society, of the 1930s in particular, when it was going through or had already gone through the launching of industrialization, collectivization, and the first five-year plans. He criticized the methods and the means by which they were carried out but continued to approve the initiatives themselves. Though Trotsky was far from immune to grand historical generalizations, he was the first to attempt to explain Stalinism on the basis not of some overall framework but of specific conflicts within Soviet society as it really was. Here we see the real breakthrough in his thinking.

For him that society was in no way socialist, as Stalin's propaganda claimed, but was still deep in a transitional period between capitalism and socialism, and therefore subject to contradictory influences.[15] The outcome of the clash between these two opposing tendencies had not yet been decided. First of all, the most serious contradiction, of which the Bolsheviks had been well aware as early as the 1920s, was still in force: with the revolution, that manifestation of "the most progressive forces in the country," Russia had made "the greatest leap forward in all of history"; but immediately afterward it had had to contend with isolation and the general backwardness of its productive capacity. With the first consistent economic successes, other paradoxes, more incidental but equally serious, were added to this fundamental contradiction—"despite these successes," according to Trotsky, "and also in large measure because of these successes."[16] And in fact, though the economy was growing rapidly, it was still far below the level at-

---

14. Ibid., nos. 58–59, p. 8. This statement appears in his essay "Stalinizm i bol'shevizm: K voprosu ob istoricheskikh i teoreticheskikh korniakh Chetvertogo Internatsionala," Trotsky's major treatment of this problem.

15. Leon Trotsky, *The Revolution Betrayed* (New York, 1972), p. 47. The first edition of this work, written between 1935 and 1936, appeared in Paris. Cf. I. V. Stalin, *Sochineniia* (Stanford, 1967), 1[14]:149–50.

16. *Biulleten' Oppozitsii*, nos. 68–69, p. 12; no. 42, p. 1.

tained by the richest capitalist countries in labor productivity and availability of consumer goods. The new nonprivate production structures demanded a constant increase in equality among individuals and social groups; in practice such equality was not yet possible—hence the strong tensions between different social strata and within each stratum. In the area of consumer goods especially, the unequal rights of the bourgeois order persisted. And overseeing this inequality was a state that, far from withering away, as Marx had predicted, was growing ever stronger and expanding its functions to embrace typically repressive measures.[17]

Therefore a second phenomenon was added to the first. The strengthening of the state had nurtured a new social group set above the others and heaped with privileges and powers: the bureaucracy. The bureaucracy, Trotsky pointed out, was not a class in the Marxist sense because even in other societies it had never been capable of giving life to a production and exchange system of its own and consequently to a specific set of social relations. Trotsky emphasized over and over that the bureaucracy performed a double function in the USSR. On the one hand, it protected the public, collective, or state ownership of the means of production established in Russia by the socialist revolution; and it did so because, among other things, that was precisely where its power base lay. But at the same time—and here was its negative function—the bureaucracy also protected its own privileges and powers. In this second role it found itself in conflict with the egalitarian strivings of the society and with the aspirations of that society's social base. What Trotsky defined as "Soviet Bonapartism"—that is, Stalin's Bonapartism—was an expression and a result of this conflict and, more generally, of the bureaucracy's double function.[18]

It must be pointed out at once that despite Trotsky's pretensions, such interpretations were still only rough probings rather than scientific findings; they were exploratory efforts to apply preexisting categories to admittedly new phenomena. In his writings of the 1930s the word "Bonapartism" frequently appears in connection with a variety of political developments in several countries. Trotsky ran into even greater difficulties when he analyzed the So-

17. Trotsky, *Revolution Betrayed*, pp. 52–56, 105–7.
18. Ibid., pp. 19–20, 234–39; *Biulleten' Oppozitsii*, nos. 36–37, p. 2; no. 41, pp. 4–5; no. 42, p. 4; no. 43, p. 12.

viet bureaucracy as a social base for Stalinism. He also seems to
have had intriguing thoughts suggesting that the word "bureaucracy" might not always be appropriate for the ruling stratum of
Stalin's society in its formative stages. But he never developed
these insights further.[19]

His historical judgment of Stalinism grew even sterner when he
dealt with that "Bonapartist bacchanalia," the mass repressions of
1936–1937. In describing the Great Terror he always spoke of "reaction." It was an "extravagant bureaucratic reaction," comparable
in scope to the revolution but diametrically opposed in direction,
the result of a conflict between "revolutionaries and Ther-
midorians at the very heart of the bureaucracy." At that point
Trotsky saw "the extermination of the old Bolshevik generation"
as "the most dramatic manifestation" of "the physical incom-
patibility of Stalinism and bolshevism," of "the contradiction between the October Revolution and the Thermidorian bureaucracy." But he remained convinced that the bureaucracy would get
rid of Stalin in the end, unless it got toppled itself by a new popular
uprising.[20]

Despite its corruption, for Trotsky the Soviet state was still a
"workers' state." And it was on this point that the major criticism
of many of his supporters focused, as it still does. The explanation
he offered seemed to betray a kind of psychological block, as if
Trotsky were reluctant to distance himself from the most glorious
page of his own biography—the revolution and the state it had created. Trotsky replied that there was no need to disturb "old Freud"
to explain his behavior, and that if anyone was guilty of "senti-
mentalism," it was not he but his critics.[21] But surely Trotsky, un-

---

19. "It is time, it is finally time to realize that a *new aristocracy* has come into
being in the USSR": Trotsky in *Biulleten' Oppozitsii*, nos. 54–55, 1937, p. 7. But
even earlier he had spoken about the "selection of a commanding order," adding
that the "need for discipline within the order" had led to a "cult of the infallible
leader": ibid., no. 43, p. 6. These ideas, which might have been linked, were not
pursued, and Trotsky continued to speak of "the bureaucracy." This fact is all the
more astonishing when one realizes that similar terms can be found in Stalin's
thought from the very beginning of his career. See Boffa, *Storia dell'Unione Sovietica*, 1:297–98, 614–15.

20. *Biulleten' Oppozitsii*, nos. 58–59, pp. 3–4; nos. 66–67, p. 21; nos. 68–69, pp.
12–13.

21. Ibid., no. 81, pp. 8–9. Even serious historians, however, have not altogether
rid themselves of the feeling that Trotsky's demeanor revealed a sort of revolution

derstandably enough, had succumbed to the self-indulgence so common in autobiography.[22] Yet in this instance his answer was far from unfounded. He did not consider the qualifier "workers'" as something "noble," never to be "sullied." In his research he tried, much more successfully than his opponents, to shun value judgments and moralizing in favor of more objective criteria. This did not prevent him from being pitiless in his denunciation of Stalinism and harsh in his struggle against it—certainly he was no less so than his critics. But what interested him most was *how* this phenomenon could have occurred in a new-model state created by the revolution; under different circumstances—that is, in the context of an old-model state—he would have taken everything much more for granted.

To rehearse Trotsky's arguments in these old disputes is not to defend them. A "workers' state," as Lenin had warned, was an "abstraction" in his time, and it still was.[23] But even as Trotsky used the expression, he tried to move from the abstract to the concrete, so that despite the inevitable simplifications built into political disputes, he would not lose sight of the uniqueness of the Soviet situation and of Soviet history. To him, as he emphasized on innumerable occasions, the expression "workers' state" meant only that certain revolutionary "conquests"—nationalization of industry, a planned economy, even collective peasant enterprises—had not gone missing. This point was of paramount importance in his eyes because he saw it as part of a worldwide revolutionary process in which sooner or later it was destined to play a role. The fact that his formulations cast this process in a very rigid mold, since he remained so firmly anchored in the Russian revolutionary model—perhaps more so than anyone else—is quite a different matter, and of only secondary importance for our reconstruction of his thought. He went so far as to say that if "Stalin's bureaucracy ever managed to destroy the economic base" of the new order—an eventuality he by no means considered out of the question—the experience of social leveling alone would be "forever part of history as an ex-

complex. See McNeal, "Trotskyist Interpretations," p. 30.

22. One instance of it can be seen in the fact that in the mid-1930s, having temporarily discarded this analysis, Trotsky returned to dating the Soviet "Thermidor" some ten years earlier, at the moment of Lenin's death and his own first defeat as the head of the opposition.

23. Lenin, *Collected Works*, 32:24–25, 48.

tremely important lesson for all humanity."[24] True, but the social differences that Stalinism was trying to stifle ended up enhanced, not diminished. The most serious difficulty was that the working class, which could be called dominant in the sense that it had laid the foundation for a possible new mode of production and exchange, was still oppressed because it was deprived of political power and reduced to a class of wage earners. This was the reality of Stalin's USSR, and Trotsky had no intention of ignoring it, though he went on to point out that this was hardly a new phenomenon in history. Other ruling classes, including the bourgeoisie, had often found themselves in equally contradictory situations in their own societies.[25]

These initial findings may have been tentative, but later developments in the Trotskyite school often do no better at advancing our understanding of Soviet history. The minor political current that later claimed to represent Trotskyite orthodoxy, having none of the Master's brilliant intellect or analytical audacity, was constrained to repeat his formulas. Certainly Trotsky's thought had its doctrinaire elements, but when it was stripped to pure doctrine, it lost its most intriguing aspects. Even the nonorthodox Trotskyites who criticized Trotsky's analysis and tried to go beyond it, convinced that they were saying what he hesitated to say, never improved it in any substantial way. Their theses, superficially more radical, actually sacrificed some of Trotsky's most stimulating insights into what really was new in Stalin's USSR. It should be said in their defense that in general they lacked that direct experience of the Soviet world and its revolutionary past with which Trotsky was so amply supplied; they all came from the ranks of communism, specifically Trotskyite communism, in countries other than the USSR.

During his lifetime Trotsky argued with many of them (Hugo Urbahns, Boris Souvarine, L. Laurat, Max Shachtman, Bruno Rizzi, James Burnham), often contemptuously. Perhaps the most interesting of them all, at any rate the one who attempted the most systematic investigation of Stalinism, was Max Shachtman, who continued to consider himself a disciple of Trotsky even when he took an extremely critical stance against Trotsky's assessments of

24. *Biulleten' Oppozitsii*, nos. 58–59, p. 19.
25. Ibid., nos. 62–63, p. 19; Trotsky, *Revolution Betrayed*, pp. 234–45.

Stalinist Russia. Yet it is difficult to find anything at all original in Shachtman's thinking. Rather than his own ideas we get polemic flashes of doubtful value that had circulated among former communists in earlier years, and with no help from Shachtman had spread among Trotskyites in the 1930s and 1940s, when the German-Soviet Pact and the outbreak of World War II made all disputes concerning the Soviet Union so bitter. The central idea of this ideological strain, and the point at which it contrasted most sharply with Trotsky's thought, was that a new kind of society dominated by a new exploitive class had come into being in the USSR, generally described as "bureaucratic collectivism." Stalinism was its most perfect expression, but it was actually a product of the revolution. At this point the dissidents usually ended up, like so many others, by drifting toward the usual (but not Trotskyite) interpretation of an unfortunate continuity in Soviet history.

The "bureaucratic collectivism" formula, still of doubtful origin, was attributed to a confused and nebulous work that eventually won some modest though bizarre notoriety for its author, Bruno Rizzi, an Italian ex-Trotskyite. It briefly described the phenomenon as a kind of society that was coming to be shared by Stalin's USSR, fascist Italy and Germany, and even the United States of the New Deal.[26] Shachtman then adopted the term and developed it with more sociological finesse, but only in respect to the Soviet Union.[27] Another former Trotskyite, James Burnham, appropriated the entire thesis, lumping together Stalinism, fascism, and Roosevelt's New Deal as so many versions of an emerging society increasingly dominated by technocrats.[28] If Burnham's book held little interest for anyone trying to interpret the various versions he was examining, Stalinism among them, still it had some influence, since it called attention to the increasing power that specialists, particularly management specialists, were acquiring in some societies.

Trotsky's influence on historical research is not limited to the

---

26. The original work—Bruno R., *La burocratisation du monde*—appeared in Paris in 1939 and would have been long forgotten had Trotsky not attacked it in *Biulleten' Oppozitsii*, nos. 79–80, pp. 4–5. The text can now be found in *Il collettivismo burocratico: Polemica L. Trotzki–P. Naville–Bruno R.* (Imola, 1967).

27. Max Shachtman's writings on Stalinism are collected in his *Bureaucratic Revolution: The Rise of the Stalinist State* (New York, 1962).

28. James Burnham, *The Managerial Revolution* (New York, 1941).

disputes his ideas later generated among his followers. Their most productive effects can be seen in the work of the historian Isaac Deutscher, who is best known as Trotsky's biographer. Deutscher came from the ranks of Trotskyism, and he never concealed his deep admiration for the "prophet" Trotsky. But he very quickly pulled away from militant politics and even more decisively from the doctrinal disputes that engaged the Master's followers. After the war—not an auspicious time for the study of Soviet problems—he started a new trend in the writing of Soviet history. His work was firmly rooted in the Anglo-Saxon tradition, since he wrote and published in London, but it was much more attuned to the dynamics of the communist movement and the Soviet revolution, to which he always felt intellectually tied. This trend was characterized by a concern not to produce some sort of interpretive framework but to explore in detail the facts and specific problems, often totally unknown, that had led to the Soviet experience.

Deutscher in particular was the first to have an opportunity to examine Trotsky's personal papers and thus to publish a mass of previously unknown information. Trotsky's thought always had great influence on his work, but he never accepted that influence uncritically. Deutscher found Trotsky's historical analyses, especially in *The Revolution Betrayed*, much more stimulating than those of his followers, whether or not they quarreled with the Master.[29] But he took care not to swallow anything whole. He did take over the idea of a Stalinist "Bonapartism," but he was more cautious about a Soviet Thermidor, tending to see more obvious links between Stalinism and Bolshevik Jacobinism.[30] Deutscher did not give the same weight as Trotsky to various elements of the Stalinist experience, such as "socialism in one country" and collectivization, but he did adopt other judgments, such as hostility toward the "right-wing opposition" led by Bukharin, Stalin's other great adversary. He added much that was original, and some of his ideas were later taken up by other schools: Stalinism as a barbarous but necessary device to wrench the country out of its backwardness,

29. Isaac Deutscher, *The Prophet Outcast: Trotsky, 1929–1940* (London, 1963), pp. 321–22.

30. A typical opinion: "What appears to be established is that Stalin belongs to the breed of the great revolutionary despots to which Cromwell, Robespierre and Napoleon belonged": Isaac Deutscher, *Stalin: A Political Biography* (London and New York, 1949), p. 566.

for instance, and the large element of nationalism in it. So Deutscher cannot be said to follow any particular interpretive path, though his ties with Trotsky permit us to speak of him in the same breath as the Thermidorian school.

One who did take over the idea of a Soviet Thermidor and make it his own, though his intellectual kinship with Trotsky is doubtful and he never acknowledged it, was the Yugoslavian Milovan Djilas. It was Djilas that gave currency to the idea of a "new class" and gave it its most thorough treatment in his book of that title.[31] One can say of this work what Deutscher said about *The Revolution Betrayed*: "For a long time the title page made a stronger impression than the book itself."[32] In fact, "new class" came to be more of an agitational slogan than a historical concept. That fate does not exempt us from careful analysis of Djilas's work, which he himself called "an inadequate synthesis of history, opinions and memoirs."[33]

His basic thesis is one we have seen before, that Stalinism was indissolubly linked to development. The party that had carried off a social revolution (unavoidable, in Djilas's opinion) had been forced to make "an industrial revolution" as well in order to "survive." It had had to "seize power in its own hands" because it had to impose policies that "exacted enormous sacrifices and involved ruthless violence, required not only promises but faith in the possibility of the kingdom of heaven on earth." This was the party's historic progressive function—the function performed in the West by the capitalist bourgeoisie a century earlier. So the socialist revolution was doomed to suffer the fate that had befallen other revolutions: the working classes had sparked all of them, only to see "their ultimate results fall to another class under whose intellectual and often organizational leadership the revolutions had been accomplished."[34]

The dissident Trotskyites, who had already signaled the rise of a "new class" in Stalin's USSR, found themselves in trouble when

31. "The Soviet Thermidor of Stalin had not only led to the installation of a government more despotic than the previous one, but also to the installation of a class": Milovan Djilas, *The New Class: An Analysis of the Communist System* (New York, 1957), p. 51.
32. Deutscher, *Prophet Outcast*, p. 321.
33. Djilas, *New Class*, p. v.
34. Ibid., pp. 16–27.

they tried to explain, in Marxist or any other terms, exactly what it consisted of. The same problem confronted Djilas, who focused not only on the Soviet Union but on East European countries as well, including Yugoslavia. He devoted a major portion of his book to an effort to define the "new class," shifting from one explanation to another; time and again, sometimes from one page to the next, he gave contradictory images of the "new class," equating it now with the bureaucracy as a whole, now with the Communist party, then with the party's directorate. His choice among these three possibilities is still uncertain at the end.[35] Djilas's search for the source of power available to the "new class" also ends indecisively, though as a Marxist he looked for it in the means of production. At times he saw it in a body of "forms of ownership," at others simply as an "administrative function [of] one specific form of ownership—collective ownership [administered and distributed] in the name of the nation and society."[36] In the end, though the book effectively denounces the injustices and forms of oppression found at that time in East European countries with state-run economies, the sociological description of the "new class" remains vague and inconclusive.[37]

Of all the ideas that sprang from the Thermidorian school, the idea of a "new class" has been one of the most sharply criticized by

35. Here are a few such conflicting explanations. At first the "new class" seems to be the party as a whole because the privileged bureaucracy "is nothing else but the party which carried out the "revolution" (ibid., p. 27). And "The communists are . . . a new class" (p. 44). But then things become more complicated: "This is not to say that the new party and the new class are identical," because "the party makes the class, but the class grows . . . and uses the party as a basis" (pp. 39–40). Thus the group seems to be expanding. "It is the bureaucracy which . . . administers and controls both nationalized and socialized property as well as the entire life of society. [This] role . . . consigns it to a special privileged position [and] this privileged class performs that function using the state machine" (p. 35). Elsewhere, however, the "new class" is abruptly narrowed to just the upper strata of the party: "The governing bureaucracy, or, in my terminology, the new class . . . is a party or political bureaucracy. Other officials are only the apparatus under the control of the new class" (p. 43). And even more explicitly: "The membership of the party, or of the bureaucracy" (p. 49). One could point to other such shifts; they are everywhere in the book.

36. Ibid., pp. 43–45. Djilas also says that the new class "is not conscious of the fact that [it] belongs to a new ownership class" (p. 59).

37. "Although it is sociologically possible to prescribe who belongs to the new class, it is difficult to do so: for the new class melts into and spills over into the people, into other lower classes, and is constantly changing" (ibid., p. 61).

Marxist and non-Marxist scholars alike. Nobody argues about the existence of a strongly privileged leadership stratum that developed in Soviet society during the years of Stalin's rule; no one outside Soviet officialdom denies it. The dispute centers on the leadership's essential characteristics and the use of the concept of class to explain them. Trotsky preferred "caste," but that was more a term of invective than a sociological identification.[38] A Western scholar observed that one was dealing here with "a new privileged stratum (although not a class)."[39] Others suggested different expressions. T. H. Rigby, for instance, used the term "estate." Stephen Cohen borrowed the Russian *soslovie* from the tsarist past, citing "the difficulty inherent in applying Western concepts, whether of the Marxist or modernization variety, to a Soviet political and social reality shaped by Russian historical and cultural tradition." *Soslovie* better renders the idea of "an official privileged class that served the state . . . more than it ruled the state." And this was the case, Cohen asserts, with the Soviet bureaucracy, particularly during the Stalin era.[40] Obviously the dispute is not simply a matter of what to call this group, since different terms imply different analytical approaches.

The most pertinent observation comes from E. H. Carr. He, too, doubts that the conceptual mechanism that Marx found useful in analyzing bourgeois society can be applied to a social reality so far removed in time and space. He observes shrewdly: "If we want to identify the ruling group in Soviet society, we have to look not for a class but for a party."[41]

Such critiques also imply different ways of looking at Soviet history and its outcomes. The whole interpretation of the Thermidorian school in all its various facets has been viewed with

38. *Biulleten' Oppozitsii*, nos. 66–67, p. 19.

39. Alexander Erlich, "Stalinism and Marxian Growth Models," in Tucker, *Stalinism*, p. 153. A similar but more thoroughly developed observation comes from a Marxist scholar who describes Djilas's theses as rather unconvincing: "Naturally the bureaucratization of our state apparatus has gone very far. But not to a point where bureaucracy would have become transformed into a new class which exploits other classes": Roy Medvedev, *L'Unione Sovietica alle soglie del 2000*, ed. Livio Zanotti (Milan, 1980), pp. 40–41.

40. T. H. Rigby, "Stalinism and The Mono-organizational Society," in Tucker, *Stalinism*, p. 65; Stephen F. Cohen, "Bolshevism and Stalinism," in ibid., p. 27.

41. E. H. Carr, *The October Revolution: Before and After* (New York, 1969), p. 91.

skepticism: it is not equipped to throw a realistic light on Soviet historical experience or on the Stalinist phenomenon in particular. "Stalin was many things," wrote Alec Nove, "but surely not the expression of the narrow self-interest of the bureaucratic elite. He feared their consolidation, and punished them without mercy."[42] Even more incisively, Cohen finds that the explanation that posits the bureaucracy as the "animating force" behind the events of the terrible decade of the 1930s, when Stalinism became established, "makes no sense, logically or empirically." He explains:

> Quite apart from the demonstrable role of Stalin, who is reduced in these theories to a replicable chief bureaucrat, it remains to be explained how a bureaucracy, which is defined as being deeply conservative, would have decided and carried out policies so radical and dangerous as forcible collectivization. And, indeed, Stalin's repeated campaigns to radicalize and spur on officialdom in 1929–1930, and after, suggests a fearful, recalcitrant party-state bureaucracy, not an event-making one. Nor is it clear how this theory explains the slaughter of Soviet officialdom in 1936–1939, unless we conclude that the "ruling" bureaucracy-class committed suicide.[43]

Impartiality requires us to recognize that these criticisms apply to Trotsky as well; he seriously underestimated Stalin and he was too close to the events he was trying to analyze to see them clearly. Yet we must also recognize that of the whole Thermidorian school, Trotsky alone was aware of those stumbling blocks and tried to avoid them.

---

42. Alec Nove, *Stalin and After* (London, 1975), p. 60.
43. Cohen, "Bolshevism and Stalinism," pp. 26–27.

8 Statism Takes the Upper Hand

In his first attempts to analyze Stalinism, Trotsky had already noted the contradiction implicit in a revolution that, according to its leaders, was supposed to initiate a gradual withering away of the state, yet that under Stalin led to an extraordinary hypertrophy of an enormously powerful state.[1] Stalin himself had publicly revised Lenin's thinking on this subject (something he seldom found it expedient to do), while some of his supporters went so far as to consider Lenin's position—though naturally they did not identify it with him personally—nothing less than counterrevolutionary.[2] What had been only a nebulous thought at the back of Trotsky's

---

1. "It is possible to hold that Stalinism is the product of social conditions that still prevent society from freeing itself from the state's straitjacket. But this theory does nothing to help us understand bolshevism or Marxism. It only points to the general level of humanity's cultural development and especially to the power relations between proletariat and bourgeoisie": *Biulleten' Oppozitsii*, nos. 58–59, pp. 11–12.

2. Stalin's famous words can be found in I. V. Stalin, *Sochineniia* (Stanford, 1967), 1[14]: 384–95. As for the Stalinists who considered Lenin's position counter-revolutionary, see the declarations of such figures as Lavrentii Beriia and Andrei Vyshinskii, cited in Giuseppe Boffa, *Storia dell'Unione Sovietica* (Milan, 1976–1979), 1:616, 731. See also Moshe Lewin, "The Social Background of Stalinism," in *Stalinism: Essays in Historical Interpretation*, ed. Robert Tucker (New York, 1977), pp. 132–33.

mind later became the principal theme of a new line of Marxist thought that developed independently of the Trotskyite school.

Like Trotsky's critique, it was born of a political conflict, the second serious conflict Stalin and his system had to face within the communist movement, after the struggle against the Bolshevik opposition. The new school arose in Yugoslavia after 1948, and Yugoslavs are still its major exponents, although, as we shall see, its influence has since spread beyond that country's borders.[3] Its matrix therefore was political and its development, at least for many years, was directly conditioned by political strife. But this was no mere debating society. The desire of the Yugoslav communists to confront Stalin's USSR not only with bold national resistance but also with a genuine political and social alternative gave it the stature of a school of thought. It envisioned a different society, one that could be called more socialist and Marxist than Stalin's USSR. This new interpretation of Stalinism found incentives rather than limitations in the political arena.

Its exponents were always men of politics and philosophers rather than historians. Only recently, with the unfolding of events in the USSR, has anyone felt impelled to take a more careful look at the ideas they set in motion. We shall return to this point, but let me say at once that several ideas of the Yugoslav school are central to the historical analysis that occupies us here.

Like Trotsky, this school stressed the rift between Stalin and bolshevism, and particularly between Stalin and Lenin's lifelong work and thought.[4] Not only, then, did these Yugoslavs adopt the

3. The year 1948 is usually seen as the starting point of a clash that was not only political but ideological and theoretical as well. One of its principal figures concurs: "Stalin succeeded in imposing a body of dogma that was violated for the first time at the beginning of 1948, in the open clash between Stalin and the Yugoslav Communist party, and later in the development of socialist-democratic self-management in Yugoslavia": Edvard Kardelj, *Le vie della democrazia nella società socialista* (Rome, 1978), p. 101; first published as *Putevi demokratije u socialistickom drustvu* (Belgrade, 1978).

4. Both have argued in singularly analogous terms with the proponents of continuity between Leninism and Stalinism. Debating Boris Souvarine, Trotsky said: "In order to explain the long series of historical misadventures, he looks for inherent, built-in defects in bolshevism. For him the real conditions of the historical process had no influence on bolshevism": *Biulleten' Oppozitsii*, nos. 58–59, pp. 13–14. And a Yugoslav source: "Attempts to represent the Russian revolution and its temporary realization in Stalinism as a necessary development, peculiar to the essence of Marxism or of Leninism, demonstrate only the low level of understanding of histor-

term "Stalinism"; they were largely responsible for giving it a legitimate place in the political and cultural debate. Unlike Trotsky
and even less like his followers, they attempted not only to analyze
Stalinism according to Marxist classical categories but to introduce
new categories that could join the mainstream of Marxist theory.
Of course, they had one advantage over Trotsky: they could call on
a longer and broader historical experience when they contemplated
developments in the USSR, and especially when they pondered the
spread of the revolutionary process that was to embrace the world,
which Trotsky had hoped for but had not lived to see. The
Yugoslav experience and the confrontation with Stalin can be seen
as a manifestation of this process.

Moreover, Yugoslav politicians and theoreticians tended to recognize some originality—wholly negative to be sure—in Stalin's
ideas. Here too they differed from Trotsky, who had always considered Stalin a mediocrity, incapable of an independent thought;
when he spoke of Stalin's "Bonapartism," for instance, Trotsky
pointed out that one need not on that account confuse him with a
Napoleon.[5] The Yugoslavs denied that Stalin's ideas had anything
to do with Marxism or "Leninism." They did not disregard the
novelty of those ideas, they simply denied Stalin his wish to be
recognized as a Marxist theoretician. They saw him rather as the
creator of a "bureaucratic revision" of Marx's or Lenin's thought,
as the main figure in a "conflict with the fundamental concepts of
Marxism," as the "theoretician" of a "system" they meant to reject precisely because they were Marxists.[6] One of the most meticulous Yugoslav scholars, Predrag Vranicki, also noted with great
insight that the core of Stalin's ideas had been exposed in the
mid-1920s and that "behind" the Stalin of that period "lurked the
future Stalin more or less entire," though of course Stalin did have
a history of his own and "became Stalin" in due course. Vranicki

---

ical processes—even if one excludes ideological preconceptions and one-sidedness":
Predrag Vranicki, *Marksizam i socijalizam* (Zagreb, 1979), p. 52.

   5. *Biulleten' Oppozitsii*, no. 43, p. 11.

   6. Vladimir Bakarič, *Le vie dello sviluppo socialista in Jugoslavia* (Milan, 1968),
pp. 105, 136; Milentije Popovič, "Appunti su alcuni problemi del pensiero socialista
contemporaneo," in *Il pensiero marxista contemporaneo nella prassi jugoslava*
(Milan, 1963), p. 215; Veliko Vlahovič, "Il programma della Lega dei comunisti della
Jugoslavia e l'inasprimento della lotta ideologica," also in *Pensiero marxista contemporaneo*, pp. 139–46.

pointed out that when Stalin spoke of "principles" or "questions" of Leninism, he was really presenting "principles" or "questions" of Stalinism, and that the "party theory," *qua* theory had in reality been not Lenin's, as he claimed and others still believe, but his own.[7] None of the Yugoslavs ever ignored the uniqueness of Stalin's ideas or the role that historical circumstances and conditions in Russia permitted them to play in determining the phenomenon that bears his name.

The new concept the Yugoslavs used as a springboard for their critical analysis was "statism." The term is generally taken to signify a widespread modern "tendency" toward "statization," which initially affects the economy but soon ends by engulfing the entire life of a community. Even in this early formulation, statism was seen as a product of the crisis of classical capitalism, as a partially "necessary and inevitable" development, and in any case as a reality that by now engulfed the whole world and that concealed grave dangers but had its good points too. Such a trend, in fact, was becoming more and more obvious in Western capitalist countries, where state intervention in the economy had grown extensively since the start of World War I. It could be seen also in the countries of the so-called Third World, where the state, usually of recent vintage, emerged as the principal instrument of economic and social development. Finally, it was seen in the so-called socialist countries of Eastern Europe and Asia, beginning, it goes without saying, with the USSR.[8] Stalinism, too, appears in this context as a manifestation, though an extreme one, of a modern and broader reality—"statism."

When the Yugoslavs introduced this concept, they opened a new perspective for a Marxist analysis of Soviet history. So long as it remained so generalized, however, the theory could not substantially enhance the interpretive capability of the analysis. "Statism" lumped together social realities the Yugoslavs themselves recog-

7. Predrag Vranicki, *Storia del marxismo* (Rome, 1972), 2:156, first published as *Historija marksizma* (Zagreb, 1971) (also available in German: *Geschichte des Marxismus* [Frankfurt, 1972]); Vranicki, *Marksizam i socijalizam*, pp. 84–85, 87–90.

8. Popovič, "Appunti su alcuni problemi," pp. 185–86; Vranicki, *Storia del marxismo*, 2:172. One of the many official documents of the Yugoslav communist party in which these positions are spelled out can be found in Josip Broz Tito, "Statism and Technocracy," a chapter of the platform prepared for the 10th Congress of the League of the Communists of Yugoslavia, in *Komunist* (Belgrade), 18 June 1973.

nized as too radically diverse.[9] The attempt to find a common de-
nominator among them was interesting and original, but what was
unique in Stalinism and in its consequences for the development of
Soviet society threatened to remain obscure. If one could indeed
speak of statism, what kind of statism was one dealing with in the
Soviet context? In Marxist terms this question inevitably spawned
a second one: Should Soviet statism be seen as "state capitalism"
or "state socialism"? Any debate couched in such contradictory
terms threatened to run aground on the same shoals where the
Trotskyite discussions had foundered, despite Trotsky's efforts to
avoid such quarrels over terms. The possibility seemed all the
more likely since the very concepts of "state capitalism" and
"state socialism" were rather ill defined in Marxist terminology.

So as not to get bogged down in a vexing linguistic debate with
obvious political and ideological implications of no concern to us
here, I shall mention only its essential points. Of the two terms,
"state capitalism" has a longer tradition in Marxist thought. In the
Bolshevik theoretical debate it was promoted mainly by Bukharin,
then a young party intellectual, who used it during World War I to
signal the growing intrusion of the state and its regulating functions into the capitalist economy.[10] In this sense it was adopted by
Lenin, particularly in reference to wartime Germany. But Lenin
broadened it to include some aspects of the Soviet economy during
the NEP, which left room for renewed capitalist activity under the
control of the Soviet state.[11] The first to apply the term to postrevolutionary Russia was Zinov'iev, during the internecine struggles of the 1920s. His intent was to emphasize how unsocialist the
Soviet economy still was.[12] Later the formula was adopted with
some alterations by a wide variety of writers, Marxist and non-
Marxist—Amadeo Bordiga, Toni Cliff, Maximilian Rubel, even

9. Popovič, "Appunti su alcuni problemi," p. 186.
10. Stephen F. Cohen, *Bukharin and the Bolshevik Revolution: A Political Biography, 1888–1938* (New York, 1973), pp. 28–33. This is an excellent analysis of
Bukharin's thought on the subject.
11. V. I. Lenin, *Collected Works* (Moscow, 1965), 32:294–98, 329–40, 352–57,
457–58; 33:277–79, 310–13, 418–21, and passim. Lenin made all of these statements in 1921 and 1922. He had mentioned a "state capitalism" adapted to Soviet
conditions, however, as far back as 1918. He often refers to these early statements
in the passages cited here.
12. G. Zinoviev, *Le Leninisme: Introduction à l'étude du leninisme* (Paris, 1926),
p. 216.

Berdiaev—to designate the Soviet social regime as a whole. This interpretation was explained by reference to the survival in the Soviet and other such economies of elements that Marx had designated as capitalist—commodities, wage labor, surplus value, alienation.[13] But more scholars rejected this notion as an arbitrary expansion of the concept of capitalism that would only sow confusion and make its obverse, socialism, appear utopian.[14]

The term "state socialism" also has a history in the Marxist debate. It was most systematically employed by the Yugoslav writers, some of whom have held that in their country the use of both "state socialism" and "state capitalism" in reference to Soviet society was conditioned by political contingencies: "state capitalism" was used between 1948 and 1953, the time of the harshest conflicts with Stalin's USSR, whereas "state socialism" was preferred after 1955, when relations between the two countries improved and the anti-Stalin debate was taking shape in the Soviet Union, along with the early Krushchev reforms.[15] Use of one term or the other became, so to speak, a thermometer measuring degrees of antagonism between the two countries and between their respective Communist parties.

There is some truth to this idea, but it hardly does justice to the

---

13. Amadeo Bordiga, *Struttura economica e sociale della Russia d'oggi* (Milan, 1966), esp. vol. 2; Maximilian Rubel, "The Relationship of Bolshevism to Marxism," in *Revolutionary Russia*, ed. Richard Pipes (Cambridge, Mass., 1968), pp. 404–7; Toni Cliff, *Russia: A Marxist Analysis* (London, 1964); Nicholas Berdiaev, *The Origins of Russian Communism* (London, 1948), pp. 146–47. An Italian writer, Arrigo Levi, considers "state capitalism" and "state socialism" to be interchangeable terms: *Il potere in Russia: Da Stalin a Brezhnev* (Bologna, 1967), p. 65.

14. I shall mention only a few of the many writers who reject this explanation. They are all strongly critical of Stalinism and of the Soviet regime as a whole: Popovič, "Appunti su alcuni problemi," p. 198; Vranicki, *Storia del marxismo,* 3:171; Norberto Bobbio, "Marxism and International Relations," in *Which Socialism?: Marxism, Socialism, and Democracy*, ed. Richard Bellamy, trans. Roger Griffin (Minneapolis, 1987), pp. 204, 209; first published as "Rapporti internazionali e marxismo," in *Filosofia e politica: Scritti dedicati a Cesare Luporini* (Florence, 1981), p. 313; Svetozar Stojanovič, *Between Ideals and Reality: A Critique of Socialism and Its Future* (New York, 1973), pp. 39–40, first published as *Izmedju ideala i stvarnosti* (Belgrade, 1969). Zdenek Strmiska observes: "These unfounded extrapolations tend to consider that every modern society that has economic, political, or class contradictions is capitalist": "Social System and Structural Contradiction in Soviet-type Societies" (Paris, 1980), p. 159 (mimeo). Strmiska expands on his critique on pp. 154–69.

15. Vranicki, *Marksizam i socijalizam*, p. 64; Stojanovič, *Between Ideals and Reality*, pp. 39–40.

complexity of Yugoslav Marxist thinking, which covered a wide
spectrum of opinion. Some Yugoslavs, for example, have spoken of
the Stalinist brand of Soviet statism as one of "various kinds" of
socialism in existence, most suitable to underdeveloped countries
and badly distorted under Stalin but still to some extent unavoidable.[16] Others have held that, at least so far as Stalinism was concerned, it was an "enormous error in historical judgment, superficial and unfair, to call this system socialist, let alone communist."[17]

Had the discussion been limited to this one set of alternatives, it
would not have gone beyond a schematic juxtaposition of a greater
and a lesser moral and political condemnation of the Stalinist
"model." But the Yugoslav interpretation, revolving as it did
around the concept of statism, is interersting precisely because it
managed to avoid such a simplistic comparison. We can thank the
political and ideological exponents of the "Yugoslav way" as well
as scholars, particularly those associated with the review *Praxis*,
who for one reason or another repeatedly found themselves at odds
with the leaders of their own country.[18]

One idea is shared by all the Yugoslav writers: a certain amount
of statism of the sort they tend to define as "state socialism" is a
legitimate and largely beneficial outcome of the socialist revolutions that have broken out in this century in economically and
politically backward countries, such as Russia, China, and Yugoslavia. The positive aspect of this phenomenon lies in the function
a state created by revolution assumes as it proceeds not only to
defend its achievements but to introduce certain "elements of socialism," such as public ownership of selected means of production. The quality of socialism implicit in such transformations,
however, is still very low and, above all, unstable. In fact, different
and indeed conflicting lines of development are possible at this
point. One would be the classical counterrevolution, with restora-

16. Bakarič, *Vie dello sviluppo socialista*, p. 62; Vlahovič, "Programma della Lega
dei comunisti," p. 126; Edvard Kardelj, *Memorie degli anni di ferro* (Rome, 1980),
pp. 128–29, first published as *Borba za priznanje i nezavistnost nove Jugoslavije,
1944–1957* (Belgrade and Ljubliana, 1980); Veliko Korač, "Il socialismo nei paesi
sottosviluppati," in *La rivolta di "Praxis,"* ed. Giovanni Ruggeri (Milan, 1969), pp.
273–83.
17. Vranicki, *Marksizam i socijalizam*, p. 84.
18. For the history of the journal *Praxis*, see Roberto Gatti, *I marxismi all'oppo-
sizione nei paesi dell'Est: Elementi per una riflessione sull'idea e sulla realtà del
socialismo* (Rome, 1978), pp. 23–48.

tion of the old order. When this menace is put down, however, a new conflict arises. One line of revolutionary development, nurtured by the consolidation of democratic values, leads to the expansion of the primary elements of socialism—workers' participation in the management of public affairs, "self-government" or "self-management" of society, the state's tendency to "wither away." At the same time, an opposite tendency leads the revolutionary state and its bureaucracies to overwhelm these potentials by growing more powerful than ever before and turning into a new oppressive Leviathan.

Toward the end of the 1950s one of the Yugoslav ideologues, Milentije Popovič, observed that Soviet development "under Stalin" had followed that sequence, moving "to consolidate the power apparatus, to bureaucratize it," and then, after the war, to spread this system throughout the world in a paroxysm of expansion. Stalinism is therefore the most dramatic form of an overpowering "statism" because it "tends toward a situation in which the state is omnipotent, omniscient, and all-regulating," like the "God of the Christians." Many other Yugoslav writers later echoed this proposition.[19]

Thorough analysis of this sort was a common heritage of Yugoslav Marxism. But individual writers later developed it in different ways. There were those who attempted to delineate the "statist" features of Stalinism. Mihailo Markovič considered six features "necessary and sufficient" to describe the phenomenon: (1) a violent anticapitalist revolution that goes no further than substituting political bureaucracy for bourgeois power; (2) a societal framework consisting of a disciplined, monolithic, and hierarchical party that has a monopoly of economic and political power and reduces all other organizations to the role of "transmission belts" to feed party interests; (3) a state that prolongs its existence beyond the annihilation of the capitalist class by setting up a dictatorship of the party or of a single leader; (4) the persistence of many forms of economic and political alienation in a society dedicated to "collective welfare"; (5) in the case of a multinational state, the subordination of the minority nationalities to the dominant one; (6) sub-

19. Popovič, "Appunti su alcuni problemi," pp. 231, 235; Stojanovič, *Between Ideals and Reality*, pp. 42, 44; Mihailo Markovič, "Stalinism and Marxism", in Tucker, *Stalinism*, p. 301.

ordination of the entire culture to the political sphere, under party control and censorship. Marković considers this list (which can also be seen as a summary of Stalinist concepts) to be the sign of a break with Marxism and a "formidable obstacle" to an effective revolutionary movement by the working classes.[20]

A second writer, Svetozar Stojanović, has denounced what he calls the "statist myth of socialism"—a myth that, he says, has dominated the twentieth century and been most fully embodied in Stalin's Russia, but should not be considered alien even to social democracy. In all cases, in fact, it makes socialist progress essentially dependent on the state. And it happens to be a myth, Stojanović declares, because its end result is anything but socialism. In the USSR especially it led not to socialism but to a "new system of exploitation and of classes" antithetical to Lenin's way of thinking and to the revolution's premises. Thus from the overthrow of capitalism emerged a new social structure, "statism," which can no longer be called capitalist but is not socialist either. Here Stojanović comes close to Djilas's idea of a "new class," but he is more cautious than Djilas; he sees the "statist class" as the dominant force in such societies, but he stops short of a thoroughgoing sociological and political analysis of that class.[21]

The most significant contribution has come to us from Predrag Vranicki, who went further than any of the others in trying to take a historical approach to these patterns of political philosophy—or, as he has said, to tackle the problem not in a "static way," merely by trying to describe it properly, but by grasping it in its dynamic unfolding.[22] We can follow the development of his thought through the succession of works he produced. He, too, started with the ideas shared by the whole Yugoslav school. "Statism" is a product of the socialist revolutions of this century. It is an "inferior phase" of socialism, "sometimes called state socialism," which, if it is to become socialism and communism, must "carry its own negation"—must, in other words, leave some space for those "social processes that predetermine the weakening of statism, its withering away, the end of the state monopoly." Stalin's ideas moved in a

20. Marković, "Stalinism and Marxism," pp. 299–300, 318–19.
21. Stojanović, *Between Ideals and Reality*, pp. 37–39, 58.
22. Vranicki, *Marksizam i socijalizam*, p. 68.

diametrically opposite direction, leading to maximal strengthening of such factors and thus to a sharp break with Marx and Lenin. Stalin identified socialism with the state, with the "statization of all the principal sectors of social life," with "state ownership and management of the means of production, with state-managed distribution of surplus." The result was not socialist progress but "the most powerful and best-organized statist-bureaucratic structure" ever seen "in the modern era."[23]

Vranicki's originality is apparent in his ability to perceive the dramatic quality of this process in the Soviet Union. If at first he had seen Stalinism as a serious "distortion" of "state socialism,"[24] his judgment later became sterner and more history-oriented. He noted that no matter which direction the Soviet Union took, it could not have become a developed nation without traumatic upheavals, and that while Stalin's ideas and even his personality were important, they were by no means the only factors. Vranicki introduced the notion of a "statist-bureaucratic counterrevolution," headed by Stalin and his faction, with some of the political organs as its social base. He also correctly identified the about-face of 1929–1930 and the massive repressions of 1936–1938 as the fracture points in postrevolutionary history; the result turned out to be a "historical innovation so far unrecognized."[25]

Events, says Vranicki, unexpectedly swerved from their revolutionary course. Not only were "social processes already set in motion" violently cut short, but the "last shreds of a socialist vision were tossed into the cupboards of historical curios." Elements of socialism present in the original "state socialism" were smothered. The bureaucratic-statist machine was strengthened through violence, by development of social relationships "typical of state capitalism" and the use of despotic controls. So far as relations between state power and culture are concerned, these are the methods of fascism. Stalin's party itself was the product of a dramatic transformation of the old revolutionary party, which turned into "the principal obstacle to the development of socialism and the chief promoter of bureaucratic-statist relations." To present all

23. Vranicki, *Storia del marxismo*, 2:148–63, 72–74.
24. Ibid., p. 74.
25. Vranicki, *Marksizam i socijalizam*, pp. 77, 81, 60.

this as "constructed" socialism was a true ideological hoax. An operation of this kind presupposed "a conception of socialism . . . completely antithetical to the idea developed by Marxism."[26]

At the same time Vranicki warned that these factors alone hardly do justice to the complexity of Stalinism, especially if they are seen too narrowly. Such terms as "bureaucracy" and "state capitalism" are particular cases in point.

> Another thing that makes Stalinism what it is, though it does not necessarily figure in every typical manifestation of state capitalism, is found in its historical origin. Stalinism was not born within an organically developed capitalist system but issued from the decline and fall of one of the first socialist revolutions. . . . Stalinsim, therefore, bears a whole revolutionary legacy, however distorted, . . . and gives it special prominence through the whole complex of moral and emotional reactions it calls forth.[27]

Similarly, the political bureaucracy of this system "plays the role of a ruling class," but this is its "only resemblance to an idea of class." True, it "does have a particular place in the production system," but "it is not a class in any clearly defined historical sense." And how could it be, "when the existence of its members—and I mean all the privileged bureaucrats, including the technocrats— seems to be so precarious that their very lives can depend on the whim of a despotic secretary?"[28] In these observations we see a concern not to bolster or weaken value judgments but to understand specific contradictions and conflicts that Stalinism injected into Soviet history.

It was just this sort of conflict that gave rise to the tragedies of the late 1930s in the USSR. Vranicki is not the only Yugoslav writer to make such charges. Stojanovič also writes that "the amount of violence Stalinism had to use attests to the strength of the socialist resistance to statist decadence." An alternative did exist, and "the Stalinists knew very well that it was a real possibility; that's why they fought their opponents with such guile and brutality."[29] Vranicki adds that this is certainly "one of the most important reasons" why a whole "generation" of Bolsheviks was "sacri-

26. Ibid., pp. 76–78, 81–84, 97. See also the entire essay on Stalinism, pp. 51–114.
27. Ibid., p. 80.
28. Ibid., pp. 98–99.
29. Stojanovič, *Between Ideals and Reality*, pp. 50, 55.

ficed." Even when they supported Stalin, the Bolsheviks of that generation "were always closely tied to the revolution. They knew how Lenin operated, and the future they fought for even before the revolution still guided everything they did."[30]

The general drift of the Yugoslav school, and its ability to point the way to stimulating lines of inquiry, was more important than the conclusions reached by individual writers. No matter what they thought about particular aspects of Soviet history, they saw the development of statism in the USSR and elsewhere as part of a universal process that in their eyes was still revolutionary. They blended its ingredients with the idea of a worldwide "transition" from one kind of society to another, from capitalism to socialism. Everything that went into the making of statism (Stalinism included), no matter how far it strayed from their idea of socialism, had to be considered within this framework. So did Western-style "state capitalism," though the Yugoslavs never saw that system as a true "road to socialism," cut off as it was from "conscious political action" in that direction. In this light it is easier to understand how they could see statist tendencies in a variety of political movements, including the social democratic parties that put so much hope in the "welfare state."[31] They stretched their framework far enough to encompass such phenomena as Stalinism—systems that many Yugoslavs considered so objectionable as to be actual obstacles to the development of socialism; but to reject them was not to lose sight of the fact that they, too, represented a phase in that process, negative though it might be.

The work done in Yugoslavia stimulated Marxist thought in other countries, focusing attention on problems of the modern state, its functions and its development. But elsewhere, too, the focus was more theoretical than historical. The French-Greek philosopher Nicos Poulantzas, who died too soon, also saw Stalinism as a form of statism—that is as a manifestation of a trend that was not exclusively Soviet, though Stalin pushed it to the extreme of "state worship." But Poulantzas never ventured beyond theoretical generalizations to a detailed investigation of Soviet history.[32]

30. Vranicki, *Marksizam i socijalizam*, pp. 53, 59.

31. Popovič, "Appunti su alcuni problemi," pp. 198–200; 187–88; Stojanovič, *Between Ideals and Reality*, p. 58. A similar opinion is expressed in even stronger terms by Nicos Poulantzas, *State, Power, Socialism* (London, 1978), p. 251.

32. Poulantzas, "State, Power, Socialism," pp. 252–56.

Another French scholar, Henri Lefèbvre, without ado has announced the spread of a new "mode of production," no longer capitalist but not yet socialist, throughout the world. Lefèbvre calls it
a "state [*étatique*] mode of production"—"something new and un-
expected" that will take the place of the capitalist mode but that is
"incompatible" with Marxist and Leninist thought; earlier Marxist
theory never even suspected its existence.[33] This mode of production would spread to every country though in accordance with a
"law of uneven development." Lefèbvre's ideas might have had
some interest for us if he had not warned us that "Stalinism,"
though he does not deal with it directly, happens to be the "objective and the meaning of his research." Stalinism, according to
Lefèbvre, achieved the status of a system between 1930 and 1940
and became the "prototype" for the state mode of production, "the
prototype for the modern state," the phenomenon that "led the
way that the contemporary world has followed."[34] State socialism
and state capitalism, "similar in some respects and quite different
in others," have divided the world between them. According to
Lefèbvre,

> the Stalinist state not only presumed to run the affairs of millions of
> people in the name of the proletarian revolution. . . . It saw its main
> task as that of enlarging the productive powers of an immense multi-
> national territory that it kept intact by violence. This, indeed, is how
> it came to be the model state of the modern world.[35]

I have quoted Lefèbvre chiefly to show how far statist thinking
managed to go. Such a vision of history, not only of the Soviet
Union but of our entire century, is hard to swallow whole. Yugoslav writers have also expressed their doubts.[36] Even so, the new
direction in which the Yugoslavs pointed is still of great interest.[37]

---

33. Henri Lefèbvre, *De l'état* (Paris, 1976–1977), vol. 2, *De Hegel à Mao par Staline: La théorie marxiste de l'état*, p. 396, and all of vol. 3, *Le mode de production
étatique*.
34. Ibid., 2:390–96 and 3:273.
35. Ibid., vol. 1, *L'état dans le monde moderne*, p. 287.
36. Vranicki, *Marksizam i socijalizam*, p. 65.
37. I seem to detect the influence of the Yugoslav school in the works of Charles
Bettelheim. Though he tries to go further, Bettelheim is still anchored to the "state
capitalism" formula. But for him "state capitalism" is part of the "transition from
capitalism to socialism" and therefore can develop in various ways. Bettelheim
holds, in fact, that there are two kinds of state capitalism— "state capitalism dominated by the working class," capable of breaking its ties with capitalism, and "state

The special virtue of their work lies in its refusal to be doctrinaire. Its starting point was a historical experience lived at firsthand—the experience of Yugoslav self-management, which always has to be opposed to Stalinism and to the various forms it has taken since Stalin's death. Everyone who sees the Soviet system as statist supports "self-management," a concept the Yugoslavs have invested with considerable authority during the whole international ideological and political debate. Of course, it is difficult to say how much these theories represent simply an emotional reaction to the growing weight the state has acquired in the world, and how much they reflect objective analysis of the course human society is taking. The policies pursued today by many more or less developed countries seem to be saying that the Yugoslav school is wrong. This is not the place to discuss that question. The case of Vranicki suggests that the productivity of this school as a whole is destined to grow in direct proportion to its willingness to turn from theoretical investigations to concrete historical analysis.

---

capitalism dominated by the state bourgeoisie," which strengthens those ties. Mao's China exemplifies the first, Stalin's Russia the second. Bettelheim's historical investigation of the Soviet process is still unfinished, however, as it stops on the eve of the "turn" in 1930. See Charles Bettelheim, *Les luttes de classe en Urss*, 2 vols. (Paris, 1974, 1977). Bettelheim's theoretical works are strongly marked by an idealization of the Chinese cultural revolution. For some time this tendency was quite widespread among sizable portions of the European left. See Charles Bettelheim, *La transition vers l'économie socialiste* (Paris, 1968) and *Calcul économique et formes de propriété* (Paris, 1970).

9 Industrial Despotism

A third interpretive approach that developed in Marxist circles hinged on an idea that Marx himself had only partially worked out and that was long overlooked by Marxist thinkers in our century: the idea of an "Asiatic mode of production." This idea enjoyed a widespread revival between the end of the 1950s and the early 1960s. At first discussion touched on the USSR and the history of Stalinism only indirectly, but eventually it developed into a lively argument about Stalin's dictatorship and the new communist experiences in government after World War II.

It seems unnecessary to reconstruct Marx's thoughts on the "Asiatic mode of production" in any detail; it's a complicated task at best, and the subject has been treated in several rewarding studies that are widely available.[1] For our purposes it's enough to recall that in his preface to *A Critique of Political Economy* Marx wrote: "Asiatic, ancient feudal and modern bourgeois modes of production can be designated as progressive epochs in the eco-

---

1. Gianni Sofri, *Il modo di produzione asiatico: Storia di una controversia marxista* (Turin, 1974) (this book is especially useful for its reconstruction of Marx's thought and the subsequent disputes); Ferenc Tökei, *Sur le mode de production asiatique* (Budapest, 1966). See also "Premières sociétés de classe et mode de production asiatique," *Recherches internationales à la lumière du marxisme*, nos. 57–58 (January–April), 1967.

nomic formation of society."[2] Several other references to the subject and numerous remarks on the characteristics of Asian society can be found elsewhere in Marx's writings. In the absence of any systematic treatment of the subject—understandable, since it never ranked high among Marx's interests—these allusions could be read in a variety of ways and sparked many arguments, when they were not being ignored. Some of Marx's thoughts on the subject remained unpublished until 1939.

After one of these long interruptions, attention was once again drawn to the Asian mode of production in 1957 by Karl Wittfogel, a German Orientalist who had emigrated to the United States. His thick volume on "Oriental despotism" is a curious work, half erudite attempt to summarize human history, half libelous political propaganda.[3] Wittfogel had devoted many years of his life to the study of Chinese history. A student of Marxism, he had been a communist in his youth, but abandoned communism in the early 1930s and so thoroughly distanced himself from its doctrines that later, in America, he became an idealogue of the Cold War. During the McCarthy years he even reported some of his academic colleagues whom he suspected of being communist sympathizers. In his past, however, one finds a vast and serious research effort that undoubtedly influenced modern Oriental studies.[4] These many facets of the man are all reflected in *Oriental Despotism*, his most ambitious work.

Venturing far beyond Marx's sparse observations, Wittfogel held that a particular kind of society had developed in a large part of the world and had remained substantially unchanged for centuries. He described it variously as a "hydraulic," "Oriental," and "agro-managerial" society. It was based on irrigation agriculture, on the impressive hydraulic constructions required by irrigation, and on a division of labor tailored to fit its needs. As entrepreneur in the business of constructing hydraulic installations, the state took

2. Karl Marx, "A Critique of Political Economy," in *Karl Marx and Frederick Engels: Selected Works* (Moscow, 1968), p. 183.
3. Karl A. Wittfogel, *Oriental Despotism: A Comparative Study of Total Power* (New Haven, Conn., 1957).
4. Owen Lattimore, in the preface to his *Studies in Frontier History* (Paris, 1962), acknowledges that Wittfogel was once a serious scholar. Lattimore's objectivity seems all the more impressive when we realize that he was one of Wittfogel's victims. See also Sofri, *Modo di produzione asiatico*, pp. 145–47.

upon itself a large number of managerial functions, and developed an extremely powerful organizational capacity that soon reached beyond the sphere of hydraulic systems to all associated aspects of life, from the military to the religious. This formidable concentration of functions would have given the "hydraulic government its genuinely despotic power." These are the origins of "Oriental despotism," a "total" despotism.[5]

According to Wittfogel, an analysis of the "hydraulic society" also required a specific "sociology of class" based not on property relations, which are extremely weak in such a society, but on relations with an inordinately strong state apparatus. The state governs by "total terror" and requires "total submission." In order to perform the necessary functions, the despot has at his disposal a segmented and vast bureaucratic apparatus that constitutes "a ruling class in the most unequivocal sense of the term; and the rest of the population constitutes the second major class, the ruled." Only the former represents "monopoly bureaucracy." Both classes, of course, are stratified: in such a system one finds "many social antagonisms but little class struggle," though more general "conflicts" between the "people" and the "men of the apparatus" do exist.[6] This type of society arose along with the hydraulic states in certain regions of the world, from ancient Egypt to China, and spread in various modified forms across huge geographic areas of the planet—to Russia, for instance.

The book betrays its pamphleteering purpose by constantly proclaiming the superiority of "Occidental" society, its history, and its system. The main political purpose of the book, and what makes it germane to my investigation, is seen in the way it sets up Soviet Russia and the People's Republic of China as a latter-day and unprecedented development in the old "Oriental despotism" combined with modern industrial capabilities; not a simple "Asiatic restoration," therefore, but a "managerial state" that differs from the old "hydraulic state" in that it is no longer based on agriculture alone but uses the same methods to manage the entire economy: an "industrial state apparatus," "totalitarian" or "communist."[7] At this point Wittfogel, despite the apparent originality

5. Wittfogel, *Oriental Despotism*, pp. 1, 8, 101.
6. Ibid., pp. 303, 265–68, 327.
7. Ibid., pp. 440–46.

of his premises, merges with the totalitarian theory so fashionable at the time, and adds his own bit to the heterogeneity and inconsistencies we have already seen.

It is not my task here to evaluate Wittfogel's ideas about the general history of non-European societies; it is enough to point to the barrage of objections that scholars have loosed against them.[8] There are other reasons why the subject of Asian societies was bound to catch the attention of numerous Marxist scholars. The Marxian concept of an "Asiatic mode of production" had already been fully debated within the communist movement in the late 1920s; the subject was even referred to in the program of the Communist International approved in 1928.[9] Wittfogel, who had direct knowledge of that debate, reconstructed and subverted its principal terms in his book.[10] China and its political struggles, a revolution looming in the Orient while it stagnated in the West, and thus the need to know and analyze the Asian societies more thoroughly had aroused interest in the subject within the Communist International and the Soviet party. Now, at the end of the 1950s, interest was reviving for the same reasons.

Once again a great insurrection of colonial peoples, this time not only in Asia but also in Africa and Latin America, led Marxist scholars in various countries to reflect again on those old ideas of Marx's that had been so long neglected. The last discussions in the USSR, in 1931, had been largely inconclusive; for a variety of reasons, none so unambiguously banal as those sometimes advanced in imitation of Wittfogel, the idea of an "Asiatic mode of production" alien to the evolutionary mainstream of European societies had run into widespread opposition.[11] As the 1930s advanced, the

---

8. Sofri, *Modo di produzione asiatico* pp. 139–47.

9. Aldo Agosti, *La Terza Internazionale: Storia documentaria*, pt. 2, *1924–1928* (Rome, 1976), p. 1026. For a little-known aspect of the debate that went on in those years within the Soviet governing circles, which makes it clear that the positions for and against the "Asiatic mode of production" did not match the preexisting divisions among the various political groups, see *XV s'ezd VKP(b): Stenograficheskii otchet* (Moscow, 1961) 1:733, 805–6, 839–40.

10. Wittfogel, *Oriental Despotism*, chap. 9, esp. pp. 397–405.

11. See Jan Pecirka, "Discussions soviétiques," in *Recherches internationales à la lumière du marxisme*, nos. 57–58 (January–April), 1967, pp. 59–78. At that time, concern that the history of Oriental countries might be reduced to a sort of second-class history was already intense. Bear in mind that as early as 1961 a scholar who was to become a major contributor to the analysis of the "Asiatic mode of produc-

political atmosphere in the USSR became less and less conducive to theoretical research. In 1938, when Stalin decided to revise Marxist philosophy in a short chapter of the official manual on party history, he proclaimed that humanity had known five "fundamental" types of modes of production: the primitive community, slavery, feudalism, capitalism, and, in the USSR, socialism.[12] From that day on, this pronouncement, which left no room for "Asiatic" forms of society that differed in any way from those listed, became dogma. It also suggested a unilinear and universal succession in the history of human societies which bore little resemblance to Marx's concepts. But not even this discrepancy could prevent the adoption of Stalin's dogmatic formulation, for to the communist movement in those days he was the premier interpreter of Marxism. A number of scholars chose instead to try to revise history to conform to Stalin's dictum.

With meager success, however. When Marxist researchers looked at the societies and history of non-European countries with greater care in the late 1950s, they discovered that Stalin's construct had no equivalent in reality, especially its rigid evolutionary line. Major portions of the history of large countries—China, Japan, India, Iran, and others in Asia, not to mention Africa—did not fit at all into that evolutionary sequence.

New discussions got under way, particularly among Marxist Orientalists in Great Britain, in France, in the principal countries involved, and later in the Soviet Union and Italy.[13] There was a prolif-

tion," Jean Chesnaux, wrote: "Marx prudently refrained from giving a systematic definition of [the Asiatic mode of production], despite what a number of American 'Marxologists' would have us believe. They were curiously concerned about doctrinal purity so long as it did not lead the people of Asia to liberation and victory": *La Pensée*, no. 95 (January–February), 1961, p. 24n.

12. I.V. Stalin, *Sochineniia* (Stanford, 1967), 1[14]:312.

13. Here are a few of the principal texts, in addition to those mentioned in n. 1 above: *Marxism Today*, July, September, October, November, December 1961 and January, February, March, June, July, August, September 1962; *La Pensée*, nos. 114 (April) and 117 (October), 1964; 122 (June), 1965; 127 (April), 129 (August), and 130 (October), 1966; 132 (February), 1967; and 138 (February), 1968. See also the contributions to the collected volume *Sur le mode de production asiatique* (Paris, 1969). And for Soviet sources: *Obshchee i osobennoie v istoricheskom razvitii stran Vostoka: Materialy discussii ob obshchestvennykh formatsiiakh na Vostoke. Aziatskii sposob proizvodstva* (Moscow, 1965); *Problemy dokapitalisticheskikh obshchestv v stranakh Vostoka* (Moscow, 1971); Iu. V. Kachanovskii, *Rabovladeniie, feodalizm ili aziatskii sposob proizvodstva* (Moscow, 1971); M. A. Vitkin, *Vostok v*

eration of translations of a manuscript Marx had written in preparation for *Das Kapital*, which had appeared in Moscow only on the eve of World War II—*Grundrisse der Kritik der Politischen Oekonomie*. There one could find a chapter on "the forms that precede capitalist production."[14] This debate continued well into the 1970s. Naturally opinions differed as to the meaning of "Asiatic mode of production," its place in the evolution of human societies, its characteristics, its geographic distribution, its degree of autonomy, its differences from the other known "social formations," and so forth. No consensus was reached in this case either, but progress was unquestionably made in the analysis and knowledge of the ways various societies developed, and it seemed increasingly more difficult to reconcile them all with a single European pattern. Attention was once again focused on a whole series of characteristics of "Oriental" or "Asiatic" development—the importance of hydraulic works, the economic and entrepreneurial functions of its archaic states, the limited distribution of private landownership, political despotism—on which Marx had touched in a number of his writings.

Although the debate contributed a great deal to the development of Marxist thought, up to this point it had virtually nothing to do with issues of Soviet history. These things were undoubtedly present in the minds and hearts of many participants, but they stayed in the background. It would have been quite arbitrary and presumptuous to go beyond this point, almost as though Marx could have foreseen Stalinism or left means handy for analyzing it. All those involved in the debate were so determined to distance themselves and their scientific concerns from the political interests of a Wittfogel that they argued against his ideas even when they went along with one or two of his insights.[15]

filosovsko-istoricheskoi kontseptsii K. Marksa i F. Engel'sa (Moscow, 1972). In Italy the debate came to encompass the whole concept of "socioeconomic formation." See *Critica marxista*, no. 4, 1970; no. 4, 1971; nos. 1, 2–3, 4, 1972.

14. Karl Marx, *Grundrisse: Introduction to the Critique of Political Economy* (New York, 1973), pp. 471–514.

15. The most significant critique comes from a Czech philosopher who was very active in the ideological renewal movement that culminated in Alexander Dubček's defeat in 1968 and who then was forced to emigrate. " 'Oriental despotism' has become a concept that embraces all of history from Genghis Khan to Stalin. In a thousand years of history Wittfogel distinguishes only two types of societies, those

If the debate had any immediate implications, they seemed to apply more to Maoist China, since many of the participants (the Hungarian Ferenc Tökei, for instance, and of course Wittfogel himself) had devoted the greater part of their research to Chinese history. Much of the documentation that supported the idea of an Asian mode of production came from that history. But the very fact that one could suspect such a direct connection, at a time when the USSR and a large part of the communist movement were deep in a political and ideological quarrel with the Chinese, led other Orientalists, such as Stuart Schram, to stay out of the debate. In the light of all that has been published, the fear that the debate might have been simply an indirect way to downgrade the Chinese revolution seems to have been quite unjustified. A French writer active in the discussion, Jean Chesnaux, explicitly denied that allegation. Chesnaux was at one time a supporter of the "Asiatic mode of production" theory and a warm admirer as well as a student of the Chinese revolution and other revolutionary movements in Asia.[16] The historians' main concern, however, was always to establish how close such countries as China had once come to social stages analogous to slavery in the ancient world and feudalism in Europe, and how much of their development had been different and unique. The controversies over these points were actually neither new nor exclusively Marxist. Historians had been aware of them even in prerevolutionary Russia.[17]

What makes these debates important for our investigation is the

---

that are heirs to European antiquity and today are part of the democratic-bourgeois world, and those that continue the traditions of the ancient Oriental despotism—the socialist countries. This notion cloaks everything in that dark in which all cats are gray. But this dark is not the night of history; it is the dark of an intellect that once was vigorous and discerning. Wittfogel paid a high price for putting his intellect at the service of primitive political interests": Lubomir Sochor, "Karl-Augustus Wittfogel: Osud jednoho intelektu," *Literarni Noviny*, 12 November 1966, pp. 8–9. Jean Chesnaux wrote that Wittfogel's work is an "odious critique of the contemporary socialist world, which in the name of a primitive geographic determinism he accuses of being nothing but a reincarnation of ancient Asian despotisms": *La Pensée*, no. 114 (March–April), 1964, p. 35.

16. H. Carrère d'Encausse and Stuart Schram, *Le Marxisme et l'Asie, 1853–1964* (Paris, 1965), p. 131. The answer can be found in Jean Chesnaux, "Où en est la discussion sur le mode de production asiatique?" pt. 2, *La Pensée*, no. 129 (October), 1966, pp. 40–41.

17. The arguments over the existence of a Russian feudalism involved such noted historians as Nikolai Pavlov-Sil'vanskii, Pavel Miliukov, and Nikolai Kareev. For a summary, see *Ocherki istorii istoricheskoi nauki v SSSR* (Moscow, 1963), 3:299–303.

spur they provided for a few Marxist dissenters in Eastern Europe
and even in the USSR to analyze their own societies and history. I
dwell on Marxist dissidents because they seem to have been the
only ones to make an original attempt to see the Soviet or Chinese
experience from an Asian point of view. Bear in mind that it was
nothing new to describe Stalinism or Maoism as an "Oriental despotism." Wittfogel aside, it was done quite often, especially by politicians prone to ready-made definitions likely to strike the public's fancy.[18] Some of the more radically anti-Marxist Soviet
dissidents have carried Wittfogel's ideas to extremes that Wittfogel
himself was never tempted to approach. Igor' Shafarevich, for example, held that socialism as such was no more than what had
existed in Mesopotamia 5,000 years ago, in the Inca empire, and in
the Egypt of the pharaohs. Many centuries and even millennia ago
there existed societies which "embodied much more fully and con-
sistently the socialist tendencies which we observe in modern
states."[19] No need, then, to go looking for anything unique in Stalin!

I shall single out two East European Marxist dissidents: the Russian Aleksandr Zimin and the German Rudolf Bahro. Both are
strongly critical of Wittfogel. Zimin describes his interpretations as
"cunningly affected, almost always one-sided, and in large part
prejudiced." He admits that one may find "striking" and "nonacci-
dental" similarities between Stalin's despotism and a "society
founded on the Asiatic mode of production," but they call for a
"genuine explanation," not "those superficial and highly colored
juxtapositions" one typically finds in Wittfogel.[20] Bahro's judgment
is even harsher: Wittfogel's book "does nothing but chauvin-
istically warn the Western bourgeois world against the 'yellow
peril.'" It was written "not in the spirit of historical objectivity but
under the thrust of an antisocialist trauma." Bahro therefore cate-
gorically rejects its "basic motivation, which inevitably leads . . .
to a total opposition to the countries where socialism already ex-

18. One example: Anthony Eden, *Full Circle: Memoirs of Anthony Eden* (Boston,
1960), p. 55.
19. Igor' Shafarevich, "Sotsialism," in *Iz pod glyb: Sbornik statei* (Paris, 1974),
pp. 34–40; published in English as "Socialism in Our Past and Future," in *From
under the Rubble*, trans. A.M. Brock et al. (Boston, 1975), pp. 31–36.
20. Aleksandr Zimin, "Il problema della collocazione storica dell'Unione Sovietica: Parallelo storico e ipotesi sociologica," in A. Zimin et al., *Dissenso e socialismo: Una voce marxista del samizdat sovietico* (Turin, 1977), pp. 156, 161, 166.

ists and to the hopes and aspirations of the people who live there."[21] Rejection of Wittfogel is really all that Zimin and Bahro have in common; in everything else they differ substantially.

Zimin's position is the more ideological of the two. He does not get involved in the subtleties of the Marxist debate over the Asian mode of production. He summarizes its features and briefly lists what he considers the "most typical" traits of such a society. Zimin accepts the idea advanced by some researchers (and rejected by others) that the Asian mode of production emerged at the dawn of the first great "turning point" in human history, the transition from a primitive tribal society to one divided into classes; it developed in those parts of the world that were "chronologically the first" to be forced by "a convergence of historical circumstances" to make that transition in order to overcome the limitations of the tribal system. In sum, this was the first improvisation along a road on which history could offer no guidance—the evolution of the classist societies. Thus was born a "bastard and deformed" type of organization destined to remain on the fringes of what Zimin sees as the "natural" evolution of a classist society, characterized by the "European" succession of slavery, feudalism, and capitalism. It's an anomaly, then, despite its broad geographic distribution, but an anomaly that could have a long life because the strong tribal imprint it inherited from its long prehistory deprived it of inner stimuli to change and doomed it to such "immobility" that it could survive even its own bloody political convulsions.[22] For Zimin this was a "stagnant" society. This view, despite its Marxist antecedents, was regarded with suspicion by many Marxists involved in the debates of the 1960s.[23]

Zimin is not an Orientalist, and his ideas diverge in many respects from those endorsed by the majority of scholars. His vision

21. Interview with Rudolf Bahro, in Angelo Bolaffi, *La democrazia in discussione* (Bari, 1980), pp. 95–96.

22. Zimin, "Problema della collocazione storica," pp. 168–69, 161–64.

23. "We have always insisted unequivocally . . . that this discussion must not be contaminated by the idea of 'stagnation.' On this point we do not hesitate to say that Marx took a pessimistic view of the ancient Oriental societies and that we dissociate ourselves from that view. We firmly believe that history does not reveal only one possible evolutionary pattern, and that the stages through which non-European populations managed to pass (particularly the 'Asiatic' stage) could also lead to more advanced forms, either alone or in combination": Jean Chesnaux, "Où en est la discussion sur le mode de production asiatique?" p. 40.

of history interests us less than the consequences he sees for our modern age. With a boldness that appears rash, Zimin sees the past repeating itself "in our present era . . . the era of the second great turning point in history," which he defines in the most orthodox Marxist terms as "the transition from a classist society to a classless society." Like any other Soviet Marxist, Zimin dates this era as beginning in October 1917.[24]

History offered us more guidance at the second great turning point than it had at the first. At the beginning of the twentieth century it offered none at all. The result in the USSR, after a promising start, was a society that was well defined but anomalous; it had sidestepped the "natural course" of history. It was neither capitalist nor socialist (as it ought to have been) nor even transitional; it was a Stalinist society, and it dared to call itself "full-blown socialism." Outside of the mainstream of history, this is a stagnant society, just as its Asian analogue had been before it; it led nowhere yet was capable of self-perpetuation and "self-preservation." Zimin does not consider this pessimistic scenario as inevitably fated to affect the future because he sees three big differences between the first and second turning points: humanity today has become "a single whole"; its parts are strongly linked by communication and contacts; and the historical process is no longer "spontaneous" because it is conditioned by strong "awareness" factors in large masses of people.[25]

Zimin's construct falls far short of a convincing historical interpretation. He admits that it "needs to be confirmed" and that it calls especially for investigation to determine how and why that anomaly came to pass in the USSR. The main problems are therefore still to be resolved. But it does suggest an approach to Stalinism that was current in Soviet Marxist circles, and probably not only among dissenters, even when discussion of such things had to be clandestine. It is still difficult to know how large these circles were. Judging by developments since the advent of Gorbachev, they must have been far from negligible, though certainly they were in the minority. In any event, while Zimin rejects Stalinism out of hand, he still defends the fundamental tenets of Marxism and sees a universal historical value in the October Revolution—a

24. Zimin, "Problema della collocazione storica," p. 183.
25. Ibid., pp. 169–78, 178–82.

judgment that, as we know today, even many members of the Soviet Communist party failed to share. Zimin said so himself, no doubt after due consideration.[26] His arrows could therefore fly in more than one direction.

"October," Zimin says, "was not intended solely to rescue the Russian people and the Russian state from dreadful backwardness and general collapse at the beginning of the twentieth century. Its significance lay in achieving salvation through a socialist revolution and in linking its redeeming mission with the world revolution that was proclaimed to usher the world through the great turning point to which history had brought it." Between Lenin on the one hand and Stalin and his successors on the other, Zimin sees not simply a break but a complete reversal: what "had to be done" became what "should not have been done."[27] As historical judgments go, this one is too hasty. Still, Zimin's position is interesting because it revives a conviction we have seen under various guises among Marxist critics of Stalinism: that escape from the predicament must be sought primarily in a worldwide revolutionary process.

Bahro, a communist active in the German Democratic Republic until he was forced into exile, offered a much more articulate analysis that bore witness to widespread cultural dissatisfaction among an even broader spectrum of Marxists in Eastern Europe. According to Bahro, the October Revolution was forced to undertake a task that Marx never imagined and that its makers never intended. The evolution of European society is a far cry from that "natural evolutionary course" of history in which Zimin believes. What becomes "generalized" in Marx's thought is only "Europe's historic role, especially in the nineteenth century." Other experiences, notably those outside of Europe, have been left out. "The key" to the solution of the modern world's problems, including those of the Soviet Union, "lies in Asia, partly in a past that is far behind our own European past."[28]

> The October revolution already was not, or was at least far more
> than, the (from our confined European perspective of waiting) 'de-

26. Ibid., pp. 185–87, 184n.
27. Ibid., pp. 184–85.
28. Rudolf Bahro, *The Alternative in Eastern Europe* (London, 1978), pp. 260–63, 43–48.

formed' representative of the proletarian rising in the West that has not taken place. It was and is above all the first anti-imperialist revolution in what was still a predominantly pre-capitalist country even though it had begun a capitalist development of its own, with a socio-economic structure half feudal, half 'Asiatic.' Its task was not yet that of Socialism . . . but rather the rapid industrial development of Russia on a non-capitalist road. Only now, when this task is by and large completed, is the struggle for socialism on the agenda in the Soviet Union.[29]

A "non-capitalist way" to develop industry and a modern economy is at the center of Bahro's whole analysis of what he agrees to call "real socialism." For him this is a "general concept" that covers all the "nominally socialist countries" and permits us to "search for the origin of the non-capitalist road in the legacy of the so-called Asiatic mode of production." That road has led to a "fundamentally different social organization from that outlined by Marx." But Bahro is less interested in the idea of the "failure of socialism" than in the "reality" of that alternative "type of society."[30] Not even a revolution in the West, in his opinion, could have modified the worldwide drama created by developmental inequality. When Western capitalist civilization reached its zenith, it "faced the entire legacy of the oldest civilized mode of production, i.e. the Asiatic." International imperialism was responsible for the revolutions whose "specific task . . . is the restructuring of the pre-capitalist countries for their own road to industrialization, the non-capitalist one that involves a different social formation from that of the European road." Thus was born what Bahro calls "industrial despotism." But it is not simply a product of the "Asiatic" legacy. It is also a new sign of the "civilizing role of the state that has been confirmed throughout world history. . . . The state as taskmaster of society in its technical and social modernization—this fundamental model can be found time and again since 1917 whenever pre-capitalist countries or their decisive minorities have organized themselves for active entry into the twentieth century."[31]

Russian society was considerably less capitalist than Lenin had assumed. Several social forms cohabited within it: the "deepest and most ancient" one, made up of the "semi-Asiatic bureau-

29. Ibid., p. 50.
30. Ibid., p. 13–14; Bolaffi, *La democrazia in discussione*, p. 96.
31. Bahro, *Alternative in Eastern Europe*, pp. 50–51, 58, 66, 126–29.

cracy"; the feudal, which had been only partially eliminated; and finally the most recent form, capitalism, with its bourgeoisie and its proletariat "concentrated in a few cities." Given the relations among the classes in Russia and its entire historic tradition, there necessarily had to appear "a different attitude towards the role of the state in the transition period than that of Marx." Then Bahro says: "The historical function of the Bolshevik 'party of the new type' consisted in preparing the apparatus for the productive overthrow of the Russian social structure it inherited, for forced industrialization. . . . When this obedient and handy tool was finished, there was no longer a Communist party. . . . There was a political administration flanked by organs of terror." Bahro therefore does not stress the differences between Lenin and Stalin. He merely points out that Lenin had always been conscious of the fact that "the way ahead was a means toward the socialist goal, however distant this lay. This consciousness was designed to survive in the party nucleus." When, on the other hand, "Stalin prematurely proclaimed his socialist constitution, while having the Old Guard shot, he both affirmed and simultaneously completed the destruction of this consciousness."[32]

It seems clear that despite his Marxist viewpoint, Bahro often comes to the same conclusions as those who base their reasoning on the idea of a "development revolution." His appears to be the Marxist version of that thinking. Of course, to say this is by no means to underestimate the originality of tackling this sort of problem in Marxist terms. This strategy permits Bahro to go on to a detailed examination of the societies said to represent "real socialism" without bogging down in a purely sociological exercise. In his hands it becomes a means to promote an authentic socialist struggle among the forces at work in those societies. At the same time, Bahro's interpretation, too, is vulnerable to the objections that can be raised against the whole development school.

Specifically, his analysis seems to be marked by a strong determinism, though he warns us that it is always difficult to draw a line between what is "evitable" and what is not. Here are a couple of examples. "The Bolshevik seizure of power in Russia could lead to no other social structure than the one now existing"; and "the Bolsheviks were driven" to collectivize the countryside. Essen-

32. Ibid., pp. 85–93, 115–18.

tially, then, Bahro espouses the idea that Stalinism was "inevitable." True, he starts from a legitimate position. He is not closing his eyes to what was going on; he wants to know the "historical reasons" for it. Such things "are not created by arbitrary caprice, and hence require in their totality neither justification nor excuse, but rather truthful description and analysis." Bahro's argument is aimed at those who want to market the final results as Socialism, canonizing them as eternal and natural.[33] We have here a political battle fought with the best of intentions and with the most serious of arguments. But the fact remains that his interpretation comes uncomfortably close to suffering from the one-dimensional fatalism we often find among non-Marxist views of a Soviet history driven by the requirements of development.

33. Ibid., pp. 90, 101, 37; Bolaffi, *La democrazia in discussione*, p. 98.

10 Other Important Contributions

Our survey of the principal interpretations of Stalinism could be concluded at this point; no other school of thought worth mentioning has emerged so far. This survey would not be complete, however, if I failed to recognize a few contributions that fit into none of the groups I have examined yet have earned a place in the historiographic debate, at least in respect to some facets of the problem. I have no intention of citing all the scholars in the Soviet Union and elsewhere who have made original contributions to one aspect or another of Soviet history and so should be included among those who have attempted a critical reconstruction of the Soviet experience. Important names may seem to have been passed over: George Kennan, Rudolf Schlesinger, Alexander Werth, Marshall Shulman, and many others in and out of academe. Obviously merit has nothing to do with the matter. The approach I have chosen obliges me to focus only on those writers who have been directly involved in the debate, or at least have enriched it in interesting ways.

Two historians—one Soviet, the other English—call for particular attention. Roy Medvedev and E.H. Carr differ considerably in origin, development, and way of thinking. The works of both have attracted attention for their novel contributions to the documentation and reconstruction of events, and therefore to our knowledge of them, rather than for any explicit or implicit interpretive scheme. But both, each in his own way, have intervened in these disputes several times and have enriched them with original ideas and fresh, well-chosen material.

Roy Medvedev must be singled out chiefly as a pioneer in his field. What he wrote about Stalin and Soviet history appeared at a time when free expression on these subjects was still forbidden. Among writers with a worldwide readership, he was the first to advance certain ideas that later reemerged at the center of the political and historical debates that finally erupted into the open in the Soviet Union of Mikhail Gorbachev (where Medvedev is now a member of the Congress of People's Deputies). We shall come to that explosion in due course. I feel obliged to focus first on Medvedev's work because of its influence on Soviet and non-Soviet scholars during that earlier phase of Soviet studies.

I do not mean to imply that other Soviet historians have nothing important to say to us. Quite the contrary. The earlier essays of such scholars as Mikhail Gefter, K.N. Tarnovskii, Viktor Danilov, and Esfir' Genkina on special moments and issues of Soviet history indicated that at least some of them would eventually have plenty to tell us in the way of broader and more comprehensive interpretations. And in fact they did, the instant they were able to express themselves freely under Gorbachev. One of the most deplorable consequences of the ironclad pre-*glasnost'* censorship was that it deprived us and the Soviets of the first-rate contributions these scholars and others like them might have made to the debate. Throughout the 1960s and 1970s, as the official interpretation of their country's history became progressively more rigid, every utterance that gave the slightest evidence of independent thought was banished. Even accurate reconstructions of Lenin's thinking were held against their authors because they could not be easily reconciled with the theory of the glorious continuity of the whole Soviet experience.[1]

Medvedev managed to avoid a similar fate only because he was able to publish his works abroad, though he still lived in Moscow. His books were forbidden in the USSR and had only a limited clan-

1. For a classic example of this kind of argument, see V. Golikov, S. Murashov, I. Chikvishvili, N. Satagin, and M. Shaumian, "Za leninskuiu parti'nost' v osveshchenii istorii KPSS," *Kommunist*, no. 3, 1969. For a summary of the discussions, see George M. Enteen, "A Recent Trend in the Historical Front," *Survey* 20 (Fall 1974).

destine distribution there.[2] It is impossible not to single out these works; they had considerable influence in promoting historical knowledge of the whole period tied to Stalin's name. Medvedev's chief contribution consists of his reconstruction of facts, disclosure of hitherto unpublished documents and information, and the gathering of valuable testimony that otherwise would have been irretrievably lost.[3] In comparison with this fundamental task, the interpretive aspect of the work recedes into the background. Medvedev's most monumental and famous book, devoted entirely to the Stalin years, is *Let History Judge.* By his title he seems to leave the verdict and interpretation to posterity. Yet we find no hint that Medvedev was anything but a true believer. The book is subtitled *The Origins and Consequences of Stalinism.*[4] Medvedev must be counted among those who most legitimated the use of "Stalinism" to designate a period and a phenomenon that cannot be identified with the rest of Soviet history in all its complexity.[5]

Medvedev's interpretations follow the Marxist-Leninist line but in a way openly at odds with the official doctrine taught in the USSR at the time. Medvedev prefers to speak of "scientific social-

2. Medvedev, like the Soviet historians quoted earlier, was a member of the Communist party. In 1969, however, he was expelled. At that time a party representative asked why Medvedev had "assumed the right to deal with and study the events of our history" and who had "authorized him to write a book about Stalin." According to him, "everything there was to say had already been said by the Central Committee in its 30 June 1956 resolution on the cult of personality": Roy Medvedev, *Intervista sul dissenso in Urss,* ed. Piero Ostellino (Rome and Bari, 1977), pp. 43–44.

3. As far as eyewitness accounts are concerned, another work did more than Medvedev's to publicize the more repellant aspects of Stalin's repressive prison system: Aleksandr Solzhenitsyn's *Gulag Archipelago* (New York, 1974, 1978), which was more widely distributed throughout the world than anything Medvedev wrote. No one has ever questioned the moral courage of this book or its value as testimony. The same cannot be said for the objectivity of its historical analysis. Roy Medvedev addressed this issue in "The Second Volume of *The Gulag Archipelago* by A. Solzhenitsyn," in Aleksandr Zimin et al., *Dissenso e socialismo: Una voce marxista del samizdat sovietico* (Turin, 1977), pp. 67–79.

4. The book first appeared in the United States: Roy A. Medvedev, *Let History Judge: The Origins and Consequences of Stalinism* (New York, 1971). Alfred A. Knopf later published an expanded edition of the book in Russian: *K sudu istorii: Genesis i posledstviia stalinizma* (New York, 1974).

5. The excellent editor of the English version, David Joravsky, observes in his Introduction: "Stalinism itself is a term that may cause confusion, for many people in the West have only a vague notion of the difference between Stalinism and the Soviet system or communism in general": Medvedev, *Let History Judge,* p. xi.

ism" rather than "Marxism" or "Marxism-Leninism," though he recognizes the roles Marx and Lenin played in creating and developing it.[6] The distinction is important. Medvedev believes that there is a correct, scientifically verifiable way of bringing a socialist society to life; that Marx, Engels, Lenin, and the others who searched for it made important but not necessarily exhaustive contributions; and that the question is still open to inquiry. He sees Stalinism as a conglomeration of deviations, errors, and profound distortions of that correct way. His analysis is therefore largely a search for accountability. He does not ignore collective responsibility; but for the most part he emphasizes the personal accountability of the tyrant, "usurper" of power in the first socialist experiment in history.[7]

For Medvedev Stalinism is not reason enough to repudiate everything that was done in his country from 1917 on to give birth to a socialist society. It does, however, represent a very heavy and unjustifiable liability that cast a black shadow over this experiment and has had fateful negative consequences that are still felt today. Beyond a few general remarks, Medvedev offers no clear vision of his own as to what the correct way to proceed towards socialism might be. He relies on what can be found in the works of Marx, Lenin, and other socialist writers. It is clear, however, that for him the correct way implies more consensus and less coercion, the participation of the mass of citizens out of conviction, broad guarantees of cultural freedoms—in other words, something altogether different from what happened during the Stalin years; as Medvedev sees it, Stalin's way was a tragic denial of all those things, imposed by cynical and systematic deception. The result was a "pseudo" or "false" socialism (*Izhesotsializm*) mixed with a few genuine socialist accomplishments that were attributable mainly to the revolution rather than to Stalin.[8]

With this general attitude, Medvedev entered into a whole series of disputes over interpretation. He rejected the idea that Stalinism was an inevitable consequence of October 1917. He rejected any form of historical determinism:

> If the political and social system created after the October Revolution engendered Stalinism, if history offered no other possibilities of

6. Medvedev, *Intervista sul dissenso*, pp. 30–31.
7. Medvedev, *Let History Judge*, p. 1.
8. Ibid., pp. 549–50.

development, if everything was strictly determined, then the October revolution must also have been determined by the monstrous system of Russian autocracy. . . . In other words, to explain Stalinism we have to return to earlier and earlier epochs of Russian history, very likely to the Tartar yoke. But that would be wrong; it would be a historical justification of Stalinism, not a condemnation.[9]

Medvedev believes that alternatives are always available for historical development, and that there were alternatives for Soviet society as it emerged from the revolution and the civil war. They were poorly understood by those who came to oppose Stalin, and those opponents became responsible for more than a few "errors" themselves. Basically, Medvedev saw the true alternative to Stalinism in something that had actually existed—the New Economic Policy—provided it could have been gradually amended to reflect the changing needs of society.[10]

Just as Stalinism "absolutely had not been" an inevitable consequence of the revolution, neither was it a child of Lenin. The contrast between Lenin and Stalin, as Medvedev presents it, takes on the hues of myth: Lenin was "the embodiment of all the best elements in the Russian revolutionary movement," Stalin "of all that was worst."[11] Medvedev and I see eye to eye on the breaking points between these two opposites in the revolutionary tradition. The first falls between 1928 and 1933: "That was the moment of a clear-cut repudiation of Leninism and transition to Stalinism."[12] The second is marked by the mass repressions between 1936 and 1938, or "the completion of a long-planned usurpation of power implemented in stages within the party and the country."[13]

Medvedev does not deny that conditions favorable to Stalinism had been created earlier, conditions that can be traced back to aspects of bolshevism or of the Lenin years. Medvedev devotes several pages of his principal work to these factors and has written some separate studies on them.[14] Nor is he unaware that a series of

9. Ibid., p. 359.

10. Ibid., pp. 349–50. For Stalin's struggle against his opponents in the 1920s, see ibid., pp. 34–47, 50–70. For a study that focuses on Bukharin, see Roy A. Medvedev, *Nikolai Bukharin: The Last Years* (New York, 1980).

11. Medvedev, *Let History Judge*, p. 362.

12. Medvedev, *Intervista sul dissenso*, p. 140.

13. Medvedev, *K sudu istorii*, p. 687.

14. Roy A. Medvedev, *The October Revolution* (New York, 1979). See also Sergei Starikov and Roy Medvedev, *Philip Mironov and the Russian Civil War* (New York,

objective circumstances deeply rooted in the Russian past or linked to world affairs in the 1920s and 1930s strongly influenced the origins and development of Stalinism. The sum total of these factors, however, never seems enough to explain the phenomenon. Here and there Medvedev contradicts himself on the "counterrevolutionary" dimensions of Stalin's power.[15] Still, the strength of his analysis lies in the contrast between Stalinism on the one hand and the revolution and original bolshevism on the other.

Not that Medvedev overlooks the complexity of Stalinism. No one was more alert than he to the support Stalin and his government enjoyed among the masses. Although the term "cult of personality" refers to just part of the phenomenon—and not the most important part, at that—it seems to him worth preserving because it expresses that strange "secular variant of religious belief" which, with Stalin's encouragement, accompanied and supported his power.[16] Medvedev also has some interesting things to say about Stalinism's "social base," which he believes had several components. The state and political organs, strongly bureaucratized and sometimes "degenerate," were an important part of this base, but still only a part. The workers, especially those who had flocked to the factories from the countryside in the rapid industrialization process, and the intellectuals of recent proletarian or peasant origin were also part of that base.[17] In other words, we are dealing here with the social strata that emerged as part of the stormy social upheaval caused by economic growth as well as by the revolution-

---

1978). This book is an excellent contribution to the study of a little-known aspect of the civil war, the role played by the Don Kossacks, and is based on the rich and previously unpublished documentation assembled by Starikov during his long study of the subject. Mironov was also the subject of a novel by Iurii Trifonov, *Starik* (Moscow, 1978).

15. "Today some communists call Stalin a counterrevolutionary and consider the events of 1936–1938 a counterrevolutionary coup. This is an oversimplification": Medvedev, *Let History Judge*, p. 375. "In many of its manifestations, Stalinism was a counterrevolution . . . , a partial restoration of tsarist autocracy camouflaged as loyalty to Leninism": Roy Medvedev, *L'Unione Sovietica alle soglie del 2000*, ed. Livio Zanotti (Milan, 1980), p. 63.

16. Medvedev, *K sudu istorii*, p. 703; Medvedev, *Let History Judge*, pp. 362–66. Medvedev also defines Stalinism as a "disease . . . that serious and prolonged disease which has been termed 'cult of personality' after one of its symptoms (by no means the chief one)": *Let History Judge*, p. xxxi.

17. Medvedev, *Let History Judge*, pp. 412–17; Medvedev, *L'Unione Sovietica alle soglie del 2000*, pp. 69–70.

ary origin of the new regime. In his care not to take too simplistic a view of Soviet society either under Stalin or afterward, Medvedev rejects the "new class" theory, though he is well aware of the emergence of a "caste system" and of "clearly defined elements of a bureaucratic oligarchy" at the upper and middle levels of the leadership.[18]

What interests Medvedev is the contradictions in Soviet society during all its developmental phases. He is guided by a historian's scruples, convinced that no good can come of forgetting or deliberately falsifying the past, or even of simply failing to put the pieces together correctly. But he is a political man as well, and as he explores his country's present and past, he is conscious of his own stake in its destiny, and so is eager to introduce radical reforms. Yet the reformer's concerns do not smother the scholar's objectivity.

E.H. Carr is a scholar of quite another sort. He, too, influenced the study of Soviet history profoundly, but in a different spirit and a different direction. Carr and Medvedev both stand for a scholarly commitment capable of bold innovations in the vastly different cultural worlds that formed them. Medvedev's voice was the first from inside the USSR to provide a comprehensive picture of post-revolutionary history at odds with the one officially sanctioned by the regime he still would not renounce. Carr worked in an atmosphere more conducive to free investigation, but he too had to challenge a scholarly tradition, in his case one that was passionate in its revulsion against the whole Soviet experience. In this sense his name has often been linked with that of Isaac Deutscher, because both men had always been "well outside the academic mainstream" in the West.[19] Linked also by ties of friendshp and mutual esteem, they brought a wholly new spirit to their work. But Carr brought even more of the "necessary detachment" to the task than Deutscher.[20] He worked meticulously for three decades. The results are impressive for the richness and accuracy of his documentation and for an analytical flair that still sets the standard for other

18. Medvedev, Let History Judge, p. 543; Medvedev, L'Unione Sovietica alle soglie del 2000, pp. 39–41; Roy A. Medvedev, On Socialist Democracy (New York, 1975), pp. 297–300, 399–400.
    19. Stephen F. Cohen, "Bolshevism and Stalinism," in Stalinism: Essays in Historical Interpretation, ed. Robert Tucker (New York, 1977), p. 9.
    20. See the author's introduction in E. H. Carr, The Bolshevik Revolution, 1917–1923, 3 vols. (London, 1950–1953), 1:v–vi.

scholars. The dispassionate clarity of Carr's thought is demonstrated by the successive modifications he made in his work as fresh discoveries came to light.[21]

Carr was associated with Deutscher also as a supporter of linear continuity in Soviet history. The two distanced themselves from that theory only in their sympathy for the revolution, not on any general interpretive issues, as some critics of linear continuity have noted.[22] But this criticism calls for a closer look. It is very difficult, for instance, to link Carr to any of the interpretive lines I have examined. In any case, the importance of his work does not rest on his interpretation. This is particularly the case in respect to Stalinism. One could even say that this problem had little to do with his research. His monumental work covers only the first twelve years of postrevolutionary history: he does not go beyond 1929, which many scholars consider to be the watershed year; Stalinism lies beyond it. The term "Stalinism" occurs very rarely in his books. One could even argue that except for some fragmentary observations in minor works, he never dealt with the problem at all, never wrote specifically about the 1930s, the true Stalin years, or about later periods.

Carr did, however, enrich the general debate over Soviet history with a number of important observations. The first concerns the Russian revolution, which he called "a turning point in history," possibly "the greatest event of the twentieth century." The revolution, "rooted in specifically Russian conditions," had "world-wide significance," represented the "first open challenge to the capitalist system, which had reached its peak in Europe at the end of the nineteenth century," and may be "thought of both as a consequence and a cause of the decline of capitalism."[23] These conclusions are not Carr's alone; other scholars share them. But it is in-

21. Cf. ibid., p. v, with the final organization of the entire work: the three volumes on the revolution are followed by *The Interregnum: 1923–1924* (London, 1954); *Socialism in One Country: 1924–1926*, 3 vols. (London, 1958–1964); and *Foundations of a Planned Economy, 1926–1929*, 3 vols. (vol. 1 with R. W. Davies) (London, 1969).

22. Cohen, "Bolshevism and Stalinism," pp. 9–10; Robert Tucker, "Stalinism as Revolution from Above," in his *Stalinism*, pp. 84–87. Isaac Deutscher seems to have addressed the problem in a different way in *The Unfinished Revolution, 1917–1967* (London, 1967), pp. 5, 21–39.

23. E.H. Carr, *The Russian Revolution: From Lenin to Stalin, 1917–1929* (London, 1979), p. 1; Carr, *October Revolution: Before and After* (New York, 1969), pp. 6–33.

teresting that Carr came to his conviction as a result of his research, rather than assuming it from the start as a premise.

Deutscher certainly agreed with Carr about the revolution,[24] but on one essential point they parted company. With some reservations, I have placed Deutscher in the Thermidor school, if only because he was so strongly influenced by Trotsky's thought, historical as well as political. I have pointed out how critical Deutscher was of the very idea of a Soviet Thermidor. The same cannot be said of Carr, and not only because his cultural matrix, unlike Deutscher's, is not Marxist. Carr makes his position on the Thermidor issue very clear: in his opinion "every victorious revolution has its Thermidor."[25] His work as a whole suggests that it cannot be otherwise. He voiced this opinion early in his career and never saw reason to change it. Only from this viewpoint can Carr be seen as a proponent of continuity in the Soviet experience. In fact, he is convinced that without Stalin's revolution from above, "Lenin's revolution would have run out into the sand," and that "in this sense Stalin continued and fulfilled Leninism."[26] This statement appears to make sense; events seem to have corroborated it; but in reality it is a reverse image of that "hypothetical history" which Carr himself despises.[27]

This approach leads to harsh judgments of individuals who opposed Stalin, especially of Trotsky and Bukharin.[28] It has also led Carr to see the differences between Lenin and Stalin mostly as a matter of character traits, and to consider "utopian" (though not in

24. See Deutscher, *Unfinished Revolution*, p. 3. Deutscher's opinion is similar to Carr's and is implicit throughout the book.

25. E. H. Carr, "Stalin," *Soviet Studies* 5 (July 1953): 3.

26. E. H. Carr, *Studies in Revolution* (London, 1964), p. 214.

27. For a repudiation of any sort of hypothetical history, see Carr, *October Revolution*, p. 122. Deutscher has given us a more moderate but more ambiguous version of Carr's thesis that a Thermidor is inevitable in any revolution; Deutscher quotes extensively from "The Legend of the Grand Inquisitor," in Fedor Dostoevskii's novel *The Brothers Karamazov*, in which Ivan tells his brother Alesha how Jesus, having returned to earth, is threatened with being burned at the stake so that his humanistic teaching may be corrected by the iron discipline of the Church, the only body capable of triumphing over the weakness of human nature: Isaac Deutscher, *Stalin: A Political Biography* (New York, 1961), pp. 361–62.

28. But he is much harsher in his judgment of Bukharin, whom he describes as "a weak, amiable and keen-witted man caught up in the turmoil of events too vast for his moral stature," than he is of Trotsky, whom he considers a heroic figure despite his "weakness of character" and lack of "political instinct": Carr, *Socialism in One Country*, 1:173, 151–52.

a pejorative sense) everything in Lenin's thought that fails to harmonize with his own view.[29] But Carr is too scrupulous a scholar to avoid problems that might shake his basic convictions. Thus he eventually noticed an even more radical difference between the two first leaders of the Soviet state. Lenin did not believe in a revolution from above; Stalin's revolution, Carr finally concludes, was just that.[30]

Carr ultimately perceived (though I think only partially) that there was a basic ideological contrast between Lenin and Stalin:

> Lenin remained in one respect rooted in the nineteenth century. While he proclaimed the need to instruct and influence the masses, he continued to believe in instruction by rational persuasion or by force of experience. By the middle of the twentieth century this belief had lost much of its validity both in the Soviet Union and elsewhere. This was perhaps the fundamental difference that marked the transition from Lenin to Stalin. Lenin regarded persuasion or indoctrination as a rational process in the sense that it sought to implant a rational conviction in the minds of those to whom it was directed. Stalin regarded it as a rational process only in the sense that it was planned and conducted by a rational elite. Its aim was to induce large numbers of people to behave in a desired way. How to achieve this aim was a technical problem which was the object of rational study. But the most effective means to employ in achieving this aim did not always, or not often, appeal to the reason.[31]

Actually, the closer Carr gets to problems of Stalinism, the more his analysis falls into inner contradictions. He saw the collectivization of the peasants, for example, as completing "the agrarian revolution which had begun in 1917 with the seizure of landlords' estates by the peasants." There is no need here to point out how questionable this statement is. In fact, Carr himself notes that the crucial decision to proceed with wholesale collectivization, which was officially announced in November 1929, contradicted all the previously proclaimed gradualism and had a "haphazard and impulsive character." The only explanation he can offer for this hypothetical impulsiveness is that in 1929 "a situation so completely out of hand bred a mood in which desperate remedies may well

29. Carr, *Russian Revolution*, p. 169; Carr, *October Revolution*, p. 61. One can find a more careful and more subtle analysis of Lenin's "utopianism" in Carr, *Bolshevik Revolution*, 1:233–49.
30. Carr, *Russian Revolution*, p. 187; Carr, *October Revolution*, pp. 95–96.
31. Carr, *October Revolution*, pp. 27–28.

have seemed the only way out."[32] One has only to recall the devastating and long-lasting consequences for Soviet society and its political life to realize that the decisions made at that time were more than "haphazard and impulsive" choices.

Much the same can be said about another of Carr's opinions. He considers Stalin "the most pitiless despot in Russian history," but also "a great westernizer." He thus joins the ranks of those for whom a comparison with Peter the Great seems unavoidable. But Carr also specifies that Stalin "westernized" Russia "through a revolt, partly conscious, partly unconscious, against western influence and authority and a reversion to familiar national attitudes and traditions."[33] Explanations of this sort bring to mind the nineteen-century quarrels between Russian "Slavophiles" and "Westernizers." Here again, Carr's interpretation was later influenced by the broader revolutionary developments of our own century, and he came to see Stalin's revolution as more appropriately identified with a resurgent Orient. No convincing support for this conclusion can be found in the available documents. "The post-Leninist reorientation of the socialist revolution implied that the final overthrow of capitalism would be the work not of its proletarian victims in the advanced countries . . . but of its colonial victims in the undeveloped countries, and that it would be the work not of an economic class, but of a political movement."[34] More convincing is Carr's observation that

> the ferment generated by the Russian revolution . . . proved more pervasive and more productive in backward non-capitalist countries. The prestige of a revolutionary regime which, largely through its own unaided efforts, had raised itself to the status of a major industrial Power, made it the natural leader of a revolt of the backward countries against the world-wide domination of western capitalism, which before 1914 had been virtually uncontested; and in this context the blots which tarnished its credentials in western eyes seemed irrelevant.[35]

32. Carr, *Russian Revolution*, p. 161; Carr, *October Revolution*, pp. 108, 109; Carr and Davies, *Foundations of a Planned Economy*, 1:269. For a critique see Tucker, "Stalinism as Revolution from Above," pp. 88–89.

33. Carr, *Russian Revolution*, p. 172; Carr, *Socialism in One Country*, 1:186.

34. Carr, *October Revolution*, p. 33.

35. Carr, *Russian Revolution*, pp. 190–91.

And so we come to Carr's best-known and most controversial judgment on Stalinism—a corollary, as it were, to his conviction that a Thermidor inevitably caps any victorious revolution: the idea that Stalin's policies were essentially impersonal. For Carr, Stalin "is the most impersonal of all the great historical figures" because "few great men have been so conspicuously . . . the product of the time and place in which they lived."[36] This was precisely the image Stalin tried to project, and it certainly served him well in the 1920s. It is therefore understandable that it might have seduced even first-rate historians. But it does not hold up under scrutiny of the events of the following decade, or even of Stalin's behavior and writings during the 1920s.

No matter how one views Stalinism, it is difficult to deny that Stalin himself played a determining role in many decisive developments during those years. The man made himself so strongly felt that some people spoke of "an era shaped most of all by Stalin himself."[37] For Carr as for Deutscher, the idea of the "impersonality" of Stalinist policies was based on the premise that Stalin, after all was said and done, had no ideas of his own; he had borrowed them all from others. Robert Tucker, one of the chief critics of this idea, has pointed out that it certainly does not apply to Stalin's fundamental concept of a "coercive revolution from above."[38] And Medvedev has noted that Stalinism provided "evidence that the individual plays a great role in history."[39] Curiously enough, when Carr had to deal with aspects of Stalin's dictatorship that were "unimaginable . . . in the days of Lenin," he, too, turned to Stalin's personality and beliefs.

Finally, Carr, like Medvedev, argues against some of the interpretive currents I reviewed earlier. We have seen that Carr, again like Medvedev, rejects the "new class" theory. He also finds untenable the notion that "what was achieved under Soviet planning [was] 'state capitalism' "; too many essential elements of capitalism, from private entrepreneurs to profits and the law of supply and

36. Carr, *Socialism in One Country*, 1:177, 186.

37. Alexander Rabinowitch, Introduction to *The Soviet Union since Stalin*, ed. Stephen F. Cohen, Alexander Rabinowitch, and Robert Sharlet (Bloomington, Ind., 1980).

38. Tucker, "Stalinism as Revolution from Above," pp. 86–87.

39. Medvedev, *Let History Judge*, p. 566.

demand, were entirely absent or played a "purely ancillary role." Carr writes: "Soviet planned economy was recognized everywhere as a challenge to capitalism [and was] a major outcome of the revolution." It would be foolish to deny that this enterprise was socialist, but it would be equally misguided to claim to find in it those elements that for Marx and Lenin gave socialism its true meaning. "If the goals could be described as socialist, the means used to attain them were often the very negation of socialism."[40]

With Carr and Medvedev I have certainly not exhausted the historians' debate on the USSR, but the picture would be incomplete without them. By including them I hope I have rounded it out in a way that will help us to understand the latest wave of dissent in the Soviet Union.

40. Carr, *Russian Revolution*, pp. 186–87.

11 Stalinism without Stalin at Home and Abroad

However one chooses to interpret Stalinism, two problems are still to be explored. The first concerns what was left of Stalinism after Stalin's death; in other words, what were or perhaps still are its more lasting features, assuming it has any? The second is more general. As we have seen, the various schools of thought have read Stalinism as primarily, if not exclusively, a Soviet problem. But can we limit it in this way? Might this not be an organism that has spread through other countries and other times? The two questions are connected, but let us look at them individually for the light they can throw on the many facets of the Stalinist phenomenon.

These are not the only questions facing historians who deal with the post-Stalinist Soviet Union, and the questions multiply when we try to trace the unfolding of the revolutionary changes of the past few decades. The last thirty years are still virtually unexplored territory as far as the Soviet Union is concerned. We await a considered evaluation of the Khrushchev decade, with its successful and aborted reforms, and of the Brezhnev years, which stretched well beyond Brezhnev's lifetime and ended only with the rise of Mikhail Gorbachev. With the exception of a few pioneering works, inevitably sketchy, the bulk of this research is still to be done. We have not yet had time to gain the necessary perspective.[1] I raise these questions now only because they reach to the very core of my investigation.

A warning is necessary. Passions are never totally laid to rest when one deals with any period of Soviet history. As one moves from its early days to the uncharted present, scholarly objectivity has to contend more and more often with political concerns and ideological bias. And the way one views Stalinism will strongly color one's view of its fate after Stalin's death. As Erik Hoffmann has said:

> Whether these current Soviet perspectives are elements of continuity or change since Stalin is a highly subjective question. Did Khrushchev and Brezhnev alter the essence of Stalinism, or merely adapt fundamental characteristics of the Stalinist system to new conditions? One's answer depends heavily on one's view of the basic features of Stalinism and the importance of certain undeniable post-Stalin changes in policy making and administration.[2]

There are, of course, points of general consensus. No one, for example, denies that Stalin's "terror," particularly in its harshest and most obsessive forms, is over. No one claims that the USSR became a liberal country after the dictator's death, or that political repression disappeared. But once this much is established, opinions as to the place these "excesses" occupied in Stalinism begin to diverge. Similarly, no one denies that economic policies have changed since Stalin's death, particularly in respect to agriculture. But discussions still grow quite heated when it comes to the magnitude, the significance, and especially the practical results of such changes.[3] While no one denies that changes have been made, no one can be blind to the survival of elements of Stalinism well after Stalin's death. The only quarrel is over the relative importance of the changes and of the Stalinist survivals. As we shall see, the clash of ideas unleashed by Gorbachev has focused on this question

1. For a more detailed discussion of these issues, see Giuseppe Boffa, *Storia dell'Unione Sovietica* (Milan, 1976–1979), vol. 2, particularly the two last chapters and the section on the Khrushchev decade.

2. Erik P. Hoffmann, "Changing Soviet Perspectives on Leadership and Administration," in *The Soviet Union since Stalin*, ed. Stephen Cohen, Alexander Rabinowitch, and Robert Sharlet (Bloomington, Ind., 1980), p. 86.

3. See Arthur W. Wright, "Soviet Economic Planning and Performance," and James R. Millar, "Post-Stalin Agriculture and Its Future," in ibid., pp. 113–34, 135–54. Both of these interesting essays have extensive bibliographies.

no less than on Stalinism itself. The problems uncovered are of more than academic interest in connection with the innovations being tried.

In the 1970s those who saw continuity in Soviet history tended least to emphasize the scope and substance of change. Foremost among them were those who formulated official Soviet doctrine. Along with the ongoing correction of "errors" and "reparation" of wrongs, they proclaimed a transition to a new "phase" in the growth of Soviet society—the "phase of developed socialism," a sort of higher rung in a ladder that the society had been ascending without interruption since 1917. The expression has appeared in official speeches and even in the 1977 Constitution, not to mention numerous sociological and popular works.[4] This novel and purely propagandistic category of "developed socialism" was difficult to reconcile with Marxist ideas on the transition from one social system to another. Soviet theoreticians conceded that in this case reality had "enriched" if not actually "modified" Marx's theory, which a century earlier had had no experimental basis on which to build.[5]

The Western proponents of both negative continuity in Soviet history and totalitarianism, who largely saw eye to eye, also failed to note significant changes after Stalin. We have seen that Brzezinski, a major exponent of the totalitarian interpretation, tended to read the changes as symptoms of crisis within a monolithic and never-changing Leninist-Stalinist system.[6] But we have also seen that these analysts found themselves in serious difficulty when they confronted developments they had considered impossible in the-

4. *Constitution of the Union of Soviet Socialist Republics* (Moscow, 1977), pp. 14, 28–31; Leonid Brezhnev, *Leninskim kursom* (Moscow, 1973), p. 12, and *On the Policy of the Soviet Union and the International Situation* (Garden City, N.Y., 1973), p. 26; M. A. Suslov, *Izbrannoie: Rechi i stat'i* (Moscow, 1972), pp. 653–57.

5. In his "Critique of the Gotha Programme," Marx writes: "Between capitalist and communist society lies the period of the revolutionary transformation of the one into the other": Karl Marx and Friedrich Engels, *Selected Works* (New York, 1968), p. 331. On this subject and, more broadly, on the transition between the two societies, see "Sull'inizio storico della società socialista," in Valentino Gerratana, *Ricerche di storia del marxismo* (Rome, 1972). To understand the official Soviet positions during the Brezhnev era, one must read Suslov, who at that time was the de facto ideological dictator in the USSR: M. A. Suslov, "Delo vsei partii," *Kommunist*, no. 15, 1979, and "Vsiakoie prizvanie i otvetstvennost'," *Pravda*, 15 December 1981.

6. Zbigniew Brzezinski, *Theory and Politics* (The Hague, 1971).

ory, and that this predicament was at the root of many contradictions noted by the more attentive among them. It would therefore be a mistake to suppose that there had to be an automatic consensus on the post-Stalin era among all those who went along with these ideas in general. Two examples will suffice.

Robert Conquest wrote one of the best books on that decisive moment in Stalinism, the year 1937, in which he saw the beginnings of a break with the Bolshevik past.[7] Yet he was skeptical of post-Stalinist changes because the moment he shifted focus from the close-up to the long view, he leaned toward the totalitarian thesis, though he saw totalitarianism not as a phenomenon typical of our times but as a tendency with age-old historical antecedents. The Soviet leaders were for Conquest "the product of centuries of history very different from our own. . . . Russia has had as its dominant political trend a despotism [claiming] total submission by its subjects and [manifesting] a tendency to unlimited expansion." Bolshevism itself, even in its Leninist phase, was nothing but "the messianic-revolutionary version of the despotic tradition." And its heirs, Stalin and others, are "soaked in [this] tradition. They cannot see the world in terms other than those of their whole history."[8]

Leonard Schapiro, who has investigated the history of the Communist Party of the Soviet Union, reached much more problematic conclusions, and not only because he considered Khrushchev to be a "great innovator." He wrote:

> Is the Soviet Union in 1977 still a totalitarian state? Certainly, a great deal of arbitrary power is still wielded both by the state and by the party with impunity. . . . The opportunity for the ordinary citizen to influence policy is negligible. This said, so much has happened since Stalin died that it may prove very difficult to reverse the process to which Khrushchev gave such a powerful initial impetus. . . . Talk of legality, of the evils of the 'personality cult,' the successful assertion of their intellectual independence by the scientists and with much

7. Robert Conquest, *The Great Terror: Stalin's Purge of the Thirties* (London, 1968).
8. Testimony of Robert Conquest in U.S. House of Representatives, Committee on Foreign Relations, *Soviet Union: Internal Dynamics of Foreign Policy, Present and Future: Hearings before the Subcommittee on Europe and the Middle East* (Washington, D.C., 1978), pp. 193–94 (hereafter *Hearings*). In opposing this idea Stephen Cohen makes an interesting observation: "We read the same history, we study the same thing and we come out completely differently": ibid., p. 241.

more limited success by the writers, the widening breach in the iron curtain—all this and much more may have started the Soviet Union along a path of evolution of which the end cannot yet be foreseen.[9]

Those who made a serious effort to revise the totalitarian interpretation by introducing the idea of Stalinism as a tendency toward "monolithism" find themselves in a more comfortable position. The Australian scholar T. H. Rigby, as we have seen, saw the Stalin phenomenon as the merging of a "mono-organizational society" with a personal tyranny. In his view, the latter was necessary to establish the former. If the mono-organizational society was to succeed, it had to change, "in a myriad ways and various degrees, the attitude and behavior patterns of a whole population."

> By the time Stalin died, however, older people had had almost a quarter-century to adapt to the system and there was a whole new generation socialized, from the kindergarten up, to its roles and expectations. In the period that followed, . . . it soon became apparent that the system had put down deep enough roots to be viable without such supports as a leader cult and massive arbitrary repression.

After Stalin, then, only the mono-organizational society was left; the personal tyranny, no longer needed, had vanished and been replaced by an "oligarchical sharing of supreme power." Yet Rigby did not exclude the possibility that the old combination might reappear in the event of a "profound or prolonged crisis": the success of Stalinism, even of "monolithism" alone, was not guaranteed forever.[10]

By and large, those who saw Stalinism as a break with earlier revolutionary and Bolshevik history were also more likely to pay attention to post-Stalinist changes. Robert Tucker, as we have seen, claimed that Stalinism was a violent substitution of the tsarist "revolution from above" model for the original Bolshevik revolutionary model. From this premise he drew a drastic but logical conclusion:

> Stalin in his macabre way remained to the end a revolutionary, albeit from above. Of few if any of those whom he chose as his associates and executors, and who survived him in power, could the same be said. This helps to explain why, in Russia at any rate, Stalinism after

9. Leonard Schapiro, *The Government and Politics of the Soviet Union*, 6th ed. (London, 1977), p. 56.
10. T. H. Rigby, "Stalinism and the Mono-organizational Society," in *Stalinism: Essays in Historical Interpretation*, ed. Robert Tucker (New York, 1977), pp. 74–76.

Stalin was going to differ very significantly from the Stalinism of his time. Without its key progenitor alive and in charge of events, Stalinism lost its very Russified revolutionary soul. There and then it became what it has remained ever since: extreme communist conservatism of strong Russian-nationalist tendency.[11]

Stephen Cohen, whose views are similar to Tucker's, draws quite different conclusions. He suggests that the post-Stalin years should be seen as a contrast and shifting between "two poles"—"a social and political confrontation between reformism and conservatism in the sense that these terms convey in other countries." Seen from this angle, the Stalinism that survived Stalin was only the extreme and "reactionary" phase of a more general conservative trend.[12] Soviet reformism, according to Cohen, has its deepest roots in the NEP, but not in the NEP alone. Like conservatism, it can be traced to the many contradictions in Stalinism:

Stalinism began as a radical act of revolution from above and ended as a rigidly conservative social and political system. It combined revolutionary traditions with tsarist ones, humanitarian ideas of social justice with terror, radical ideology with traditional social policies; the myth of socialist democracy and party rule with the reality of personal dictatorship; modernization with archaic practices; a routinized bureaucracy with administrative caprice.[13]

Later conflicts were similarly fed by these "dualisms." The reformist movement after Stalin, according to Cohen, gained the upper hand under Khrushchev, but his fall "ushered in . . . a far-reaching conservative reaction" that substantially colored the whole Brezhnev regime.[14]

The division of the post-Stalin years into alternating periods of innovation and stagnation, if not outright return to Stalinism, was a prominent feature of the early, and inevitably rather sketchy, research done on the pre-Gorbachev period. Like Cohen, Alexander Rabinowitch finds the Khrushchev phase to be substantially "reformist," if "erratic," and it seems "undeniable that between 1964 and 1967, the reformist impulse in the Soviet Union declined

---

11. Robert Tucker, "Stalinism as Revolution from Above," in ibid., p. 108.
12. Stephen F. Cohen, "The Friends and Foes of Change: Reformism and Conservatism in the Soviet Union," in Cohen et al., *Soviet Union since Stalin,* p. 12; *Hearings,* pp. 210–11.
13. Cohen, "Friends and Foes of Change," p. 20.
14. Ibid., pp. 16–17; *Hearings,* pp. 214–19, where we find a detailed analysis of the motivations and manifestations of the Soviet conservatism of that time.

sharply" and a long period of conservative reaction set in.[15] A writer of different background and orientation, the Englishman Alec Nove, who tends to see both Khrushchev and Brezhnev as in a sense inevitable "products" of their times, agrees: after Khrushchev's fall, "gradually but inexorably, the 'conservative' and cautious line triumphed."[16] Thus one even heard talk of "neo-Stalinism," though most scholars considered the term inadequate.

Not everyone endorsed the idea of a Khrushchevian reformism balanced by a Brezhnevian conservatism. The entire development school, which had seen Stalinism as a product of industrialization, tended to think it had become obsolete now that the "moderniza-tion" of the country was for all intents and purposes completed. Whatever was left of Stalinism was therefore only a survival from that period, inadequate to deal with the new economic and social problems facing the regime. Marxists would say that the Stalinist "superstructure" was no longer in harmony with the social struc-ture and therefore was in conflict with the growth of productive forces, yet it lived on through inertia, with a few modifications and adaptations. From this viewpoint some scholars saw Khrushchev's reforms as tentative, and held that the Brezhnev years, far from being a reaction to those innovations, had continued and even en-hanced the reform process.

These views were most forcefully expressed by Jerry Hough, a meticulous student of the more minute movements in Soviet soci-ety. In Brezhnev's USSR he saw the process of change advancing in at least three directions: a broader diffusion of decision-making power; more freedom to discuss problems of public life, which led to more open discussion of general issues; and greater egalitarian-ism. Of course Hough saw all these improvements as relative, but they did represent developments that fitted the requirements of an industrialized country.[17] Erik Hoffmann offered a more subtle but

---

15. Alexander Rabinowitch, Introduction to Cohen et al., *Soviet Union since Sta-lin*, pp. 5–7.

16. Alec Nove, *Stalinism and After* (London, 1975), p. 159.

17. Testimony of Jerry Hough in *Hearings*, pp. 267–69. Hough emphasized that "the political structure of the Soviet Union remains essentially unchanged, that organized opposition still is not tolerated, that the elections to the soviets are still a fraud, and so forth" (p. 265). He did, however, "think that the Soviet Union has become more egalitarian than the United States in the distribution of income and privileges, and I do think that mobility from a lower status background into the top political-economic elite is more open" (p. 269).

basically similar opinion. In Brezhnev's "administration" he saw a broadening of policy-making procedures generated by efforts to "improve the central party organs' capacity to lead and manage society in the era of the scientific and technological revolution."[18] And finally, even among those who viewed the Brezhnev period as a "conservative reaction," some observers, such as George Breslauer, saw the difference between Khrushchev and the subsequent "collegial administration" as mainly a matter of "approach" to the same continuing problem of "mass political participation in public life"—"populist" and "anti-elitist" under Khrushchev, "managerial" and "bureaucratic" under his successors.[19] Both variants, however, were a far cry from the Stalinist pattern.

These themes were repeated, though less optimistically, by some dissident Soviet émigrés, not all of whom embraced the linear interpretation of Soviet history so dear to the heart of Solzhenitsyn. One of the most influential of the émigrés was Aleksandr Yanov. He, too, detected a factional struggle in the post-Stalinist USSR, but he saw it as crystallizing mainly about a "new Russian right," nationalistic, isolationist, and messianic, to be found both in Stalinist official circles and in the multifaceted world of dissent. Starting from seemingly opposite poles, the two strands of this tendency could eventually merge to produce a new type of Stalinism. For Yanov, then, what was left of the old Stalinism, and what conceivably could rise again, was basically the nationalism of imperial Russia. It had survived Stalin and all the other forces arrayed against it on both the right and the left because it was rooted in the society and in its history.[20]

Finally, a whole spectrum of opinions can be found among those Marxists who did not accept the story of "developed socialism" sanctified by the party. The Chinese, publicly at least, retired from the fray when they embarked on a reform program and found

18. Hoffmann, "Changing Soviet Perspectives," pp. 76, 78, 85.
19. George W. Breslauer, "Khrushchev Reconsidered," in Cohen et al., *Soviet Union since Stalin*, pp. 50–51, 66–67.
20. Aleksandr Yanov, *Détente after Brezhnev: The Domestic Roots of Soviet Foreign Policy* (Berkeley, 1977). Yanov sees Russian history as an alternation of "Stalinist" phases with periods of disorder and "Brezhnevist" phases of "soft authoritarianism." It seems that the kind of political organization predominant in Russia since the middle of the sixteenth century—an "autocracy" quite distinct from "Oriental despotism"—never permitted "rigid, Stalinist" regimes to survive beyond the lifetime of any particular tyrant.

themselves taking steps that they had once scorned as symptoms of "restored capitalism" in the USSR.[21] But their new study of Soviet history was still in its infancy, and its initial findings were set forth with caution.[22] No other scholars who called themselves Marxists entertained any doubts that Stalin's legacy was still strong in the USSR, though they could not always say exactly what that legacy was. Their analyses are so generalized that they shed very little light on the problem.

Thus for all those who saw the Soviet Union as a traditional class society—whether they saw it as straightforwardly capitalist or state capitalist or bureaucratic-collectivist or Djilas's "new class," whether they traced it to the revolution or the NEP or Stalin—that's what Stalinism was and always would be. After Stalin was gone, the shift from his ways of governing, considered downright terroristic, to the more legalistic ways of his successors represented nothing but consolidation of the new dominant class, of its power and its mechanisms to exploit the other strata of the population.

But we have seen that not all Marxist observers shared this reductive view. The orthodox Trotskyites, who in the mid-1950s fervently hoped to see the final "collapse" of Stalinism, have not really contributed much to our understanding of subsequent developments.[23] Here again, as in their grapplings with Stalinism, we see the sterility of blind adherence to the letter of the Master's writings without the vigor of his critical spirit. Deutscher's original contributions have proved much more stimulating. Deutscher was always so convinced that Stalinism had survived Stalin that he repeatedly called attention to the "limits" or even the "failure of the official de-Stalinization." But he was also convinced, as

---

21. See, e.g., how the Chinese had presented articles selected from the Soviet press: "Speculators at Large in Moscow" and "What a Collective Farm!" *Peking Review*, no. 34, 1963, pp. 21–22; "Cucumber Plague" and "Private Hotels Mushroom in Orenburg," ibid., no. 35, 1963, pp. 28–29.

22. Cf. Frane Barbieri, *Il Miliardo* (Milan, 1981), pp. 34, 123–24. Chinese scholars have been interested participants at various international conferences, such as the meeting organized in Rome in June 1980 by the Gramsci Institute on the topic "Bukharin in the History of the Soviet Union and of the International Communist Movement." The most important papers delivered at this meeting were published in *Bucharin tra rivoluzione e riforme* (Rome, 1982).

23. Robert McNeal, "Trotskyist Interpretations of Stalinism," in Tucker, *Stalinism*, p. 40.

Trotsky had been, that much of the original revolutionary spirit remained alive in the USSR. For him the idea of continuity served to keep in sight the part of that spirit which had never died since the "abolition of private property and the complete nationalization of industry and banking." Like Trotsky before him, Deutscher always watched eagerly, sometimes overoptimistically, for signs that through all the "malaise, the heart-searchings and the gropings of the post-Stalin era," the continuity with the revolution might be winning out over the continuity with Stalinism.[24] In this respect the Master's influence over Deutscher never waned.

With hopes running high in Belgrade after Khrushchev's early reforms, the Yugoslavs, too, noted the persistence of Stalinism in the USSR, in the form of a "bureaucratic statism" based on the total statization of the means of production. They contrasted this phenomenon with what they perceived as a Soviet movement toward "self-managed socialism" in response to both domestic needs and foreign influences. But very few Yugoslav theoreticians were ready to say that such a movement, however desirable or necessary, could become firmly established under Brezhnev, let alone prevail, when it had not managed to do so even under Khrushchev.[25]

Roy Medvedev was readier to believe that the post-Stalin changes in the Soviet Union represented a real break with the past: "The regime based on the cult of Stalin had ceased to exist after the 20th Congress."[26] Like some American scholars, Medvedev tended to believe that in this sense the Brezhnev years were more fruitful than the Khrushchev period, and he pointed to certain reforms whose real significance sometimes escaped observers far from the scene. These reforms were among the less sensational ones, but they had a lasting impact on Soviet society. "The issuance of internal passports to agricultural workers, so that they can now move from one part of the country to another, was a true

24. Isaac Deutscher, *The Unfinished Revolution, 1917–1967* (London, 1967), pp. 101, 36, 39.

25. See the Belgrade journal *Socialism in the World*, nos. 22, 23 (1981), for a transcript of the Cavtat round table debates in September 1980 on the subject "Socialism, Participation, Self-management."

26. Roy Medvedev, *Intervista sul dissenso in Urss*, ed. Piero Ostellino (Rome and Bari, 1977), p. 21.

social reform. Foreign observers were wrong to underestimate its importance."[27]

Not that Medvedev thought Stalinism had vanished. "Many elements of the pseudo-socialist system created by Stalin remained more or less intact, and they are still with us [in the 1970s]. The struggle against Stalinism and neo-Stalinism in all its manifestations, whether open or veiled, continues to be one of the most important problems."[28] Medvedev has had considerable influence on many foreign scholars because he has always emphasized the complexity of post-Stalinist society. He finds there remnants not only of Stalinism and of revolutionary traditions but of earlier social institutions.

> I see our society as a contradictory combination of socialism and pseudosocialism, something in its own way quite extraordinary. In this society of ours, behind the facade of socialism and couched in socialist phraseology, we can still find palpable connections of a capitalist type and even semifeudal relationships and institutions.[29]

This brief survey hardly explains why Stalinism survived so long without Stalin, and it may even seem irrelevant in view of the hurricane Gorbachev's *perestroika* has unleashed over Soviet studies, not to mention world politics; yet it should help us understand the stage those studies had reached when the new and more radical turnabout came and Soviet scholars got a chance to enter the fray with their own insights. It should also help us to understand the extreme diversity of reactions, from the utmost skepticism to the most exhilarating hopefulness, with which the "experts" greeted Gorbachev's innovations. And finally it can tell us something about that underground spiritual preparation in the USSR which allowed those new ideas to bloom at the end of the 1980s.

We come closer to understanding these matters when we look into the international aspects of Stalinism. The research carried

---

27. Roy Medvedev, *L'Unione Sovietica alle soglie del 2000*, ed. Livio Zanotti (Milan, 1980), p. 37.
28. Roy A. Medvedev, "The Stalin Question," in Cohen et al., *Soviet Union since Stalin*, pp. 48–49.
29. Medvedev, *L'Unione Sovietica alle soglie del 2000*, p. 5.

out in that direction, however, is even sketchier and more fragmentary. Everything I have examined focuses on the problem as it
affects the USSR. To concentrate on Soviet history is of course legitimate. No matter how one looks at Stalinism, there is no doubt
that it was born and grew to maturity in the USSR and from there
spread its influence abroad. But so long as research is confined to
the USSR, two important questions will continue to be neglected:
the specific weight of Stalinism in the communist movement as a
whole and the recurrence of some of its features in other countries.

The communist movement was Stalinist for a good part of its
history, from the beginning of the 1930s to the middle of the
1950s. It not only exalted Stalin's authority and joined his "cult,"
it also accepted his political leadership, his ideas, orientations, and
directives. This is not to say that the communist movement understood what Stalinism really represented in Soviet history. A large
body of credible evidence tells us that it was in fact quite ignorant
on this score.[30] But the matter cannot be reduced to a simple mis-
understanding. The movement's conception of Stalinism may have
been purely mythical. Yet the Stalinist blueprint, embellished by
clever propaganda, did exercise an undeniable fascination for the
movement. The revisionist process that arose within the Communist parties in the mid-1950s also has a long and tormented history; in a few instances, particularly in the weaker national organizations, it withered quite quickly.

The problem lies elsewhere. The movement had always harbored
dissent and opposition. But even when opposition to Stalin was
most tenacious, as in the case of Trotskyism, it was parried with
relative ease at the fringes of the movement's organized cadres and
even outside them. The first genuine exception was the Yugoslav
rebellion in 1948, which showed vitality of quite a different order.
But it had behind it an indigenous revolution and the vigor of a
nascent state. And here lies the crucial point. In all the analyses I
have examined, Stalinism emerges from an initial revolutionary
experience to form a new economic and political system, a new
type of social organization, even a new political "culture." It always is identified with a state. Outside of that state and the society
it represents, Stalinism or anti-Stalinism in the communist move-

---

30. See Eric J. Hobsbawm, "Gli intellettuali e l'antifascismo," in *Storia del marxismo*, vol. 3 (Turin, 1981).

ment can be only tendencies, hopes, programs, perhaps myths, always a bit impractical if not pure fantasies. The picture changes dramatically when we come to new states that have emerged from their own revolutionary matrix.

At this point the analysis becomes more complex. True, a communist state—Yugoslavia—did successfully revolt against Stalinism, but other states copied the Stalinist "model" fully or in part, fitting their economies and the whole of their social life into the parameters worked out by Stalin's USSR. In the countries penetrated by the Soviet armies in World War II the problem may seem simple, because there Stalinism essentially was "exported" or "transplanted" from the USSR.[31] This "forcible transplantation" has been seen as a typical element of latter-day Stalinism, as the "externalization of the Stalinist revolution from above"—revolution not only from above but from a foreign land.[32] This conclusion is supported by the facts and is widely shared, at least in the case of several countries in Central and Eastern Europe after 1947–1948.

But this interpretation can be misleading if it is oversimplified. It tends, for example, to ignore internal stimuli that supported the importation of Stalinsim into those countries.[33] Immediately after the war, a stimulus of this kind was also present in Yugoslavia. For several years after the war the Yugoslav communists had tried on their own account to conform to the Stalinist pattern. Only later did a search begin for a different path to development.[34] Thus elements of Stalinism could be found even in countries that were never occupied by Soviet troops. Yugoslavia can be counted as one of them because the Soviet armies went through only the northern portions of the country and stayed only a short time. But the situation becomes even more intriguing when some of these elements are discovered in countries whose experience with revolution or simply with reform had nothing directly to do with the communist movement.

31. Boffa, *Storia dell'Unione Sovietica*, 2:396–419.
32. Tucker, "Stalinism as Revolution from Above," p. 106; Rabinowitch, Introduction to Cohen et al., *Soviet Union since Stalin*, p. 2.
33. Cf. Karel Kaplan, "Formation of the Communist Power Monopoly in Czechoslovakia, 1948–49" (Paris, March and May 1979), pts. 1 and 2 (mimeo), part of the research project "Experiences of the Prague Spring, 1968," directed by Zdenek Mlynar.
34. Boffa, *Storia dell'Unione Sovietica*, 2:345–46.

Until just a few years ago it was official Soviet doctrine that in
its essentials the Soviet system was to spread to other countries
everywhere; it was a sort of historical rule. Naturally Soviet ideologues did not talk about the diffusion of Stalinism, let alone its
exportation, since for them there was no such thing. The spread of
their system simply proved the universal value of "Marxism-Leninism." In the Khrushchev and Brezhnev years they were willing to
admit what they would not under Stalin: that the socialist experience can vary from country to country. But they also insisted that
to be truly socialist, a system must obey certain "universal laws."[35]
True, these laws were formulated in such general terms that they
could be taken to imply a variety of options. But the formulations
were always perfectly reconcilable with the readings given to those
so-called laws in Stalin's time and after, the readings that in practice regulated Soviet daily life.[36]

The problem presents little difficulty for the non-Soviet proponents of totalitarianism and Bolshevik continuity. For them the
question is not so much Stalinism as communism. Given certain
ideological and organizational premises, one arrives at certain results—in this case, what one found in the USSR under Stalin. Of
course not all countries governed by communists are or were uniformly identical; yet the variations, however obvious, are still seen
as less important than what they have in common. Whether the
chosen label—"totalitarianism," say—is then applied to any particular instance of this single reality often depends, as we have
seen, on political expediency. Such maneuvers do not alter the general trend of the analysis.

The situation is not so simple for scholars of other persuasions.
Those who have emphasized the typically Russian factors in Stalinism—the Russian revenge—cannot help mistrusting the explanations that solve everything by simply invoking the evils of communism. They tend to give greater weight to external factors when
the "model" is transferred to other countries. Moshe Lewin writes:

> The later events in Eastern Europe help clarify this proposition.
> There was no internal reason, e.g., in Poland, to stop the "nepien"

35. *XXVI S'ezd Kommunisticheskoi partii Sovetskogo Soiuza: Stenograficheskii
otchet* (Moscow, 1981), 1:22, 27, 34; Brezhnev, *Leninskim kursom*, 2:377.
36. *History of the Communist Party of the Soviet Union: Short Course* (Moscow,
1960), p. 735.

policies. They could have contributed but were interrupted by the imposition of re-Stalinization by external intervention. The switch to a fully fledged Stalinist model rather than the continuation of a more relaxed experimentation resulted from this intervention of a powerful external factor which also ensured the feasibility of the imposed model.[37]

Robert Tucker goes so far as to suggest an embryonic global theory: that beyond the Soviet borders Stalinism must inevitably clash with phenomena in the communist movement which are similar in origin but different or even opposite in meaning. He views Stalinism within the broader framework of the communist movement and of communisms, which he sees not only as parties—that is, political forces that want to govern a country and therefore generate certain "systems of power"—but as "culture-transforming movements" that create, or attempt to create, "socio-political systems" that represent a "new form of culture," or at least of "political culture." Even after such revolutionary movements are securely in power, according to Tucker, they all face serious obstacles because the cultural ways of the past are bound to live on in the minds and habits of the population. No matter how impressive and diverse the means used, no sociocultural change can be more than partial. What emerges, says Tucker, "is some sort of amalgam of the pre-revolutionary culture with the socio-cultural innovations that the revolutionary regime has succeeded in implementing." Since the preexisting cultures are essentially national cultures today, "there will take place a certain nationalization of the revolutionary new way of life."

As Tucker sees it, Stalinism was the first instance of this tendency, since it transformed bolshevism into a "form of Russian national communism," though it did not "shed its international expansionistic impulses." Tucker believes that this "nationalization" of communism, as of any revolutionary movement in power, "can even be formulated as a rule, though not as an iron law." He points to the fact that "the revolutionaries themselves were acculturated under the old regime and hence bear elements of the old culture within their own personalities, and, finally, the further fact that *some* of the revolutionaries—for example, a Stalin—are more

---

37. Moshe Lewin, "The Social Background of Stalinism," in Tucker, *Stalinism*, pp. 116–17. For the difficult times of which Lewin speaks here, see Boffa, *Storia dell'Unione Sovietica*, 2:338–42, 407–16.

inclined than others to become imbued with nationalist feeling
and to find things in the national cultural past, Russian in this
case, which seem worth preserving or reviving."[38] For Tucker, then,
where no foreign coercion intervenes, the revolutionary culture becomes intermingled not so much with Stalinism as with forces
that, though similar, lead to very different results. Tucker explains
in the same way that mixture of revulsion against and strong attraction to Stalinism which he sees in Maoist China: revulsion
against the element of Russian nationalism in it, attraction to a
"revolution from above aimed at transforming Soviet Russia into a
great military-industrial power capable of fully defending its independence and interests in the world."[39]

Even some of those who do not accept the continuity theory are
convinced that Stalinism is a genuine worldwide phenomenon of
our times. An idea that seems diametrically opposed to Tucker's
on this issue is offered by Gilles Martinet. Admittedly it focuses
not so much on Stalinism as on some of its "essential traits." But
these traits don't strike Martinet as peculiarly Soviet, still less as
exclusively Russian or even communist:

> Stalinism is a worldwide phenomenon to this day. An economy that
> identifies itself with state power, which in turn identifies itself with
> a hegemonic party, gives us an equation we find not only in Russia
> and in East European countries but also in various countries of the
> Third World where the communist party has not played an impor-
> tant role. Stalinism is therefore still a vital phenomenon even
> though it no longer takes the extreme forms it assumed in some
> periods.[40]

Elsewhere Martinet finds that Stalinism is even "gaining ground
in the Third World . . . often independently of any association with
. . . the international communist movement." On another occasion he has spoken of Stalinism as present in China and in the
"so-called socialist" Far Eastern countries. He identifies its main
features as "statization of all means of production; identification of
state and party; absolute party hegemony; authoritarian and centralized planning; administrative management of all public enter-

---

38. Tucker, *Stalinism*, pp. xvi–xviii.
39. Tucker, "Stalinism as Revolution from Above," pp. 106–7.
40. Giuseppe Boffa and Gilles Martinet, *Dialogo sullo stalinismo* (Rome and Bari,
1976), pp. 1–2.

prises."[41] Of course it remains to be seen whether these characteristics adequately define Stalinism.

Rather than contradict each other, Tucker and Martinet simply point to different aspects of Stalinism: some tend to spread and be repeated outside the USSR, sometimes in original ways; others not only are not repeated but trigger a growing differentiation even within a political culture that was intended to be unique and universal. It's the two viewpoints that differ. But are they incompatible? The picture is complicated by the presence of a whole series of ideas that fall somewhere between.

Of all interpretive approaches, the development school is certainly the most likely to see Stalinism as not an exclusively Soviet phenomenon. Since these observers consider Stalinism to be a probable result of the effort to modernize a backward economy quickly, they naturally maintain that it is reproduced (with some variations) wherever the same conditions prevail. China immediately comes to mind. And China is the example most frequently cited, because the size of the country and the strong ideological family ties between the two revolutions make the comparison so tempting, and also because the tensions and violence of the last twenty years of Mao's rule are reminiscent of the Soviet experience. Many people have therefore called China a second case of Stalinism, this time not imported but arising from the same historical circumstances. A. F. K. Organski lumped the two cases together and called them both "Stalinism."[42] Alex Inkeles pushed the analogy beyond China and declared that the Stalinist experience in Russia could serve as a "model" for all of Asia and for the Third World in general.[43] Jerry Hough saw just one substantive difference between the Soviet case and others found all over the underdeveloped world: the greater stability and the greater success of the Soviet regime and of all others that sprang from communist revolutions. Hough cites China, Vietnam, Cuba, and, "to a certain degree," Yugoslavia.[44]

41. See the introduction to the French edition of Boffa and Martinet, *Dialogue sur le stalinisme* (Paris, 1977), p. 8; Gilles Martinet, "Sociétés staliniennes et persistance des modèles," in *Feux croisés sur le Stalinisme* (Paris, 1980), p. 97.

42. A. F. K. Organski, *The Stages of Political Development* (New York, 1965), p. 99.

43. Alex Inkeles, *Social Change in Soviet Russia* (Cambridge, Mass., 1968), pp. 383–84; more generally, pp. 383–98.

44. *Hearings*, pp. 260, 265.

When one approaches the problem from this angle, such conclusions seem quite logical, even when the analysis is based on Marxist premises. Rudolf Bahro's assessment, in fact, moves in the same direction: "With the revolution in Russia and China and with the revolutionary process in Latin America, in Africa, and in India, humanity is taking the shortest route to socialism." The process does not stop there, however. One fundamental aspect of Stalinism, "the state as taskmaster of society in its technical and social modernization," is also a "model" that is followed time and again

> wherever precapitalist countries or their decisive minorities have organized themselves for active entry into the twentieth century. From this standpoint the Soviet Union is identical not only with China, but also with Burma, Algeria or Guinea, and not only with Guinea, but recently also with Peru or Zaire, and not only Zaire, but even Iran. . . . This only underlines the fundamental value of the state in this context.[45]

This reasoning need not be confined to the so-called Third World. If a Yugoslav could call Albania "a peculiar form of Stalinism in miniature"; if a Soviet dissident could link Albania and China on the same Stalinist dimension;[46] if, finally, the same model could be involved for Ceausescu's Romania (though not in public, for diplomatic reasons), then everything will inevitably be traced to the development problem. These are countries where development is imperative; they are quite different from such states as Czechoslovakia and Poland, where one senses no strong homebred Stalinism and where reaction to the imported brand was notoriously harsh.

Stalinism as an international rather than a peculiarly Russian or Soviet phenomenon was also a primary theme of the Yugoslavs, though they tended to consider it a product of Soviet supremacy over the communist movement in its Comintern and Cominform phases. "Bureaucratic Stalinism as a political entity actually became dominant for a while because of Stalin's influence not only in the Soviet Union . . . but also . . . in a majority of communist

---

45. Rudolf Bahro, *The Alternative in Eastern Europe* (London, 1978), pp. 61, 129.
46. Predrag Vranicki, *Marksizam i socijalizam* (Zagreb, 1979), p. 93; Roy A. Medvedev, *Let History Judge: The Origins and Consequences of Stalinism* (New York, 1971), p. 544.

parties."[47] The Yugoslavs saw China in the 1960s as an instance of Stalinism revisited. But bear in mind that these assessments were not free of political motivations even when they were offered in a historical or sociological context. Some scholars saw the Chinese phenomenon, like the Soviet experience under Stalin, as a complication of that "state socialism" through which all socialist revolutions of this century have passed.[48] Only a few of these writers have linked it directly to the development problem.

> The fact that the so-called cult is not an exclusively Russian product, though some of its details are Russian, is demonstrated clearly enough by the revival of Stalinism in China. The way Stalinism is adapted to and assimilated by the backwardness of Chinese society shows the vulnerability of the socialist revolution in an underdeveloped country to the influence of a backward praxis.[49]

Still in the Marxist camp, the various Thermidor strains proved less fruitful. Trotsky had agonized over the first attempts to export Stalinism at the beginning of World War II, in 1939 and 1940.[50] But he had very little time to develop these thoughts, as he was assassinated by the Stalinist machine in August 1940. Orthodox Trotskyites always had trouble with the revolutionary experience outside the USSR because the ideas the Master never had a chance to revise did not fit these novel situations.[51] As for the heterodox observers, they usually drowned the problem in a sea of generalities about restored capitalism, bureaucratic regimes, or the "new class." On the other hand, Deutscher's more detailed investigation of revolutionary episodes in this century took note of Stalinism's revival outside the Soviet orbit. Without discounting what was unique in the Chinese revolution, Deutscher wrote, "Even their image of socialism bears the Stalinist imprint: it is the image of a Socialism in One Country, enclosed by their own Great Wall." Ac-

---

47. Milentije Popovič, "Appunti su alcuni problemi del pensiero socialista contemporaneo," in *Il pensiero marxista contemporaneo nella prassi jugoslava* (Milan, 1963), p. 214; Predrag Vranicki, *Storia del marxismo* (Rome, 1972), 2:159.

48. Vranicki, *Marksizam i Socijalizam*, pp. 71–72; Svetozar Stojanovič, *Between Ideals and Reality: A Critique of Socialism and Its Future* (New York, 1973), p. 42.

49. Veliko Korač, "Il socialismo nei paesi sottosviluppati," in *La Rivolta di "Praxis*," ed. Giovanni Ruggeri (Milan, 1969), p. 275.

50. Isaac Deutscher, *The Prophet Outcast: Trotsky, 1929–1940* (London, 1963), pp. 457–62.

51. McNeal, "Trotskyist Interpretations of Stalinism," pp. 40–44.

cording to Deutscher, "Maoism, like Stalinism, reflected the backwardness of its native environment, which it would take the revolution a very long time to digest and overcome."[52]

After reviewing the various positions, I am left with the impression that once again we have taken only a few tentative steps toward resolving the problem. Comparative studies of the revolutionary experiences of our time, including those that arose under the banner of communism, have barely begun. They have long been hindered by ideological bias and by concern with political alignments. To a large extent these obstacles are still there. So we can't be surprised that no one has yet ventured beyond a few probings and interesting perceptions. If we want to understand Stalinism, clearly we must examine it as an international rather than a merely Soviet problem. But we are still far from a satisfactory solution. Which well-identified elements of Stalinism and the entire Soviet experience were duplicated outside the USSR? Exactly where were they repeated, with what variations, in what subjective or objective circumstances? The investigative effort in this whole area is barely getting under way. No satisfactory answers are possible without further careful investigation, and unless one goes beyond the most obvious comparisons, the phenomenon will once again be stretched so far that it loses all specificity. That would hardly be progress. The work to be done is still considerable.

52. Deutscher, *Unfinished Revolution*, pp. 95, 90.

12 The *Perestroika* Debate

With the coming of *perestroika* after decades of forced silence, the controversy over Stalinism erupted in the USSR with volcanic force. It is fair to say that this was the first time the subject had really been aired. In the past, even during the comparatively lively Khrushchev years, the tone of the discussions had been muted. In fact, the debate did not begin at once even after Mikhail Gorbachev became leader of his country in March 1985. Signs of dramatic changes in the lives of Soviet citizens appeared very quickly, but it took historians, perhaps burned by previous experiences, about three years to plunge headlong into a free and uninhibited analysis of their country's predicaments.

Historians later were criticized for their tardiness; once they had joined the fray, they regretted it themselves.[1] And it is true that the first impulses to reopen the Stalinist question came from literature, the theater, films, and journalism rather than from historical

---

1. See A. Iskenderov, "Istoriia sovetskogo obshchestva v novom osveshchenii," *Voprosy istorii,* no. 6, 1988, p. 50, and no. 10, 1989, p. 62; Viktor Danilov in *Voprosy istorii,* no. 3, 1988, p. 22; M. Reiman, "Perestroika i izuchenie sovetskoi istorii," *Voprosy istorii,* no. 12, 1989, pp. 145–46; G. Bordiugov and V. Kozlov, "Vremia trudnykh voprosov: Istoriia dvadtsatykh i tridtsatykh godov i sovremennaia obshchestvennaia mysl'," in *Urok daet istoriia* (Moscow, 1989).

research.[2] In this case as in so many others, however, the primary stimulus was political. The true turning point was a speech delivered by Gorbachev in Moscow on 2 November 1987 to commemorate the seventieth anniversary of the October Revolution. Such a speech had never been heard before on an occasion of that sort. In a risky attempt to summarize the seventy years since 1917, Gorbachev expressed some highly unorthodox judgments on many episodes and figures of the past, beginning with Stalin's famous adversaries; he harshly accused the dictator of unforgivable crimes; and he exhorted scholars to fill the all too numerous gaps, or "white spots," that kept Soviet citizens from knowing their own history.[3] And for the first time the speech did not claim to offer an official version of that history, not even a new one; it simply threw the door open for scholars to pursue their own investigations. A few months later the country's leading historical journal, whose editorial board had meanwhile been revamped from top to bottom, opened its pages to discussion of problems that had been untouchable for years.[4]

Late start or not, the debate over history—and not just among historians—quickly became explosive. In a very short time the conditions essential for unhindered progress in the scientific world had improved dramatically. The mass of information about the past grew, and this time it was not circulated through rumors, indiscretions, or secondhand news but was supported by documents and reports from authoritative commissions that worked with original sources. During recent years anyone interested has been able to find in the specialized press a huge amount of data that earlier had been blocked by maximum secrecy.

One after another people who had crossed Stalin or whom he had targeted for whatever reason were rehabilitated—victims of the notorious trials in the 1930s, party leaders and rank-and-file alike, all the way down to people who had never caught the public eye but who had had their parts to play in the events of those years. Unlike

2. Literary figures joined historians at one of the first round tables organized by the new editorial board of the USSR's foremost historical journal. See *Voprosy istorii*, no. 6, 1988, pp. 3–114.

3. See Mikhail Gorbachev, *Oktiabr' i perestroika: Revoliutsiia prodolzhaetsia* (Moscow, 1987).

4. "Kruglyi stol: Istoricheskaia nauka v usloviiakh perestroiki," *Voprosy istorii*, no. 3, 1988.

the rehabilitations of the 1950s and 1960s, the new wave was marked by disclosures of many previously unknown details of past persecutions.[5] The rehabilitations also touched off a spate of extraordinarily interesting memoirs. The most fascinating were the reminiscences of Bukharin's wife, Anna Larina, and the secret notebooks of the writer Konstantin Simonov.[6] These records do not deal exclusively with Stalin's persecutions, but this theme clearly dominates their pages. The renewed interest in the cast of characters in Soviet history, beginning with Stalin himself and his iconoclastic successor, Khrushchev, has sparked a search for further testimonials by supporting actors in the dramas of the past.

The areas that were closed to researchers for such a long time— "the painful questions of our history," in the words of one scholar[7] —have now been opened to public scrutiny: the famine that followed collectivization in 1932 and 1933, and the simultaneous depopulation of Kazakhstan; the events leading to World War II, including the Molotov-Ribbentrop pact; the mass graves at Katyn; the persecution of Soviet prisoners of war as they returned home; the anti-Semitic repressions of the late 1940s, carried out under the guise of a "struggle against cosmopolitism." Efforts are being made to arrive at a rough estimate of the number of victims left behind by Stalin's regime, particularly of those who perished in its most tragic episodes or their aftermath.[8] Lenin and the revolution, though largely sheltered from this revisionist tidal wave, are receiving more dispassionate scrutiny. The need for a critical approach to Lenin and his achievements has been proclaimed even in the theoretical writings of the Communist party press.[9]

Periodicals and publishing houses now welcome a vast assort-

5. In 1989 a new CPSU journal, *Izvestiia TsK KPSS*, began to publish the reports of the Special Commission of the Politburo of the CPSU for the study of "materials related" to Stalin's repressions.

6. Anna Larina (Bukharina), *Nezabyvaemoe* (Moscow, 1989); Konstantin Simonov, "Glazami cheloveka moego pokoleniia," *Znamia*, nos. 3–5, 1988.

7. Viktor Danilov, "Kollektivizatsiia: Kak eto bylo," in *Urok daet istoriia*, p. 158.

8. L. A. Gordon and E. V. Klopov, *Chto eto bylo: Razmyshleniia o predposylkakh i itogakh togo chto sluchilos' s nami v tridtsatye i sorokovye gody* (Moscow, 1989), pp. 157–65, 177; "O Staline i stalinizme: Beseda s D. A. Volkogonovym i R. A. Medvedevym," *Istoriia SSSR*, no. 4, 1989, p. 98.

9. O. Volobuev, S. Kuleshov, and V. Shelokaev, "Istoriko-partiinaia nauka: Usloviia razvitiia," *Kommunist*, no. 16, 1989, p. 41.

ment of writers, and the "rehabilitated" Bukharin and Trotsky are not the only ones to get published. The "dissenters" of yesteryear have seen their work recognized; so have émigrés, both those who left the country in the long-ago years of the revolution and civil war and those who sought refuge abroad in more recent times, beginning with Solzhenitsyn and his *Gulag Archipelago*; so have foreign writers, historians and otherwise, not all of whom are moved by goodwill toward the Soviet people and their problems, sometimes not even by excessive respect for the facts.

The declassification of archives is proceeding more slowly, and some historians have already complained.[10] Yet here, too, change is very noticeable, partly because journals have begun to publish original documents, partly because several scholars in privileged positions were able to gain access to important dossiers, even some of the most secret ones, without having to contend with the censorship regulations that once made such sources virtually inaccessible.[11] Thus we have a biography of Stalin by a writer who had the singular good fortune, unique until now, to examine Stalin's personal papers as well as those of some of his closest collaborators.[12]

The historians' work cannot be isolated from the broader debate that has shaken Soviet society to its roots in the past few years. We cannot look at it as a discussion strictly among historians because it never was that. Its motivations were often ethical, philosophical, sociological, and even psychological. The arguments over Stalinism therefore involve scholars of many disciplines, as well as literary figures and artists of all kinds. In such an environment the moral commitment is particularly strong, partly because it fits traditional characteristics of Russian culture but also because this time, in contrast to the 1950s, the debate over history's primary influences has been coupled with a desire, particularly among the intelligentsia, to expiate the collective responsibility for the darkest pages of the past. Witness the devastating effect on many

10. "Problemy istorii i sovremennost'," *Voprosy istorii KPSS*, no. 2, 1989, p. 62.

11. On these regulations see Volobuev et al., "Istoriko-partiinaia nauka," p. 39.

12. Dimitrii Volkogonov, *Triumf i tragediia: Politicheskii portret I. V. Stalina*, vol. 1, *Oktiabr'*, nos. 9–12, 1988; vol. 2, ibid., nos. 7–10, 1989. In book form: Dimitrii Volkogonov, *Triumf i tragediia: Politicheskii portret I. V. Stalina*, 2 vols., 4 pts. (Moscow, 1989). An abridged version of this work is available in English: *Stalin: Triumph and Tragedy*, ed. and trans. Harold Shukman (London, 1991). On the previously inaccessible sources that Volkogonov was able to use, see his "O Staline i stalinizme," *Istoriia SSSR*, no. 4, 1989, pp. 90, 97.

viewers of a film such as *Pokaianie (Repentance)*, which lingered throughout the first phase of the debate on Stalinism. The closing line in the film: "What meaning does a life have if it does not lead to the temple?" has become the opening line for many an essay on the subject.[13] Such expressions as "It's not just Stalin, it's us" also come from the film, as well as the assertion that "Stalin's actions can be judged objectively only from a position of unconditional repudiation of violence, starting with the principle that no one has the right to threaten the life of another person." Alas, at least for the present, it is difficult to imagine how this can become a valid criterion for historical investigation.[14]

Politics, however, has set the tone of the discussions. From the beginning it has been inextricably entangled in the clashes among the various leanings that have emerged bit by bit in Gorbachev's USSR. People debate ever more passionately over what happened yesterday, under Stalin or after Stalin, searching for directions to point their way today. They realize full well that they are discussing "the history of a recent past tied by a thousand threads to our present."[15] The blindest, most unshakable convictions are justified by a concern to prevent a "repetition" of the errors so abundant in the past, by the need to understand what is being done to reform Soviet society now ("If we change things, we must understand very clearly what it is we are changing"),[16] and by outrage against anyone who defends anything connected with the Stalin years, whether in resistance to change itself or in dismay at the suddenness of change.

To separate pure history from the heady political, social, and cultural emulsion that is drenching Soviet life even as I write would be a hopeless endeavor; to include everything would carry us much too far afield. What follows is an attempt to pinpoint those ele-

13. Bordiugov and Kozlov, "Vremia trudnykh voprosov," p. 233; N. Moiseev, "Zachem doroga esli ona ne vedet k khramu," in *Inogo ne dano* (Moscow, 1988), pp. 51, 54–55; I. Kliamkin, "Kakaia ulitsa vedet k khramu?" *Novyi mir*, no. 11, 1987.

14. Aleksandr Tsipko, "Istoki stalinizma," *Nauka i zhizn'*, no. 12, 1988, p. 44. This essay has appeared in two versions: the first in *Nauka i zhizn'*, nos. 11 and 12, 1988, and nos. 1 and 2, 1989; the second under the title "O zonakh zakrytykh dlia mysli" in *Surovaia drama naroda: Uchenye i publitsisty o prirode stalinizma* (Moscow, 1989). My quotations are from the first version, except as noted.

15. Gordon and Klopov, *Chto eto bylo*, p. 9.

16. V. Frolov, "Chtoby eto ne povtorialos'," in *Inogo ne dano*, pp. 392–94; G. Vodolazov, "Lenin i Stalin," in *Osmyslit' kul't Stalina* (Moscow, 1989), p. 135.

ments that in my opinion define the Stalin phenomenon most directly and specifically.

By now the word "Stalinism," once so doggedly avoided, has found its rightful place in the new discussions. The old expression "cult of personality" has not disappeared, but it is no longer so simplistic and is used mostly to convey the pseudoreligious aspects of the Stalin phenomenon.[17] New turns of phrase have appeared to signify the kind of government and political machine organized by Stalin and kept going after his death; thus one speaks routinely of an "administrative (or bureaucratic) command system." Still, the term used most frequently today is "Stalinism," sometimes replaced by or compared with the typically Russian word *stalinshchina*, a locution currently favored by Gorbachev.[18] The *-shchina* suffix gives proper names a strongly pejorative coloration and in this case implies a desire to deny Stalin the esteem that *-izm*, appropriate for an intellectual or political doctrine, seems to suggest to Soviet minds. Several writers who use both terms have tried to identify more subtle shades of meaning.[19] But there is no consensus among them and the nuances do little to clarify the problem. The two expressions may be used interchangeably; as one authoritative source has said, both terms "have by now entered our consciousness as something incompatible with socialism and democracy."[20]

The dispute over terminology, however, is a first step toward full-blown conflicts between differing interpretations. It also directs our attention to the more specifically indigenous elements of the Soviet debate, in comparison with those found elsewhere. It is not only a matter of a stronger emotional charge, understandable in someone who argues about one's own history, lived, experienced, and suffered at firsthand along with loved ones and compatriots. Beyond the political questions that are at the bottom of the debate lie more profound questions that only the Soviet people could

17. D. Furman, "Stalin i my s religiovedcheskoi tochki zreniia," in *Osmyslit' kul't Stalina*, pp. 402–26.

18. Antonio Rubbi, *Incontri con Gorbacev* (Rome, 1990), p. 232.

19. Volkogonov, *Triumf i tragediia, Oktiabr'*, no. 10, 1989, pp. 80–81; in book form, Volkogonov, *Triumf i tragediia*, vol. 2, pt. 2, pp. 136–37; Tsipko, "Istoki stalinizma," *Nauka i zhizn'*, no. 11, 1988, p. 40; Gordon and Klopov, *Chto eto bylo*, p. 303; V. Lapkin and V. Pantin, "Chto takoe stalinizm," in *Osmyslit' kul't Stalina*, p. 238; *Voprosy istorii KPSS*, no. 2, 1989, pp. 60–61.

20. *Surovaia drama naroda*, p. 3.

ask—indeed, had to ask: Where are we? What sort of society do we live in? What kind of country is this? For decades the dominant ideology held that the USSR was a socialist nation, and this belief became part of a common consciousness that transcended any doubts that might have surfaced in recent years, transcended even the values that individuals might have attributed to the very idea of socialism, whether positive or negative. But now people are asking themselves something more: Is Stalin's regime compatible with any idea of socialism as we have come to know it in theory and practice? And what are its consequences for us today? Only in the Soviet Union is the debate over Stalinism propelled by such painful singlemindedness.

Many people, particularly in the early discussions, referred to what developed in the USSR after the revolution and especially under Stalin as socialism or communism "in the rough." Others, using an expression that became fashionable, spoke of "barracks socialism."[21] Someone else spoke in more cultivated tones of "paleosocialism," to indicate a still shapeless, "immature," or even "premature" phase through which any new society must pass in the course of its development.[22] Some people see in Soviet society, or at least in Stalinist society, an odd mixture of social organizations, and so we get the oxymoron "feudal socialism."[23] Everyone is concerned about the ideological aspects of the problem. Given the context of Soviet life we can understand why, but preoccupation with ideology gets in the way of a genuine effort to understand Stalinism. From the historian's point of view, none of these expressions explain Soviet society; all of them tend to identify tendencies that developed in postrevolutionary times and culminated in Stalin. And this is where the real debate begins.

So far there is nothing to indicate that the Soviets have anything unique to contribute. It is probably too early for that; after all, only

21. L. Anninskii, "Monolog byvshego stalintsa," in *Osmyslit' kul't Stalina*, p. 65; Bordiugov and Kozlov, "Vremia trudnykh voprosov," p. 236; V. Kiselev, "Skol'ko modelei sotsializma bylo v SSSR," in *Inogo ne dano*, p. 364. The writer who called the expression "fashionable" is Mikhail Gefter, "Ot anti-Stalina k ne-Stalinu: Ne proidennyi put'," in *Osmyslit' kul't Stalina*, p. 532.
22. G. Shakhnazarov, "Obnovlenie ideologii i ideologiia obnovleniia," *Kommunist*, no. 4, 1990, pp. 46–59; Gordon and Klopov, *Chto eto bylo*, p. 7.
23. A. Butenko, "O revoliutsionnoi perestroike gosudarstvenno-administrativnogo sotsializma," in *Inogo ne dano*, p. 554; Bordiugov and Kozlov, "Vremia trudnykh voprosov," p. 236.

a few years have gone by since the debate started in earnest, though it had been simmering quietly for some time. Yet the Soviet writers do represent almost all of the views we have been examining. Some of them manage to hold more than one position at the same time. Simple ecclecticism? In some cases, undoubtedly so. But for others the matter is more complicated. One-dimensional explanations no longer satisfy, and the interpretive effort is driven to move in more than one direction. But the Soviet debate is an extension of the one already in progress elsewhere. There is no break, no interruption between the discussions now going on in the Soviet Union and the ones that are engaging scholars everywhere else. Nor can we speak of a sharp contrast between Marxist and non-Marxist interpretations in the USSR. Marxist views are more in evidence, of course, if only because of the sheer weight of Marxist thinking on all aspects of Soviet history. But as the search for the forces that gave birth to the Stalin phenomenon proceeds, Marxism itself—as we shall see—is subjected to critical questioning. Besides, the re-evaluation of the Soviet past covers too much ground and digs too deep to remain within the confines of any one theory.

The fundamental dilemmas that marked the debates on Stalinism in the West have of course now emerged in the USSR. Foremost among them is the clash between supporters and opponents of linear continuity in Soviet history from the revolution on. Advocates of the continuity theory, for whom Stalinism is nothing but the "logical conclusion" of the revolution, of bolshevism, and of Lenin's mission, are found among these historians, too.[24] But in Gorbachev's USSR, as everywhere else, these views seem designed to further political ends rather than objective inquiry. Few works of serious history support continuity, but a great many political commentators rely on it in a simplistic form, most of them at the extreme left or right of the political spectrum. At one end stand those who defend the basic rightness of everything that has been done in the country from 1917 on, as of course they must do if they are to minimize the worst features of Stalinism and deny the need for radical reforms now. At the opposite end we have those who see the whole revolutionary and postrevolutionary history of the

24. For an example see Andrei Siniavskii, "Stalin—geroi i khudozhnik stalinskoi epokhi," in *Osmyslit' kul't Stalina*, pp. 112–25.

country as a tragic error and demand the complete abolition of the established order. In either instance the search for the original sin or the primordial merit, as the case may be, seldom stops with Lenin and October; it encompasses the entire revolutionary movement, particularly in Russia, and Marxist thought in general, with all its cultural premises.

When the scene shifts to an authentic historical debate, these ideas subside, and even when they appear to be gaining strength, they are seldom so rudimentary. In the first place, the Soviet people are well aware that their history is far from simple; most of them have lived and suffered through it, not learned about it from books. Second, it is precisely here that some distinctive characteristics of the Soviet debate begin to appear. Thus, even for those who see continuity in Soviet history, the starting point is still a search for the "historical sources" of Stalinism. As soon as the analysis crystallizes, it becomes clear that these sources cannot be reduced to any one factor or bound by a chain of iron determinism. In any case, this is not the primary strand of the search. The discussion in the USSR, even when it has been politically motivated, has been driven from the start by an effort to identify what Soviet scholars call "alternatives" to Stalinism—other roads that might have been taken at one time or another in the past. The search for "alternatives" had by its very nature to focus on the "turning points" and "breaks" in the course of postrevolutionary events. The primary strand of the discussion therefore could not follow the continuity theory in either its positive or its negative version. Let's not forget that rejection of the continuity theory was the starting point for the courageous opposition to all the official glorifying ideology of the preceding decades, which clung to continuity for dear life.

Probably the most radical and therefore most controversial event in the search for "sources" was the publication of an essay by Aleksandr Tsipko. Tsipko traces Stalinism to both Russian revolutionary extremism and Marxism, not only in its more leftist variants but in all those variants that spread farthest and lingered longest; Tsipko's barbs don't spare even Karl Kautsky.[25]

Even more deadly in Tsipko's eyes was Marxism's alliance with the "radical traditions" of the "Russian revolutionary movement."

25. Tsipko, "O zonakh zakrytykh dlia mysli," p. 188.

His harshest indictment is reserved for the Russian intelligentsia of the left—its maximalism, its perpetual "infantile disease" of extremism, its "abstraction" drenched with messianism and never alleviated by the antidotes that the Western intelligentsia had had the time to manufacture. For Tsipko, then, Stalinism springs from the "tragedy" of the civil war, from its "butchery," its "terror." But in practice, Stalinism is only a variation of "leftist extremism" and therefore essentially the "tragedy and drama of the Bolshevik guard, its disease"; the Bolsheviks relinquished power to Stalin out of "impatience." Tsipko sees no real difference between Stalin and Trotsky, yet he rejects the idea of deterministic inevitability. He writes: "I don't insist that Russian revolutionary radicalism, the traditions of spiritual maximalism, and messianic hopes led inevitably to Stalinism. I am deeply convinced that in history nothing is inevitable, there is nothing that could not have been different or turned out differently."[26] Yet he is not always true to his convictions.

Tsipko's ideas about the "origins" of Stalinism have been contested by numerous writers. Some have pointed to several other national and international factors that led to the phenomenon, beginning with Russia's "epochal" economic and social backwardness in comparison with the more advanced countries.[27] But more important, explanations of the sort Tsipko offers were discarded or explicitly opposed by the greater part of the investigations into the "alternatives" in history. For many notable writers the 1917 revolution, including its October developments, had in fact been necessary.[28] But the revolution, bolshevism, and the Russian revolutionary movement could have gone in any of several directions. An attempt to reconstruct the possibilities a posteriori would be only a theoretical exercise, but they were evident at decisive moments in postrevolutionary history and were to emerge again after their defeat. The majority of participants in the debate tend to view all of Russia's revolutionary history, before, during, and after Stalin, as

26. Tsipko, "Istoki stalinizma," *Nauka i zhizn'*, no. 1, 1989, pp. 50–56; no. 2, 1989, p. 53.
27. Gordon and Klopov, *Chto eto bylo*, p. 154.
28. "Was there a choice in 1917? I have thought a lot about this question, and I say with no hesitation: There was no choice": Mikhail Gefter, "Stalin umer vchera . . . ," in *Inogo ne dano*, p. 310. See also O. Latsis, "Perelom," in *Znamia*, no. 6, 1989, p. 126.

one continuous struggle among several tendencies, or at least between two basic ones, which for the sake of convenience may be identified as "democratic" and "authoritarian."

Many scholars believe they can pinpoint the exact moment when the authoritarian tendency, with Stalin as its most radical promoter, achieved a decisive victory over its democratic rivals: 1929, with the end of the NEP and the switch to the accelerated (or frenetic) tempo of industrialization and its corollary, forced collectivization.[29] This idea is endorsed by a majority of historians, especially by those who, like Viktor Danilov and V. S. Lel'chuk, were deep in a critical analysis of the past as far back as the 1960s but could not publish their findings and were forced to keep their thoughts to themselves. These scholars set the tone of the debate from the beginning; eventually they were joined by younger historians more directly involved in the study of Stalinism.[30]

Almost all the schools of thought we examined earlier trace their origins back to some strand of Russian culture. The "alternatives" school, too, has its distant forerunner, one dear to the hearts of many Soviet researchers and too long neglected by their Western colleagues. Nikolai Bukharin was a major participant in the ill-fated battle to save the NEP from the extremist tendencies that Stalin immediately co-opted. Danilov was the first to speak of a "Bukharin alternative" to Stalinism, and he was one of the few who insisted that other viable alternatives had been available at the time. But Stalin had destroyed them all. This typically Soviet line of thought sees Stalinism principally as a violent suppression of the other road to development represented by the NEP. Later, faced by the dramatic consequences of that first choice, Stalinism deteriorated into a despotism that grew progressively more cruel. Some people even see the NEP as a sort of golden age. Various scholars, including some foreigners, have criticized this attitude in

29. Two writers assure us that this coincidence is part of the "historical memory" of the Soviet people: Bordiugov and Kozlov, "Vremia trudnykh voprosov," p. 239.

30. Danilov, "Kollektivizatsiia," pp. 147–48; S. Lel'chuk, A. Il'in, and L. Kosheleva, "Industrializatsiia SSSR: Strategiia i praktika," in *Urok daet istoriia*, pp. 209, 222–24; N. S. Simonov, "V predverii 'Velikogo pereloma': Prichiny svertyvaniia novoi ekonomicheskoi politiki," in *Voprosy istorii KPSS*, no. 3, 1990, pp. 56–72; G. A. Bordiugov and V. A. Kozlov, "Dialektika teorii i praktiki sotsialisticheskogo stroitel'stva: K voprosu o deformatsiiakh sotsializma," in *Istoriia SSSR*, no. 6, 1989, pp. 3–22.

the Soviet press.[31] They are not in the majority, however; most historians are well aware of the contradictions that eventually led to the crisis of the NEP at the end of the 1920s.

Politically, the advocates of this interpretation are interested mainly in proving wrong those who, in their eagerness to preserve the old Soviet order, maintain that Stalin had no possible choice except the one he made at the time. But their motivations are not exclusively political. They are trying to look more carefully at the fundamental problem of Soviet history, the relationship between Lenin and Stalin, or—it amounts to the same thing—between Stalin and the revolution. Bukharin is reevaluated as the continuator of the line of thought and action developed by Lenin, especially after the civil war. These writers identify the Lenin-Bukharin axis as most representative of the democratic potential of the Russian and Bolshevik revolution. They see Stalinism not as the continuation of the task Lenin started but as its total negation, its opposite, a complete break with the leading figure of October 1917 and with the democratic, even libertarian elements of the revolution's climactic phase.[32]

These writers are the first not to make a latter-day cult figure of Lenin. If anything, they are determined to "historicize" him, to study the evolution of his thought, even to point out the contradictions in it. The opposite position, the one that promotes substantial continuity and identification between Lenin and Stalin, has been supported in the USSR less by traditional scholarly studies than by an admirable novel, *Vse techet (Everything Flows)*, by the late Vasilii Grossman.[33] The young and not so young historians who have set out to refute Grossman's thesis understand that any simplification would be fatal to their own. For precisely this reason their line of thought is perhaps the most interesting and well bal-

31. For one example, see V. Popov and N. Shmelev, "Na razvilke dorog: Byla li al'ternativa stalinskoi modeli razvitiia?" in *Osmyslit' kul't Stalina*, p. 284. For critiques, see M. Reiman, "Perestroika i izuchenie sovetskoi istorii," in *Voprosy istorii*, no. 12, 1989, pp. 153–54; "Nep i sovremennost'," *Kommunist*, no. 8, 1990, pp. 76–79.

32. Evgenii Plimak, *Politicheskoe zaveshchanie V. I. Lenina: Istoki, sushchnost', vypolnenie* (Moscow, 1988).

33. Published earlier in several Western countries, it has now been released in the USSR: *Oktiabr'*, no. 6, 1989. For a comment that approaches the novel from the viewpoints of philosophy and sociology as well as history, see Vodolazov, "Lenin i Stalin," pp. 126–59.

anced in current Soviet historiography. To them Stalinism becomes the "Stalin alternative," the reclaiming and stifling of the
democratic soul of a revolution that had found its greatest representative in Lenin, and therefore the abandonment and disavowal
of Marxism itself.[34]

Some people who follow this line of thought tend to grant Stalin's ideas a modicum of originality, however anti-Leninist, anti-
Marxist, antidemocratic. (Writers in this camp speak of *stalinizm*
rather than *stalinshchina*.) This is the most delicate part of their
task, for anyone who agrees with such a claim may be suspected of
being soft on Stalin, since the image of Stalin as thinker was blown
so out of proportion for so many years. Other writers, in fact, indig-
nantly reject any suggestion that Stalin might have been capable of
conceiving a political doctrine.[35] Yet it is precisely the current of
thought most sensitive to the idea of Stalin as original thinker that
is making the greatest effort to get to the bottom of history, even
the history of Stalinism, to understand its evolution in all its
stages, to distinguish an "early" from a "mature" Stalinism, and
both from "late Stalinism."[36] Hence the eagerness to search out and
give credit to all those who resisted the advance of Stalin's ideas
and practices, with special attention to the political struggles of
the 1930s, particularly the Riutin case of 1932, the fate of the
Bukharin faction, and resurgence of Leninist and anti-Stalinist feel-
ings toward the end of the war and in the aftermath of victory.[37]

The tendency to identify Stalinism with Trotskyism was a cu-

34. Lel'chuk et al., "Industrializatsiia SSSR," p. 222; P. Volobuev, "Muzhestvo
samopoznaniia," in *Urok daet istoriia*, p. 311; see also E. Ambartsumov's comments at the round table "Partiia i perestroika: 'Kruglyi stol' v Institute marksizma-
leninizma pri TsK KPSS," in *Urok daet istoriia*, p. 330.

35. For discussions on this point, see Butenko, "O revoliutsionnoi perestroike,"
p. 556; Latsis, "Perelom," p. 124; Vodolazov, "Lenin i Stalin," p. 39; A. Burganov,
"Istoriia mamasha surovaia . . . ," in *Surovaia drama naroda*, p. 50; I. V. Bestuzhev-
Lada, "Amoral'nost' i antinarodnost' 'politicheskoi doktriny stalinizma,'" in *Istoriia SSSR*, no. 5, 1989, pp. 78, 84.

36. Vodolazov, "Lenin i Stalin," pp. 142–59.

37. "It is our duty to resurrect all the instances of resistance to the *extremism of
Stalin's power*, to reconstruct the destinies of all those who refused to join it and
even more the destinies of those who had the courage to protest directly or to try to
change the course of events by replacing individuals at the top of the party pyra-
mid." So wrote Mikhail Gefter, "Stalin umer vchera . . . ," p. 534. The list of works
dedicated to this kind of research is too long to be cited; interested readers will find
pertinent material in all the journals mentioned in the notes to this chapter.

rious, perhaps simply immature manifestation of the same sort of problematic research—curious because, as we know, Trotsky was the head of the clan that drew a sharp distinction between Lenin and Stalin, bolshevism and Stalinism.[38] The more discerning historians have therefore rejected any comparison between the two celebrated antagonists, and many an argument has sprung up among Soviet and non-Soviet scholars.[39] But this tendency must be kept in mind all the same, even by those who do not share it (and I am one of them), for at least two reasons. The simpler and less important reason is that those who consider Stalin incapable of original thinking tend to emphasize the old notion, now out of favor even among Western historians, that Stalin simply borrowed Trotsky's ideas. The second reason is more serious, for this way of thinking springs from one of the most singular interpretations of Stalinism ever proposed in the Soviet debate: that Stalinism was a repressive and violent reaction unleashed by urban intellectual Russia (represented by both Stalin and Trotsky) against the rural community, its values, its culture; it was an authentic "antipeasant war" that reached its climax in collectivization, with the *"raskrest'ianivanie"* or "depeasantification" of Russia.[40]

This interpretation was promoted less by historians than by one of the most important literary movements in the contemporary USSR, represented by such talented writers as Boris Mozhaev, Vasilii Belov, Sergei Zalygin, Andrei Bytov, Fedor Abramov, and Valentin Rasputin. Its heritage goes far back, to the populist culture of the *Trudoviki* and even the Slavophiles, which was so influential in prerevolutionary Russia and was far from extinct in the post-1917 period, when it was assiduously though clandestinely

38. "There is an abyss between Lenin and Stalin, and at the bottom lies an enormous mound of corpses": ibid., p. 515. This image reminds one of the "river of blood" Trotsky accused Stalin of putting between himself and bolshevism. I have reason to believe that the coincidence is unintentional, and for that reason all the more significant.

39. For a comparison of the various positions in this dispute, see Tsipko, "Istoki stalinizma," *Nauka i zhizn'*, no. 3, 1989, pp. 49, 51, 54; V. Sirotkin, "Ot grazhdanskoi voiny k grazhdanskomu miru," in *Inogo ne dano*, pp. 370–91; Lel'chuk et al., "Industrializatsiia SSSR," p. 220; Danilov, in *Voprosy istorii*, no. 3, 1988, p. 22, and no. 9, 1988, pp. 8–9; Reiman, "Perestroika i izuchenie," pp. 155–58.

40. "Kollektivizatsiia: Istoki, sushchnost', posledstviia: Beseda za 'kruglym stolom,'" *Istoriia SSSR*, no. 3, 1989; V. A. Razumov, "'Raskrest'ianivanie'—termin i soderzhanie, vremennye ramki," *Voprosy istorii KPSS*, no. 10, 1989.

nurtured in the years of collectivization and urbanization. We also find it in the work of some historians as a reaction against those who saw Stalinism as an expression of patriarchal "petty bourgeois" Russia staging a comeback under the thin veneer of Russian intellectual Marxism. "Petty bourgeois" had long been considered synonymous with "peasant."[41]

At this point we enter the area where the more familiar interpretive strands meet and intertwine in the Soviet debate. Since I have said that representatives of almost all the schools of thought I discussed earlier have taken part in the Moscow debate, let us review them briefly to see what parts they have played.

The totalitarian interpretation has had its supporters in Leonid Batkin, A. Etkind, L. Gozman, and Mikhail Kapustin.[42] By and large they have repeated what has been written by the school's theoreticians in the West. If anything, they have simplified their Western colleagues' analysis of the contemporary world. They describe the system simply as a traditional dictatorship that becomes particularly powerful through the use of modern means of communication and mass repression.[43] Their main adversaries are those who consider any comparison with Nazism misleading.[44] But this is not the most important point. This current of thought has wielded influence beyond the historical field through the widespread use, mainly political, of its terminology, especially the words "totalitarian" and "totalitarianism." Popular and academic writers, even when they start from different positions, use these words as synonyms for more traditional words (despotism, dictatorship) to telegraph disapproval. The words are occasionally used with similar connotations even in official documents of the Communist party.[45]

---

41. Tsipko, "Istoki stalinizma," *Nauka i zhizn'*, no. 12, 1988, pp. 44–66.

42. Leonid Batkin, "Son razuma: O sotsio-kul'turnykh mashtabakh lichnosti Stalina," in *Osmyslit' kul't Stalina*, pp. 9–11. We find a typical if extreme expression of this tendency in Mikhail Kapustin, "K fenomenologii vlasti: Psikhologicheskie modeli avtoritarizma. Groznyi, Stalin, Gitler," in ibid., p. 373: "It is becoming more and more obvious today that Nazism and *stalinshchina* are, so to speak, the two faces of the twentieth-century Satan, come to trample all the six thousand years of civilization and to reject and violate history."

43. The most effective summary of the classical totalitarian theory comes from L. Gozman and A. Etkind, "Kul't vlasti: Struktura totalitarnogo soznaniia," in *Osmyslit' kul't Stalina*, pp. 337–71.

44. *Voprosy istorii KPSS*, no. 2, 1989, p. 61.

45. The political resolution of the 20th Congress of the CPSU (*Pravda*, 11 July 1990) speaks of a "Stalin totalitarian system."

The interpretation of communism as "Asiatic despotism" can also be glimpsed on the pages of some periodicals, but not insistently and never with the original variations developed by some Marxist writers in the West and in Eastern and Central Europe.[46] These references to "Asiatic despotism," often in tones of contempt, hardly constitute an analytical trend. The explanations tend toward the ecclectic and are usually couched in simplistic terms that evoke the country's Asian heritage, which is almost equated with barbarism and therefore with something alien, if not downright repugnant, to Russian culture.

The poor showing made by the vision of Stalinism as "Russia's revenge"—or better, the revenge of the Russia the Bolsheviks thought they had defeated in 1917—may seem a bit more puzzling. But bear in mind that such grand overviews of their land's history are of only relative interest to Soviet scholars; they do not altogether ignore Stalinism's strong Russian roots, but they evoke them largely in their search for the "sources" of the phenomenon. They are therefore considerably more prone than Westerners to get tangled in the countless nuances of the continuity-versus-break problem.

Stalinism as an expression of developmental policies designed to wrench the country out of its backwardness—policies foreign to the socialism in whose name the revolution was made—does appear with some regularity in the new Soviet debate. The two writers who have developed this concept most cogently in the Soviet Union, V. Lapkin and V. Pantin, have repeated a substantial part of the analysis that Alexander Gerschenkron formulated thirty years earlier in the United States. Stalinism is supposed to have adopted and brutally carried through the characteristics of the drive for industrialization that had been evident in prerevolutionary times and had quickly reappeared in the 1920s, after the hiatus of World War I and the civil war.

> Stalinism is therefore a developmental stage in which forced industrialization without a market is carried out by a coercive apparatus that uses extraordinary methods, pumping resources from a premer-

46. E. Starikov, "Marginaly, ili razmyshleniia na staruiu temu 'chto s nami proizoshlo?'" *Znamia*, no. 10, 1989, pp. 142–50; Anninskii, "Monolog byvshego stalintsa," p. 65; V. Kiselev, "Skol'ko modelei sotsializma bylo v SSSR," in *Inogo ne dano*, p. 364.

cantile economy. This stage of development occurred not only in our country but in a whole series of other countries with premercantile economies whose governments resorted, as ours did, to forced industrialization, taking real socialism for their model.

Lapkin and Pantin had no wish to justify the past; they were trying "to understand that era as a historical choice made by Russian society, but with the groundwork already laid by the developmental process in other nations throughout the world; to understand it as part of a natural and global process."[47]

Even this interpretation drew lively criticism. V. Popov and Nikolai Shmelev saw the "choice" as "logical and natural" only insofar as it was a "consequence of the growth of a bureaucratic apparatus that had arrogated all power, political and economic, in that order."[48] The great historian Mikhail Gefter is more cautious: "Look at the cycles and convulsions of the 'third world.' We are their precursors." Then he simply wonders: "Couldn't things have gone differently?"[49] He is much too wise to give a categorical answer. Elsewhere we find the same thought expressed in a more traditional fashion: "[What was supposed to have been] the broad highway leading to the construction of socialism in all countries of the world turned out to be a typical road in a relatively backward country—and even that wasn't built to the best specifications."[50]

Now let us go over the same interpretation once more, this time as it is seen by a follower of Aleksandr Solzhenitsyn. Igor' Shafarevich picks up another of the development school's ideas—the one that draws a parallel with industrialization in the West, no less. But Shafarevich's aim is to condemn both experiences, because, he says, both are tainted by the falseness of their objectives. He makes use of the most modern (and most radical) ecological theories to broaden his argument. But the real matrix is the same as Solzhenitsyn's: rejection of all modern civilization from the Renaissance on. For Shafarevich the conflict is not between Stalinism and democracy but between Stalinism and liberalism on the one hand and "peasant civilization," the "millenary civilization of the

---

47. Lapkin and Pantin, "Chto takoe stalinizm," pp. 334, 336. L. Gordon and E. Klopov tend to agree. See "Stalinizm i post-stalinizm: Neobkhodimost' preodoleniia," in *Osmyslit' kul't Stalina*, p. 469.
48. Popov and Shmelev, "Na razvilke dorog," pp. 320, 323.
49. Gefter, "Stalin umer vchera . . . ," p. 317.
50. *Voprosy istorii*, no. 12, 1988, p. 4.

Russian countryside," on the other. Shafarevich writes: "Western technological civilization, like Stalin's leadership system, chose a technocentric ideology over a cosmocentric civilization." In Stalin and Western technology we see two different paths to the same utopia: "nature and society" organized according to the "mega-machine principle," from which every "human" and "vital" element is totally excluded. Shafarevich, of course, is inspired by these bold comparisons to join Solzhenitsyn in denouncing European progressive liberalism as one of the main props of Stalinism.[51]

Another well-known interpretion to be considered is that of the Thermidor school. So far it has found few supporters among Soviet scholars, perhaps because of its Trotskyist origins. They are aware of it but they are extremely cautious about using its arguments. Thus even those who do detect Bonapartist elements in Stalin are reluctant to see his success as another Thermidor.[52] But there are others who do not hesitate to recognize Thermidorian features in Stalin's power. One of them is Dimitrii Volkogonov, Stalin's latest biographer, but he avoids making a final choice even among the interpretations he endorses, merely setting forth the possibilities. In this case he says simply that "every revolution carries the seeds of a Thermidor."[53] The same thought is expressed more stimulatingly by Gefter, who quotes Lenin's wise opinion to the effect that a Thermidor is indeed a "necessity," an "implacable norm," but that in Russia the "Jacobin workers" would have the "wisdom and courage to Thermidorize themselves."[54] Obviously Lenin was not thinking about what Stalin and Stalinism were to become.

The idea that Stalinism might be considered a counterrevolution was also largely discarded, along with the Thermidor, as "too one-sided and sketchy." It is interesting that this judgment comes from an outstanding historian, Viktor Danilov, who does not miss the epoch-making significance of the year 1937 in the history of Stalinism. The repressions of that period, Danilov has written, "destroyed the portion of the Communist party that had taken a direct part in the revolution, was charged with the ideas and principles of true socialism, preserved the memory of Lenin's phase of the

51. Igor' Shafarevich, "Dve dorogi—k odnomu obryvu," *Novyi Mir*, no. 7, 1989, pp. 154–56, 158.
52. Plimak, *Politicheskoe zaveshchaniie V. I. Lenina*, pp. 117–24.
53. *Istoriia SSSR*, no. 4, 1989, p. 102.
54. Gefter, "Stalin umer vchera . . . ," p. 313.

party's development, and had or was in a position to have its own idea about how this society was supposed to grow."[55]

The last interpretive current to be considered sees Stalinism as the triumph of total and all-consuming statism, or more incisively as a "cult of the state." Earlier I described the Yugoslav origin of this theory. Now we find it again in the writings of a Soviet author, Andranik Migranian, who has defined the phenomenon as "total removal of the people from ownership by means of its complete statization."[56] As absolute statism triumphant, Stalinism also becomes absolute supremacy of the "bureaucracy." In the 1930s, Migranian says, "our political system became completely bureaucratized as the whole population came to have no part in the political sphere." It was in those years that "the conflict between the spheres of democracy and bureaucracy . . . ended with the complete victory of the latter." The system escaped petrification only because the massive repressions of the "terror" allowed the "charismatic leader" to get the results he wanted even at the expense of the bureaucracy. But as soon as those methods were abandoned, the struggle between the "charismatic leader" (by now Khrushchev rather than Stalin) and the bureaucracy ended with the leader's defeat and bureaucracy's total triumph.[57]

A similar opinion was once expressed by Andrei Sakharov in what is perhaps his only written statement on Stalinism. I mention it here because I don't wish to ignore a man of his stature or to minimize his long battle for democracy in the USSR, though others voiced the same ideas before him, and still others have contested them. According to Sakharov, the USSR had already witnessed the coming to power of a "special social stratum," the bureaucracy. Stalin was the "representative" of this "new social force." Not that the bureaucracy had an easy life under Stalin. A "personal dictatorship" was formed, "enhanced by Stalin's cruelty and his other distinguishing traits. But the mandate for power came to him from the bureaucracy, though not exclusively from it."[58]

---

55. Danilov, in *Voprosy istorii*, no. 12, 1988, pp. 13, 15.
56. Andranik Migranian, "Demokratiia v teorii i istoricheskoi praktike," *Kommunist*, no. 1, 1990, pp. 33–42. The quotation is on p. 36.
57. Andranik Migranian, "Mekhanizm tormozheniia v politicheskoi sisteme i puti ego preodoleniia," in *Inogo ne dano*, pp. 103–7.
58. Andrei Sakharov, "Trevoga i nadezhda," in *Trevoga i nadezhda* (New York, 1978); in English in *Alarm and Hope*, ed. Efrem Yankelevich and Alfred Friendly, Jr.

Before we conclude this brief survey I must draw special attention to the contributions of two Soviet historians who are difficult to fit into any interpretive category. The first is Dimitrii Volkogonov, the latest biographer of Stalin. Since he is the only scholar to have gained access to a large mass of documents that were always considered secret (and are not easily accessible even now), his work is particularly notable for its abundance of hitherto unpublished information and unknown details. The result is the first "political portrait" entirely critical of Stalin written and published in the Soviet Union. The two volumes of this work have already become indispensable for anyone seeking knowledge on the subject. The interpretive aspect of the book seems less original to me. Volkogonov posits the problem very explicitly by asking: "What is Stalinsim and what is its nature?" The answers cover a broad spectrum: "an anomaly of history," "a variant of Caesarism," "the disease of immature socialism," "a kind of secular religion," and so on. For Volkogonov Stalinism is "one of the possible (and extremely negative) means of realizing the ideas set forth by Marxist theory" and at the same time a "distortion of the theory and practice of socialism," "a forsaking of Lenin," and "a dictatorial form of alienation of the workers from their right to make use of the state government and their own resources." As one can see, the information is abundant; the final interpretive choice is not so clear.[59]

Mikhail Gefter's contribution to the analysis of Stalinism is altogether different and perhaps more profound. Gefter was not permitted to study unpublished documents. His solitary and agonized reflections on the past are always highly original, never obvious or trite. Gefter feels no inclination to soften his critical commentary on the past. Far from it. But neither does he wish to simplify it. He sees Stalinism as a collective tragedy—Russian, above all Soviet— but also something much broader in scope. His allusion to Shakespeare as a touchstone has been criticized by people who prefer more banal opinions, under the impression that they are more radi-

---

(New York, 1978), a collection of Sakharov's political writings. The article appeared under the title "Neizbezhnost' perestroiki" in *Inogo ne dano*, pp. 122–34; and in book form: *Trevoga i nadezhda* (Moscow, 1990).

59. Volkogonov, *Triumf i tragediia, Oktiabr'*, no. 10, 1989, pp. 66–99; in book form, Volkogonov, *Triumf i tragediia*, vol. 2, pt. 2, pp. 114–37 and, more broadly, all of chap. 5.

cal.[60] But for Gefter it is simply one of many instruments to be used in the effort to understand the past, "to understand those who cannot speak, the defeated ones of 1923, of 1928, of 1934, . . . without foolish and offensive patronizing, but also without the homage of a 'rehabilitation' that arrived shamefully late"; ultimately, to understand Stalin himself. Because, as Gefter says, "It's not just Stalin, it's us." In fact, "is Stalin perhaps not closer to us, as we are today, than Lenin himself?" In that "Stalin is us" there is no moral judgment, no repentance or atonement, but rather awareness of the need for historical understanding. Gefter rejects out of hand the old commonplaces, the "zigzags of history," the "diabolical personality," the "omnipotence of the apparatus." His investigation of Stalinism is a continuous interrogation of the collective conscience. No one is absolved, neither the Bolsheviks nor the Soviet people nor the West, for its share of responsibility in the Cold War and for the "capitalist encirclement" that "was not the ravings of a maniac." So far Gefter has not given us a finished interpretive theory of the phenomenon. Here is his most precise formulation: "Stalin put in motion a mechanism of permanent civil war, which in my opinion is his most substantial contribution to what is called Stalinism."[61] Clearly more a note than an analysis. But then everything Gefter writes can be described as "notes"—notes for that new and more enlightening interpretation of Stalinism, for that authentic quantum leap that we have the right to expect from contemporary Soviet historiography.

"Stalin Died Yesterday," the title of Gefter's best-known essay, has already acquired emblematic significance in the Soviet debate. That title helps to remind us of the answers the Soviets give today to my question concerning the temporal and spacial limits of Stalinism. This brief overview of the debate should make it clear that so far as Soviet scholars are concerned, the phenomenon is not limited to the deeds and life of Stalin. Some of its most fundamental

60. In an interview with Gleb Pavlovskii, Gefter was asked: "Do you see Stalin as a tragic figure?" Gefter replied: "Shakespeare would have answered in the affirmative." See Gefter, "Stalin umer vchera . . . ," pp. 318–21. The rather banal criticism of this reference to Shakespeare runs as follows: "Here is a very revealing conversation between two contemporary intellectuals who obviously hate Stalin with all their souls, but . . . consider it inadequate and frivolous to treat him with *contempt*": Batkin, "Son razuma," p. 27.
61. Gefter, "Stalin umer vchera . . . ," p. 305.

characteristics have survived until recent times; some people say they have not entirely vanished even today. But I believe the words I have quoted also make it clear that most Soviet writers do not see Stalinism as something confined within the borders of their country. More than foreign scholars, perhaps, they tend to view it as a phenomenon that has ramifications throughout the twentieth-century world.

13 A Summing Up

The time has come to put the pieces together. It is also time to spell out my own thoughts on the subject. To some extent I have already attempted to do so. In analyzing the various schools of thought, I have taken care to describe them as objectively as I could without limiting myself to an arid exposition of their hypotheses. I have tried to point out their origins, development, merits, and shortcomings. And I have tried to indicate not only the criticisms leveled against them by scholars of various persuasions but also the principal objections that I personally believe they invite. Even so, a few remarks of a more general nature do not seem out of place.

When one examines the interpretations given to Stalinism, it is impossible to avoid the conclusion that none of them is really satisfactory—but also that all of them, when they are stripped of the factiousness that so often mars them, have contributed to the study of the phenomenon, though certainly not in equal measure. Within the individual schools some writers have delved deeper into the problem than others. Some lines of research, in my opinion, have wandered off in the wrong directions. But all in all, one cannot call any of them altogether inconsequential. In each of them some fertile seed can be found, sometimes buried under piles of dust.

This judgment should not be mistaken for an attempt to take refuge in eclecticism. Rather it is an invitation to reflect on the complexity of the subject. Any one-sided approach, no matter how serious, is destined to prove inadequate. At best it will draw attention to one factor while inevitably it neglects others of equal importance. We are faced with one of the most important phenomena of modern history, and we must examine all its elements and all its implications. The debates it has triggered are still far from exhausted. All the political and moral condemnations, however justifiable, were not enough to put the matter to rest.

The history of Stalinism, with all the circumstantial evidence of its role in the development of Soviet life, is much better known today than it was a decade or two ago; even so, much remains to be done in this area as well. I have repeatedly pointed out the obstacles that have stood in the way of the reconstruction of the Soviet past, and not all of them have disappeared.

But now at last the seals on the archives are being broken. In just a few years the situation has changed dramatically. We may hope that even more progress will be made in this direction. Such progress would be profitable to us in the West and even more so to those who are most directly involved, the Soviet people.

I am convinced that despite the controversy it still generates, the term "Stalinism" is useful and legitimate, for it designates an important historical phenomenon that cannot simplistically be identified with the bolshevism from which it sprang, or with the world communist movement, which is yet another descendant of bolshevism, or of course with all those authoritarian governments and movements that have filled our century. It has its own peculiarities. For the same reason it cannot be classified with earlier forms of despotic or dictatorial power, unless the category is made so inclusive that all historical perspective is lost. The term "Stalinism" is therefore not just a convenient invention or a device to twist an argument. Scholars have outlined its substance quite clearly; further research will fill in the picture.

The Stalin phenomenon belongs to that tumultuous maelstrom of revolutionary transformations that in a single century took on such unprecedented rhythms and intensity that it spread virtually throughout the planet. It would be difficult to deny that Stalinism is a part of this process: it emerged in the wake of the Russian revolution, at a critical moment in its history, and it was inextricably tied to other phenomena involved in the process and influenced them in turn. To deny Stalinism a place in this picture out of political or moral revulsion or out of fear of corrupting the idea of revolution beyond repair is an exercise in futility; like it or not, it is to go against too many facts.

The revolutionary process that has engulfed a world grown smaller under our very eyes—more "interdependent," as they say—has not been an unambiguous development. Many people have tried to tie all the elements together and point them in a single direction. The most famous and probably still the most consistent attempt was made by Lenin and translated into the agitational slogans of the Bolshevik revolution. But the road from intentions to reality is always long.

Revolutionary movements and changes in real life, though they merged in a process that altered society and politics all over the globe, have appeared in contradictory guises. The constant resurgence of internationalist ideals, fed by the ever-growing internationalization of the economy and of politics, confronted a new and often furious nationalism among nations that had long been relegated to subservient roles. The desire, born in the more developed West, to overthrow or go beyond capitalism became tangled with the desire in larger portions of the globe to avoid precapitalist stages of development and find new ways to attain the societal growth that capitalism had produced in most of Europe and North America. The entrance of formerly alienated masses into the political arena—the birth of "mass societies," itself a manifestation of fundamental democracy—clashed with a widespread inability to forge a collective will except by means of monolithic structures closed to democratic interplay. The list of contradictions could continue, but this overview should make the point.

The Russian revolution and the Soviet experience owe their significance for the rest of the world to the fact that they became a sort of crossroads for all these contrasting tendencies. And it is here that Stalinism too found its international strength and that ability to influence which sparked imitations elsewhere in the world. Stalinism was an answer to the Third World's problems— often a drastic answer, promoting nationalism over internationalism, developmental imperatives over socialist ideals and the socialist way of life, maximum authoritarianism over democratic participation. This stark description, however, should not make us forget that throughout its historical evolution Stalinism always bore the mark of the contradictions that had encouraged its emergence. No matter how harshly repressed, they never entirely disappeared.

Stalinism is a phenomenon of our time precisely because it represents an answer to the new problems that we still see all around us. The interpretations that have focused on the reemergence of earlier Russian "models"—the Russian revenge—have done much to stimulate an analysis that sweeps away the more primitive patterns into which the phenomenon was first cast and grasps an important component of Stalinism. And this component is found also in the contemporary histories of other emerging nations—often in different guises, because the national cultures with which the individual revolutionary experiences must deal are also quite different. But important though it is, this interpretation alone does not permit us to understand Stalinism. Stalinism was certainly a Russian phenomenon, deeply marked by the country's history; yet precisely because the Russian revenge was mixed with socialist idealism to form a larger whole, it was not exclusively a Russian phenomenon at all, and we see it reappearing in other situations in other parts of the modern world.

Naturally it is also not enough simply to note that Stalinism was part of a broader revolutionary process. By itself, in fact, this assertion obscures Stalinism's undeniable counterrevolutionary features. By "counterrevolutionary" I do not mean "restorational." For reasons I shall try to explain shortly, Stalinism was not a restoration of any earlier system, but a new system. It was, however, an offensive (we don't yet know how conscious, but certainly well defined) against fundamental features of the Bolshevik revolution. Because I do not trust analogies that have had a misleading ideological role in the investigations I described earlier, I find the Thermidor idea sterile. Yet it is true that Stalinism involved a vast assault on the ideas, ideals, and political orientations of the Russian revolution in general and of October 1917 in particular. The climax of this offensive, the crucial moment that permitted it to consolidate its position, was "the year '37" with its "river of blood."

But Stalinism is also the whole complex of new norms that emerged at the end of this stormy voyage. "New" is not a value judgment. We are talking about social, economic, political, and institutional norms. Why are they considered part of Stalinism? Because in fact they came into being with Stalin's "revolution from above," through an often bloody struggle against the norms that had been emerging during the first postrevolutionary decade. Most of them remained in effect after Stalin's death, well past the offensive against his "cult" in the Khrushchev era. They underwent a series of more or less significant, more or less successful reforms. So we need carefully considered evaluations rather than hasty judgments when it comes to estimating how much of Stalinism survived in the USSR in recent decades or survives there even today. But these evaluations cannot avoid the conclusion that essential elements of the system are still alive even after the shocks and blows it sustained, thus revealing its resilience.

Stalinism is made up of a variety of elements. Some of them have been studied more thoroughly than others—its economic policies, for example, or more accurately its "development" policies, and the terrorist methods with which it laid low all opposition. Other elements have been studied very little. Curiously enough, among the most neglected we find Stalin's political and social ideas in all their inventiveness, although these are the very ideas that still have considerable influence in the USSR and in other countries, even in some not ruled by communist parties or movements.

But here again we must not leap to conclusions. When one speaks of Stalin's ideas, one risks being misunderstood—as if one sought to rehabilitate that old image of Stalin the "Marxist theoretician" which once was so central to the iconography of the "cult." The two issues should not be confused. Marxist ideology was in fact an instrument of power for Stalin—as others have already pointed out—and he manipulated it with easy abandon, in accordance with the ever-changing requirements of politics. Concern with theory was discernible in Stalin only insofar as he needed it to justify praxis. But this does not mean that he had no ideas of his own about socialism, the state and its structures, the party, the functions of ideology, the collective organization of society. These were the ideas he forced on the country by every means available during his days in power. And precisely in this sense it is legitimate to speak of Stalinism.

I shall simply list here Stalin's principal ideas: the need for the maximum strengthening of the state as the supreme, and in practice the only, expression of society; the statization of the entire economy, and therefore of every aspect of life associated with it, as an integral manifestation of socialism; the idea of the party as a sort of military-ideological order that came to be recognized as identical to a state institution, the most crucial one for the state, its central support; all other social organizations, from administrative bodies to the mass communications media, from the armed forces to citizens' associations (trade unions, youth organizations, whatever) seen as transmission belts for directives from above. The sum total of these belts, beginning with the most important one, the party, constituted the all-encompassing and monolithic state, itself the expression of a monolithic society—that is, a society free of internal antagonisms. This state has its own official ideology, the only one acknowledged and taught, equipped with its own seminaries and guardians, and the only one granted any kind of expression. Only a state so conceived can guarantee the adoption of socialist principles in either production or distribution. Any questioning of this questionable axiom in theory or in practice, even any request for systematic control of its functioning, is harshly repressed. When one looks to see how far Stalinism spread abroad, one should probably begin by considering which of these concepts have been transplanted and in what form.

Another problem is to establish just how compatible these ideas really are with Marxism and with Lenin's thought and actions. I am convinced that they have nothing in common, in fact are antithetical. One of Stalin's most successful political-cultural operations consisted in presenting his own ideas as the quintessence of Marxism-Leninism. This strategy had lasting influence not only within the Soviet world or the communist movement but also among the most determined of their opponents. Nor can we be surprised when we remember that by any estimate "Marxism" and "Leninism" enjoyed their widest influence between the 1930s and the 1950s, the period when Stalin was spreading his gospel—and that gospel was Stalinism. Seen in this light, these ideas have also proved effective in practice, for they provided answers to the problems unleashed by the revolutionary process in the USSR, problems that later surfaced in other countries. Hence their hegemonic effectiveness outside as well as within the Soviet Union. That this effectiveness was limited in time and exorbitant in price is also true, and helps us to understand the crisis that followed.

Another issue that has received too little attention is the social foundation of Stalinism. In crucial periods that foundation took on a mass character, though Stalin's rule had staked its very existence on brutal conflicts with vast strata of the Soviet population. In analyzing the various interpretations one can see that the most traditional explanation, the one that places this foundation within the ill-defined contours of a strongly heterogeneous bureaucracy, falls short. For this reason I pointed out the most interesting suggestions made by various writers. They all seek to locate the social underpinnings of Stalinism in the great social mobility made possible first by the revolution and then by the "revolution from above." Personally, I am convinced that this is where we should dig. Unfortunately, this is also one of the areas where the gaps in the available Soviet sources have always been most plentiful. The gaps, of course, are not accidental. Stalin's government suppressed every social analysis that failed to conform to the official theory of "monolithism"—in practice, all analysis.

Knowledge of Soviet society in its Stalinist phase is not only a historical problem. It is also the basis for our knowledge of Soviet society today, no matter how much that society may have changed; it helps us to understand the significance of Stalin's system, of those parts of it that survived for so long in the USSR after his death and still survive, tenaciously resisting all efforts to change them. The character of this system has been discussed at great length, especially among those with a Marxist point of reference. These discussions never were and never could be primarily historical. In practice they kept pace with the entire process through which this system was formed; it is enough to think of the debates and the arguments that went on within the Socialist International and between the Socialist and Communist Internationals between the two world wars, and involved communists and socialists in various countries, Marxists of other political shadings, and leftist intellectuals in general after World War II. The discussions always had strong ideological overtones and immediate political implications. Even today they continue, often on the same level. Thus one goes from the official Soviet position, which sees the system as "real socialism"—the position that was born the day Stalin decreed "constructed socialism" in the USSR—all the way to the assertions that reduce Stalin's ideas to a simple variant of capitalism, perhaps disguised as "state capitalism." But all too often such explanations signify only that one is "in favor" or "against" the Soviet regime past or present, more in favor or less in favor than somebody else.

The problem would not arise if this were not a different and therefore new kind of system. It cannot be reduced either to socialist ideals such as those that arose in the European democratic culture or to any of the familiar social models of the past, not to capitalism and not even to the old "Asiatic despotism." And so we had the multitude of names that purported to describe it: "transitional society," "bureaucratic collectivism," "state mode of production," "pseudosocialism," and so on and on. Unfortunately, instead of explanations we too often got labels hastily manufactured from generalizations based on meager and even casual personal experiences.

Let me suggest how I think we should proceed in our search for the place Stalinism occupies in the events of our century. I assume everyone agrees that the decades after World War I witnessed profound changes in values, lifestyles, social organization, and international relations. Among the theoretical lines of thought humanity has pursued in its attempt to make sense of such changes, the Marxist is certainly one of the most important, less because of its wide appeal among nations of diverse cultures than because it has served as a stimulus and a guide to action, and thus has been an active factor in those changes. Marxism understood those changes as signifiying a crisis in capitalist society and the progression of a new mode of production and distribution, a new "social formation"—the socialist-communist. This is an interpretation one can certainly accept or reject, but we have seen that it is shared today even by scholars who are not exactly of the Marxist persuasion (remember E. H. Carr).

What a person who shares this interpretation cannot do, I think, is to see the change as a linear process, so that in a particular country at a certain point in time a well-defined line is crossed where one stage of society's development ends and another begins. A breakdown of an old way of life and the establishment of new forms of social organization is more intricate and dramatic by far, with advances and even a breakthrough in one direction, a headlong reteat in another, mixtures of old and new social forms in one country or another. This scenario is even more certain in the case of a process that has literally spread throughout the world.

Stalinism and all of Soviet history can be analyzed only within this framework. It is within this framework that the various attempts at interpretation reveal their usefulness, great or little, through their ability to identify at least some of the many elements that went into the making of the phenomenon in its entirety, with all its sharp discords. And this is also the way history can best help us understand the contradictions of the present, especially those of Soviet society—contradictions that arose through the various layers of the past, among which Stalinism is still the most important but certainly not the only one. I believe the same criterion is useful when one investigates how much of Stalinism has been reproduced in other countries and what contradictions, national or international, its spread has in turn provoked in the USSR and elsewhere.

To emphasize these requirements for fruitful research is not to assume an attitude of Olympian detachment in the hope of escaping the more specifically political debate that still goes on about these matters. I have said from the beginning that I could not do so even if I tried. I could never get rid of the political dimension that is part of each of us. I certainly never intended to do so. Even a good political battle, however, cannot get very far without reliable knowledge of the historical phenomena it inevitably must contend with and a precise analysis of the contradictions in the world we live in, which those phenomena have spawned. The battle against Stalinism is no exception to this rule. Formulas and simplifications will do for a speech or a polemic, but their fabric is soon seen to be threadbare.

Consider the Soviet experience. The 1917 revolution can still inspire individuals and movements (it would seem strange if it did not), just as other crucial events in history have done. Its objective value lies in the inspiration it has provided for masses of people in countries of all sorts. But for this very reason a vast variety of things have flowed from the revolution of 1917, in the USSR and elsewhere, many of them mutually contradictory. The appeal of the Russian revolution therefore cannot take the place of an analysis of the specific phenomena that are historically linked to that event; even less can it be used as a kind of cloak that covers everything, explains everything, absolves or condemns everything. No matter what its bias, such an approach cannot take us far. Yet some of the recent Italian discussions of "Leninism," for example, are still riddled with these vices.

One concluding remark is in order. For all the reasons I have brought out, I do not believe a fresh look at Stalinism is anachronistic just because the term figures less frequently in today's political debates. If anyone is tempted to dismiss Stalinism as a thing of the past, I need only point out that the historians' debate analyzed here is enough in itself to show that matters are not quite that simple. But there is another consideration that seems to me even more pertinent. In Stalinism European culture found itself facing a phenomenon that, though it had a few ties with European ideas, was a product of a world emerging outside the political and cultural confines of Europe, a world that Europe still viewed with a supercilious eye. This century was destined to present Europe and indeed the world with several phenomena of this sort, and it probably will present it with several more. But Stalinism was the first and probably is the most important. This is reason enough for us not to let our attention to it flag.

Index

Library of Congress Cataloging-in-Publication Data

Boffa, Giuseppe.
    [Fenomeno Stalin nella storia del XX secolo. English]
    The Stalin phenomenon / Giuseppe Boffa ; translated by Nicholas
Fersen.
        p. cm.
    Translation of: Il fenomeno Stalin nella storia del XX secolo.
    "A book from the Center for the Humanities and Social Sciences,
Williams College."
    Includes bibliographical references and index.
    ISBN 0-8014-2576-X (alk. paper). — ISBN 0-8014-9799-X (pbk. :
alk. paper)
    1. Stalin, Joseph, 1879–1953. 2. Kommunisticheskaia partiia
Sovetskogo Soiuza—Purges. 3. Soviet Union—Politics and
government—20th century. I. Title.
DK267.B585513   1992
947.084'2—dc20   91-813